Handbook for Academic Authors

Handbook for Academic Authors

Fourth Edition

BETH LUEY
Arizona State University

PUBLISHED BY THE PRESS SYNDICATE OF THE UNIVERSITY OF CAMBRIDGE
The Pitt Building, Trumpington Street, Cambridge, United Kingdom

CAMBRIDGE UNIVERSITY PRESS
The Edinburgh Building, Cambridge CB2 2RU, UK
40 West 20th Street, New York, NY 10011-4211, USA
477 Williamstown Road, Port Melborne, VIC 3207, Australia
Ruiz de Alarcón 13, 28014 Madrid, Spain
Dock House, The Waterfront, Cape Town 8001, South Africa

http://www.cambridge.org

First published 1987
Second edition 1990
Reprinted 1991, 1992, 1994
Third edition 1995
Reprinted 1996, 1997, 1999
Fourth edition 2002

Printed in the United States of America

Typeface Palatino 11/13 pt.   System QuarkXPress™   [HT]

A catalog record for this book is available from the British Library.

Library of Congress Cataloging in Publication Data available

ISBN 0 521 81477 4   hardback
ISBN 0 521 89198 1   paperback

For Mike and Nora, again

Contents

vii

Contents

Contents

Illustrations

Preface

In 1980, after ten years as an editor of scholarly books and textbooks, I began teaching scholarly editing and publishing. I soon learned that my faculty colleagues regarded me as a window onto a mysterious and often frustrating publishing world. They asked my advice on questions ranging from semicolons to royalties, from en dashes to remainders. At the same time, they informed me of a number of publishers' practices – many admirable, some reprehensible – that I had never encountered.

As a teacher, I met daily with students who were curious about aspects of publishing that I had avoided. I have little artistic ability, for example, and had always regarded book design as magic. That explanation was clearly inadequate for bright, curious graduate students. My expertise in the dollars-and-cents area of publishing was equally sad; to correct my deficiencies, I even went so far as to take an accounting course so that I could use the proper terms in explicating the financial arcana.

In 1982 I began to worry that my theoretical knowledge, though apparently sound, was untested. Besides, I had some ideas for books that needed to be written. I formed a small publishing company and, with the assistance of my husband on legal and financial matters, learned firsthand the realities of what I was teaching. There is no better way to learn the economics of publishing than to invest your own money. Nor is there any better motivation to improve your marketing skills than to have your closets taken over by unsold books.

Preface

Having been editor, indexer, publisher, production manager, marketing manager, and shipping clerk, I decided it was time to try being an author. The result is this book. I have tried to test my advice by following it, and so far it has worked. I have also discovered that I am not immune to authorial paranoia and irrationality. Although Colin Day, my editor at Cambridge, diligently kept me informed of the manuscript's progress, I was periodically convinced that it had been sucked into a black hole. And although the copyediting was tactful, the green deletion of every little comma nevertheless caused a twinge of psychic pain. I have added empathy to my professional skills.

Finally, a word about this book and Cambridge University Press. Relations between author and publisher are always complex. They are doubly so when the book is about publishing. The book is not an official Cambridge guide for authors. It describes the general range of publishing practices, not all of which the Press follows. I sent a prospectus to a dozen presses. I submitted the completed manuscript to Cambridge and received a contract four months later. Only after acceptance did they offer generous assistance and suggestions. More than a half-dozen people in the New York and Cambridge offices commented in detail on the manuscript, but at no time did anyone attempt to dictate content. I incorporated their suggestions happily – when I agreed with them. But the ideas and opinions in this book are my own.

I am grateful to many employers, colleagues, and friends in scholarly publishing who have shared their ideas, pleasures, and frustrations, especially Margot Barbour, John Bergez, Georges Borchardt, Louise Craft, Fred Hetzel, Naomi Pascal, Elizabeth Shaw, and Phyllis Steckler. My colleagues at Arizona State University have helped me understand authors' problems and puzzlements.

I must especially thank Brian Gratton, who not only commented extensively on several chapters but also convinced me to learn to use a computer so that I could finish the book promptly. I have edited books for more than a hundred authors, and I have learned something from each of them. I must thank my students, who have taught me a great deal. Finally, Cambridge University Press – personified in Colin Day, Rhona Johnson, Brigitte Lehner, and Christopher Scarles – has been prompt, courteous, helpful, and enthusiastic: an exemplary publisher.

Preface to the Second Edition

Soon after the first edition of this book appeared, it became clear that publishing practices were changing so rapidly that I needed to begin thinking about a new edition. The most significant change has been in the expanded use of computers for composition and desktop typesetting. A clear majority of academic authors write with computers, and the practice of typesetting from authors' disks has moved beyond the experimental stage.

This edition therefore has a new chapter, Chapter 10 (Chapter 11, in the third edition), about using the computer and about electronic publishing: databases, CD-ROMs, and the like.

Another change has occurred in the structure of the publishing industry, which has become increasingly global. Commercial scholarly publishing has a greater presence in the United States because of the expansion of British and European houses into the U.S. market both through the opening of new offices and by the acquisition of U.S. firms. Although the long-term implications of internationalization remain unclear, it seems important to provide more information about commercial scholarly publishing and about the practices of transatlantic publishers. You will find most of this information in Chapter 4, but it appears throughout the book wherever it is relevant.

My own experience has expanded over the past three years to include editing the journal *Book Research Quarterly*, retitled *Publishing Research Quarterly* in 1991. As a result I have expanded Chapter 2 to add what I have learned. I am also working on a book about grants for publication, and I have provided an introduction to that subject in Chapter 5 and in the appendix. I have updated the bibliography and incorporated some of the suggestions made by reviewers of the first edition, to whom I am grateful.

Preface to the Third Edition

The five years since the second edition of this book appeared
have witnessed economic and technological changes in scholarly publishing and in the academic world. The nation's economic recovery has not been reflected in the budgets of
colleges and universities. The anticipated improvement in the
market for Ph.D.s has not occurred, and academic jobs remain
scarce. Library book budgets have shrunk, reducing the sales
of scholarly publishers. University press budgets have suffered along with those of academic departments, and presses
are more than ever tightening their belts and seeking new
markets. There are some brighter spots, however. Personal
computers have made it easier for authors to prepare manuscripts and cheaper for publishers to manufacture them.
Electronic networks and CD-ROM technology have created
new products and more efficient distribution methods. The
technology is young, and neither publishers nor authors are
entirely comfortable with it, but it is promising. For example,
although university presses are not putting their books online, you will find their catalogues on the Internet.

For the academic author, these changes mean that publication is more important than ever, more difficult than it has
been, and likely to take new forms. In this edition, I have
tried to help authors adjust to this new climate by providing
current information on both the state of new technologies
and their meaning to authors. I have revised Chapter 12 to
reflect the changing costs associated with reduced print runs.
Most important, I have added a chapter on writing for

general readers. I did so not only because scholarly publishers are eagerly expanding into this market, but because the understanding of scholarship that such books generate may be the best way to maintain and extend public support of education and research.

Preface to the Fourth Edition

This edition brings advice to authors fully into the age of the Internet, the World Wide Web, and the electronic book and journal. Although many technological, economic, and professional issues about electronic publishing remain unresolved, confusion is beginning to give way to clarity. The last chapter of this book, which is entirely new, is meant to describe current practices and, perhaps more important, to encourage authors to explore technology not only as a way of communicating knowledge but also as a way of generating it.

The rest of the book brings readers up-to-date on the processes of finding a publisher, producing journal articles, working with journal and book publishers, and preparing a manuscript. I have also evaluated the economic impact of electronic publishing.

In preparing this edition, I have benefited from discussions with book and journal editors, documentary and textual editors, historians of the book, and my colleagues and students at Arizona State University. Contemplating the possible "death of the book" has clarified the value of print and the meaning of books and reading in our lives. The medium is not the message, but it shapes the message and the impact of its delivery. I hope this edition will help authors convey their messages effectively by choosing the appropriate media and using them wisely.

Chapter 1

The Publishing Partnership

I promise to do all I can to make you a great publisher even
as I expect you to do all you can to make me a great author.
Robert Frost to Alfred Harcourt

Faculty members are always writing or talking about writing
and of necessity are always thinking about publishing. Each
has an article nearly finished, about to be started, or stuck
somewhere in the middle. Many have a book manuscript
under way or under consideration at a press. And some are
complaining, half-sincerely, about the tedium of reading page
proofs. Although writing and publishing are discrete processes, they are interdependent. Why write if no one will
publish? And what is there to publish if no one writes?

Despite this interdependence, academic authors and publishers of scholarly books and journals do not always understand each other very well, and they sometimes find it
difficult to coexist peacefully. Publishers and journal editors
lose sight of the tremendous pressure to publish that is
exerted on scholars, particularly young, untenured scholars.
Authors, for their part, are guilty of not understanding either
how publishing works or how to use the system to their
advantage.

Publishers' indifference to the scholar's plight, although
perhaps regrettable, does serve a purpose. The editor considering a manuscript who remains conscious at every moment
that the fate of another human being is at stake may not make

the best decision. Especially in this period of scarce academic jobs and often unrealistic administrative demands for "productivity," failure to publish early and often may force a scholar to resort to driving a cab or designing web pages. But the editor who too generously takes that into account and publishes too many marginal manuscripts may also end up driving a cab. Authors' ignorance of publishing, however, is both self-imposed and self-destructive. It is not difficult to learn how the world of scholarly publishing works, and it is foolish not to make the effort. Once you understand what publishers want from authors, it is easy enough to provide it and thereby improve your chances of publication. That is what this book is designed to help you do.

Publishing What You Write: How to Use This Book

In an ideal world, people would write only when they had something important to say. Discovery or inspiration would be the driving force. In the real world, though, this is only one of several worthy motives. Academic authors do write for the pure joy of communicating ideas, but they also write for tenure, money, and fame.

Let us assume for the moment that you are writing because you want to get tenure, be promoted, or get a raise. Perhaps you want to publish so that you can find another teaching job at a more hospitable institution. In these cases, depending on your field, you are going to have to write articles for scholarly journals and possibly a book or two for scholarly presses. Because university administrators believe that the refereeing procedures of these journals and presses guarantee the scholarly value of the works they publish, they accept such publication as evidence of the author's scholarly accomplishments. Chapter 2 explains how to find an appropriate journal for your work and how to speed up the refereeing process; it also offers some suggestions about effective article writing and about revising talks and speeches for publication. Chapter 3 is devoted to the problems of revising a dissertation for book or journal publication. Chapter 4 describes the various sorts of book publishers and tells how to decide which publisher would be best for your book. It also suggests ways to make acceptance more likely. Chapter 5 tells how to work with a publisher, including an explanation of how to read your contract and a discussion of how to seek grants for publication costs. In Chapter 6, I offer advice on editing multiauthor books and compiling anthologies.

Perhaps you are not concerned about tenure or promotion but do want to make some money. In that case, skip the journals and monographs and get to work on a textbook. (Either that or shift to romance fiction, apocalyptic novels, or diet books.) Journals do not pay authors, and few scholarly books generate significant royalties. Writing textbooks, however, can be profitable. As you will learn, the money is not quick or easy. Writing a textbook usually will not help you get tenure, because many deans and other administrators mistakenly exclude textbook writing from scholarly activity. Although writing a textbook does not require original research, it does demand a comprehensive knowledge of the field and an original, well-thought-out perspective on it. Chapters 7 and 8 will help you write a textbook, find a publisher, and see the project through to completion.

If it is fame that you seek, you need to write a book that nonacademics will read, that will be reviewed in newspapers and popular magazines, stocked in bookstores, and achieve a respectable sales rank on Amazon.com. This is not as easy as it sounds and requires authors to involve themselves in the publishing process in new ways. And although writing books for general readers is more profitable than writing monographs, it is typically less lucrative than writing textbooks. Chapter 9 discusses the writing, publishing, and economics of trade books.

Chapter 10 explains the mechanics of authorship, regardless of whether you are writing a journal article, monograph, textbook, or trade book: how to prepare a typescript for a variety of production methods, obtain permission to quote and to reproduce illustrations, proofread, and index a book.

Because money is so often a bone of contention, I have summarized the economics of book publishing in Chapter 11. There you will find an explanation of why books cost so much and where the money goes, along with an analysis of the impact of online publishing on costs and prices.

Chapter 12 discusses the various forms of electronic publishing and their value in research and teaching.

Finally, the bibliography, which is briefly annotated, lists books on writing, guides to journals in various fields, style guides, and further information on most topics covered in the book. It is organized topically, following the order of the text.

In addition to the pleasure and pride of seeing one's ideas and words in print, publishing can lead to security, status, wealth, and (occasionally) fame; surely it is worth the effort to learn a bit about it. This book is an introduction to scholarly publishing. The serious writer needs several other books as well.

The Scholar's Bookshelf

Anyone who writes should own *The Elements of Style* by William Strunk Jr. and E. B. White. This brief paperback solves the most common difficulties of grammar and diction and offers sound, memorable advice on clear writing. I read it once a year without fail. (Full information about this and all other works mentioned in this book is provided in the bibliography.)

You must also own a good dictionary. Although the Merriam-Webster dictionaries (the third edition of the unabridged or the latest collegiate edition) are the most generally accepted, I prefer the *American Heritage Dictionary* because it provides good usage notes and has a more pleasing layout. Its optional CD-ROM version provides spoken pronunciations. Other popular dictionaries are the *Oxford American Dictionary* and the *Random House Dictionary*. If you plan to write a book, you must own *The Chicago Manual of Style*. Nearly every book publisher relies on it, and it is the authority for many fields on note and bibliography style. It also tells you how to proofread

4

and index your book. It is fairly expensive, but it is worth buying. If you deal with British publishers or journals, Judith Butcher's *Copy-Editing: The Cambridge Handbook* will be helpful. The writer about to revise a dissertation may find *The Thesis and the Book*, edited by Eleanor Harman and Ian Montagnes, useful. It is available in paperback.

If you become interested in the world of academic publishing, you many want to subscribe to the *Journal of Scholarly Publishing* (formerly *Scholarly Publishing*), published by the University of Toronto Press, and to *Publishing Research Quarterly* (formerly *Book Research Quarterly*), published by Transaction Publishers. If you do not subscribe, make sure your library does and take time to browse through the journals occasionally. *The American Scholar* includes at least one article a year on some aspect of book publishing, and the *Chronicle of Higher Education* frequently includes news and feature stories on scholarly publishing.

The Publishing Partnership

While authors are worrying about getting their books published, editors are out busily acquiring manuscripts. It is the same process viewed from different angles. The reputations of authors and publishers ride on the same books. When a book is well reviewed or even wins a prestigious award, both author and publisher share the glory. The book that succeeds commercially puts money into both the publisher's coffers and the author's pocket. When a book fails – critically, financially, or aesthetically – author and publisher share the disappointment. Why, then, is there conflict between partners? Ignorance is one source of conflict. The author who does not understand the refereeing process, who does not read the contract, and who does not learn to proofread is bound to be unhappy with how long it takes to get a book accepted, to feel cheated on discovering that the publisher will not provide an index, and to become outraged when a reviewer points out typos.

Illusions about money are another source of friction. An author whose book is priced at $40.00 and whose royalty is 10 percent figures "$4.00 per book, and they're printing 1,500, so I should get $6,000." Unfortunately, the royalty may be paid on net receipts (20 to 40 percent less than gross), at least 100 copies will be given away free for reviews and publicity, and not all the other copies will be sold. When the first royalty check arrives and the author gets, say, $1,500 – knowing that the first year is probably the best – disappointment sets in. With disappointment comes suspicion. Where does the rest of the money go, anyway? Authors who do not know what it costs to produce a book and who do not understand prices and discounts are apt to think mistakenly that presses are getting rich from their labors. They are not. University presses do make money on some titles but rarely more than the authors do. Successful trade books make money, but authors should not be misled by the six- and seven-figure advances paid to a handful of best-selling authors and celebrities. For most serious nonfiction books, royalties are respectable but far from extravagant. Textbooks, too, should make money for both author and publisher, with the amount depending on the number of students who enroll in the relevant courses, the book's share of the market, and the book's longevity.

Some authors and librarians, irritated by what they view as exorbitant prices for journals and books, are hoping that electronic media will eliminate the need for publishers, or at least reduce prices. Electronic media will certainly play an increasing role in scholarly communication, but it is unlikely that either publishers or high prices will disappear. Paper, ink, and postage represent a small part of journal costs, and the value added by publishers in acquiring, reviewing, selecting, and improving articles and books is too often overlooked. Publishers must also meet readers' expectations that electronic media will have useful features not available in print media, adding further to publishing costs. Readers' attachment to the codex form is also proving to be more enduring than anticipated.

Throughout this book, I explain the financial implications of various policies and technologies. Chapter 11 discusses the economics of scholarly publishing in some detail, and Chapter 12 explains various electronic media. I hope that this will reduce one source of mistrust and perhaps contribute to constructive discussion of new media and their uses.

Editorial changes can lead to disputes. Most writers have worked hard on their manuscripts, and many resent any attempt to alter their words and punctuation. They view the editor's suggestions as attempts to take over their books, and they see editorial queries as questioning their authority. The editor, however, is trying to correct errors, clarify meanings, and eliminate clumsy constructions in order to make the author's book better. I hope that the sections in Chapters 5, 8, and 9 on working with your editor will help you to develop happy and productive relationships with those who labor to improve your writing.

Some authors also fear that their publishers are not doing enough to sell their books. The level of marketing effort, and the types of marketing activity undertaken, will depend on the nature of your book and the publisher's estimate of the size of the audience. Chapters 5 and 9 explain the marketing strategies of scholarly and trade publishers and suggest ways authors can cooperate in reaching the largest possible market. Much of the conflict between authors and publishers is rooted in the very interdependence that also makes them partners. Authors resent having their professional stature and even their livelihoods rest in the hands of nonacademics. And just as faculty members often comment on how great teaching would be if it weren't for the students, publishers occasionally long for the day when books would magically appear without authors. With a little understanding, however, the two sides can get along quite nicely.

This book is, in a sense, an effort at making peace as well as informing. The writer who understands publishers will be more successful in dealing with them and will make the publisher's life much easier. Writers may view my effort as one-sided, because all the instruction is directed at them.

7

Throughout the book, though, I have set a high standard of behavior for publishers and have suggested ways authors can hold publishers to these standards. For most authors, publishing is rewarding and even fun. Needless to say, the same is true for most editors, or they would be in a better-paid field. I hope that this book will make publishing easier for both authors and publishers and that it will reduce the friction that often seems inevitable.

Chapter 2

Journal Articles

He put his hand into the well-known nook under the pillow: only, it did not get so far. What he touched was, according to his account, a mouth, with teeth, and with hair about it, and, he declares, not the mouth of a human being. . . . "Gayton, I believe that alchemist man knows it was I who got his paper rejected."

M. R. James, "Casting the Runes"

Journals are the medium most frequently used by academic authors for disseminating the results of their research. In some fields, particularly in the natural and physical sciences, book writing is rare. A biochemist may publish hundreds of journal articles and never think of writing a book. Journals are also the least professionalized of the publishing media. In the humanities and social sciences, journals are often edited on the side by academics with regular teaching and research assignments and without professional staff.[1] (This is far less common in the physical and natural sciences.) The advent of personal computers, relatively inexpensive phototypesetting, and desktop publishing has led to the creation of numerous small, specialized journals run out of faculty offices. Electronic journals that are "printed" only after they reach subscribers'

---

[1] Should you ever become a journal editor, you will want to consult *Journal Publishing* by Gillian Page, Robert Campbell, and Jack Meadows (New York: Cambridge University Press, 1997).

computers are becoming plentiful; these are even easier to start and cheaper to distribute.

The growth of specialized journals since the 1960s has expanded opportunities for publication. At the same time, the end of the academic hiring boom of that decade and the stabilization of the size of the academic community have decreased the number of submissions received by many journals. This adds up to improved possibilities for getting good articles published, even if they are on very specialized topics. It also means that mediocre work can be published in less prestigious journals that need to fill their pages. To make sure that their work is published in the best possible place, authors need to write well, select carefully the journals to which they submit their work, prepare their manuscripts properly, and communicate clearly with journal editors.

Writing Well

Good academic writing is clear and succinct. (To use myself as an example, I first wrote that sentence: "For the purposes of academic writing, writing well is writing clearly and succinctly." I read it, saw that it was neither clear nor succinct, and rewrote it. Reading and revising are essential to good writing. Had I not spotted the problem, the manuscript editor would have fixed it, after a good laugh at my expense.) If you can move beyond clarity to grace and elegance, you are to be congratulated. Editors will happily settle for clarity, however.

Many fields have formal conventions about article writing: All articles are organized in the same way, with subsections covering specified topics (e.g., title, abstract, introduction, method, results, discussion, references). Because disciplines vary, you should familiarize yourself with the conventions of the field in which you are publishing. If this is the field in which you have done most of your research, you probably have absorbed such conventions subliminally. You will have to make a special effort, though, if you are writing in an area outside your usual territory (e.g., a historian venturing into a medical journal or a lawyer writing for a psychology journal). The bibliography of this book includes the official style manuals for a variety of disciplines. If your discipline has a generally accepted style manual, you should own and use the current edition. The bibliography also includes several general guides to writing, guides to writing for specific fields, and dictionaries.

Intelligent readers are impressed by ideas and clear expression, not by elaborate constructions and excess words. If your writing is obscure, vague, and verbose, readers will translate what you have written into plain English and wonder why you did not write it that way in the first place. There are two possible answers, neither of which is flattering. First, perhaps you did not know how. More damning, perhaps you realized that reduced to plain English your idea did not make sense or was so obvious that it wasn't worth saying. Good writing saves the reader's time and your reputation.

Beyond the basic advice on writing offered by Strunk and White in *The Elements of Style,* I can offer a few suggestions that may help you avoid errors common in academic writing.[2] A frequent error is the use of jargon. The lingua franca of many disciplines frequently departs from standard English. However, it is rarely necessary to use a word that is not in the dictionary. This does not mean that you should avoid technical language, because a technical term often expresses an idea most economically and will be understood by your readers. In writing for specialized journals you need not worry about whether a layperson will read it. To determine whether you are using technical expressions appropriately or are simply resorting to jargon, ask yourself whether you are using the plainest word that will say precisely what you mean. Do not use technical words merely to impress. It sometimes can be helpful to define technical terms precisely, within your article, to ensure that you are using them properly and that your

[2] If English is not your native language, you will find assistance in Gregory A. Barnes, *Communication Skills for the Foreign-Born Professional* (Philadelphia: ISI Press, 1982).

readers will understand exactly what you mean. Technical terms can take on a life of their own if not used carefully.

Bureaucratic language is a form of jargon that easily creeps into one's writing and provokes the special ire of editors and careful readers. Do not use *finalize, monies,* or *debrief* when you mean *finish, money,* or *question.* Equally to be avoided is trendy language, which rapidly becomes overused and then dated. "Excellence," "the best and the brightest," and "the right stuff" all fell victim to this phenomenon, but even words that have not been used in book titles are vulnerable. Try not to use business jargon: by the time your work appears, no one will be putting things on the table or thinking outside the box. Some of these expressions – though not all – were acceptable at one time, but overuse has worn them out. If you feel you must choose between being stuffy and being trendy (a false dilemma), choose stuffy.

Also avoid cuteness, especially in titles. Your title, of course, should be brief and should tell the reader what your article is about. Occasionally a title can be used to attract attention but usually not in a scholarly journal. If a title is not clear, your article may be indexed incorrectly and will not turn up in computer searches, so that it may languish unread and uncited.

Another frequent fault in academic writing is the repetition of certain words, notably qualifying adverbs and abstract nouns. *Rather, quite,* and *somewhat* can usually be omitted without sacrificing meaning. Similarly, you should rewrite sentences to avoid using such phrases as "friendly by nature," "in terms of," "on a weekly basis," "generous in character," and "for the purpose of."

Even if you are deaf to the beauty of language, you can be accurate. Check and recheck all quotations. A literary scholar once quoted *Macbeth*'s hags on the heath as chanting "Double bubble toil and trouble." The failure of referees to catch such mistakes should not be taken as license to butcher the Bard – or anyone else. Also be accurate and complete in the citations you provide in notes and bibliographies. Any of the style manuals in the bibliography – including, of course, *The*

Chicago Manual of Style – will assist you in this task. Some journals and a few book publishers routinely check citations, but you should not rely on this. The reader who cannot find an article using your citation has good reason to doubt your reliability.

In sum, you can write well by being clear, direct, precise, and accurate. If you can accomplish this apparently modest goal – and if you have something new and important to say – you will be on your way to publication in a reputable journal.

Selecting a Journal

Few journals tolerate multiple submissions. In fact, some regard this as a sin so serious that they report it to the author's department chair. Because you can send your work to only one journal at a time, you should choose carefully. The best way to decide where to submit an article is to look through the journals you read regularly. As long as you are writing in the mainstream of your own discipline, one of these journals will probably be the place to start. However, when you venture into new territory, you will have to do some exploring. Investigate journals cited in your manuscript first. Many field-specific guides to journals are published (see bibliography), and you should consult them. This rooting around will produce a list of journals that cover your subject area. The guides will often provide further information, such as maximum length of articles, usual time for review, preferred style, percentage of submissions accepted, and time between acceptance and publication. (Such information is usually based on the editors' self-reporting and may not be entirely accurate or up-to-date.) Because journals frequently change editors and addresses, and because policies change, you should always consult the latest issue of the journal or the website to verify its current location, staff, and editorial policy.

Most journal editors do not welcome query letters, so it is up to you to decide whether a journal is appropriate or not. A journal that regularly publishes articles in your field and of the same length and scope as yours is appropriate. Do not, for example, submit a bibliographical review to a journal that never includes such reviews, even if it does include other sorts of articles in the same field. When you have a list of journals, look at the current issue of each. Many journals include a description of editorial requirements; some post these on websites; all provide an address to write to if such information is not published. You may have to eliminate some journals from your list because your article is too long or too short or because your article is illustrated and they do not publish graphic material. Perusing a few issues may also disclose an ideological or theoretical bias that renders the journal unsuitable. You may decide to eliminate others because they seem sloppily produced or edited. Take a look at the date of the current issue to see whether the journal is hopelessly behind schedule.

When, contrary to the norm, the journal's note to contributors or directory listing indicates that the editor does expect a query letter, compose a brief one that includes the subject of your article, why you believe it is suitable for the journal, and why it is worth publishing. Also include a physical description (length, illustrated or not, how many notes, and so forth). If your manuscript is available in electronic form, say so. You may send such query letters simultaneously to as many journals as you like; the single-submission rule applies only to the full manuscript.

In deciding where to submit, you first may want to figure out whether to choose a less prestigious journal that you think will probably accept your article and publish it quickly or to begin by trying for one of the big names. This decision will depend on your own impression of how administrators evaluate publications, on how much of a hurry you are in, and of course on how much you yourself value publication in a major journal. Do not automatically assume that a lesser journal represents your best bet. Journals are quirky, and you may find your work rejected in the minor leagues and accepted in the majors. However, remember that more prestigious journals may take longer to get your work into print because of backlogs of accepted articles. They may also demand more extensive revisions than lesser journals. Whenever possible, choose a refereed journal – that is, a journal whose submissions are reviewed by outside readers in addition to the editor. Most universities distinguish between articles in refereed and nonrefereed journals when awarding tenure and raises. But many do not distinguish among refereed journals. You can find this out from your colleagues and department chair.

Your colleagues are also a good source of information on how prompt a journal is about refereeing, how quickly articles are put into print, and how well promises are kept. You should take much of this information with a grain or two of salt, because horror stories abound. (For an entertaining fictional account of how bad things can get, read Kingsley Amis's marvelous academic novel, *Lucky Jim.*) Consistent accounts of mistreatment by a journal should put it low on your list.

Colleagues can also warn you away from journals whose quality or reputation is questionable. Having your work published in the journal of last resort may lengthen your publications list, but it will not enhance your reputation. If your work is rejected by several journals, especially if a number of referees point out substantive problems, you should consider radical revisions before continuing to submit it. If your only remaining hope is a journal with a reputation for publishing almost anything, you need to decide whether publication will help or hurt your career.

You may want to ask one or two colleagues to read your article before you send it off. You probably know who is likely to be helpful in providing suggestions on content, organization, and writing. Be prepared for criticism and accept it graciously. If you just want a pat on the back or uncritical encouragement, read the article to your dog.

After reading the manuscript, your colleagues may suggest a journal that you had not thought of. Do not follow the suggestion without checking the journal yourself for appropriateness and editorial requirements.

Another way to get criticism of your work is to present the paper at a national or regional meeting or at a less formal colloquium. Some writers regard such public presentation as insurance against plagiarism by referees. Such dishonesty is too rare, however, to make this a genuine concern. The real value of public presentation lies in the opportunity to receive criticism and suggestions.

Some authors achieve lengthy publication lists by recycling their research. They change the emphasis slightly, alter the length, rephrase, add a section or two, and submit two or three articles instead of one. Although journal editors and subscribers may initially be unaware that they are being victimized in this way, eventually word gets out. Both editors and colleagues read more than one journal. Although this practice is legal, it is ethically questionable and wastes the time of editors, referees, and readers. In the medical sciences, it can have serious consequences for patients. A researcher doing a meta-analysis (a synthesis of several studies on, for example, nonsurgical treatment of a specific cancer) may unknowingly be counting the results of a single study more than once, if its authors have published it more than once. This duplication will alter the statistical results and may mislead practitioners into thinking that a treatment is more (or less) effective than it really is.

On the rare occasion when republication of material is appropriate – for example, if the first appearance was a brief note in a journal with very limited circulation, or in another language – you should nevertheless tell the editor the circumstances of the first publication. Enclosing a copy of the original article or manuscript will enable the editor to verify the differences and make an informed decision.

A variant on duplicate publication is "salami publishing," in which each bit of research is divided into the thinnest possible slices (sometimes referred to as "LPUs," for "least publishable units"), with each slice submitted as a separate article. This is marginally more ethical than duplicate submission, but it is equally wasteful. Nor is it clear that it does the slicer much good. In any serious review of a scholar's work (for tenure, promotion, a new job, or major grants), reviewers look at all the applicant's work as a body. If there is only one ounce of salami there, slicing it thin doesn't make it any weightier. One significant article in a major journal almost always benefits a researcher's career more than four or five trivial pieces scattered in lesser publications.

Another way that lengthy bibliographies are built is by overstating the number of authors. In the humanities, where single authorship is the rule, this rarely happens. But when scientists work in research teams, each team (or sometimes each department or institution) sets rules for who may be considered an author. (In a few cases, more than a hundred authors have been listed for a single article.) Some professional societies are trying to establish standard definitions of authorship, but so far none has been widely adopted. Most standards revolve around two issues: knowledge and responsibility. To be listed as an author, one should have direct knowledge of the conduct and results of the entire study and should be willing to take responsibility for its conduct, data, and conclusions. In the absence of accepted standards, each author must follow the guidelines of institution and conscience.

Preparing the Manuscript

The general rules for preparing an article manuscript for publication are very simple: print out neatly on high-quality white 8½- by 11-inch paper, double space (text, notes, and bibliography), and leave ample margins on all four sides (at least 1 inch). Use 12-point type. Print the article on a laser or ink-jet printer. It is usually all right to send a photocopy if it is of good quality. Some people argue that sending the original assures the editor that you are not submitting the article elsewhere. The fallacy of this argument is obvious, particularly in the era of computer-generated "multiple originals."

Beyond these commonsense requirements, be sure to follow the instructions provided by the journal to which you are submitting the paper. Specifically, if the journal's format includes notes in a particular place and in a particular style, comply with these conventions. Conforming to a given footnote style can be a nuisance if journals in your field do not agree on which style to use, but it is worth taking the trouble. If the editor wants two copies of the manuscript, send two copies. If the journal publishes abstracts, prepare one. If quotations must be in English, provide translations. If the journal follows the style book of the Modern Language Association, American Psychological Association, Council of Biology Editors, or some other professional organization, or if it has its own style sheet, get the style guide and follow it. (See the bibliography for a list of style guides.)

Proofread and correct the manuscript carefully (see Chapter 10). Make sure you have a printed copy of your own, even if the manuscript is also on a computer disk and your hard drive. Keep a backup disk as well as hard copy.

Unless you are told otherwise, be sure to provide a separate title page with your name, address, and article title. Repeat only the title on the first page of the text. Do not put your name on each page, because this makes it difficult to implement blind reviewing, in which referees are not told the author's identity. Mail the manuscript flat, not folded. If you are also sending a disk, place it in a rigid container within the envelope. Enclose a self-addressed envelope of appropriate size with return postage. Send it first class. If you want reassurance that the manuscript arrived safely, send it by certified mail with a return receipt or enclose a self-addressed, stamped postcard. Journals should automatically acknowledge receipt of submissions, but not all of them do. When submitting articles to journals outside the United States, enclose International Reply Coupons for return postage. They can be purchased at the post office.

A brief cover letter is adequate unless you have something specific to tell the editor. For example, if you have sent photocopies of artwork, you might want to let the editor know that you have the originals and will obtain permission to use them. (On illustrations and permissions, see Chapter 10.) Let the editor know what software you have used. Some journals use authors' disks for typesetting, and a few give precedence to such manuscripts in scheduling. Some specify acceptable software and require that you provide disks.

When the editor prefers to receive manuscripts electronically, send yours as an e-mail attachment. The e-mail message becomes your cover letter and should indicate the software used and the title of the file or files. Tables, figures, and notes are sometimes best transmitted as separate files. You can use the acknowledgment feature of your e-mail program to confirm the manuscript's safe arrival.

Refereeing

On refereed journals, experts review submissions; for nonrefereed journals, the judgment of the editor or the editorial staff suffices. Thus, editors of nonrefereed journals can make decisions faster, but publication in these journals does not offer the prestige or the assistance provided by the refereeing process. The notion that refereeing provides a service to a would-be contributor may be alien to the author busily collecting rejections or requests for revision. Nevertheless, it is a service. Referees can save an author from mistakes of fact, poor logic, ignorance of sources, and other embarrassments. Their purpose is not merely to screen out bad articles but also to recognize good ones and help move articles from the unacceptable category into the acceptable. Although you should not expect referees to correct minor details or rewrite bad prose, they will often give general advice on further sources or weaknesses in your argument whose correction would make your work publishable. Certainly not all criticism is constructive, but much of it is. As an academic writer, you are likely to wear the hats of both referee and author during your career. To perform both jobs well, you should try to keep in mind what it is like to be under the other hat.

Most articles are read first by an editor who determines whether they are appropriate for the journal and good enough to be sent to a referee. "Good enough" may mean sufficiently original and interesting, adequately researched and documented, clearly written, or all of these. Articles that survive this initial scrutiny are then sent to at least one referee, who is either a member of the editorial board or a specialist unaffiliated with the journal except as an occasional reviewer. Journal editors may ask referees specific questions about the article or ask them to fill out a form; some ask for a letter grade in addition to comments and recommendations. More often, however, the referee is asked merely whether the article should be published in the journal and why or why not. The major scientific and medical journals have a more elaborate refereeing process that may include review by a statistician or other technical experts in addition to review by outside referees.

Referees have a great responsibility, and no one who is unwilling to take the job seriously should agree to review an article. A referee must be competent in the field (and that includes being familiar with current research), able to judge other people's work objectively, willing to spend the time it takes to evaluate the article and make useful suggestions, and committed to doing all this under a deadline. As a contributor, you expect this of referees. When you yourself are asked to be a referee, make sure you meet your own standards.

Because most people who write articles also judge other authors' work, you may need some more advice about what to do when wearing the referee's hat. As you read an article, you will be asking yourself a number of questions: Is the topic worth investigating? Is the author's research sound? Have the relevant sources been tapped? Is the thesis clearly and convincingly argued? Does the evidence support the thesis? Is the article adequately documented? Is the writing clear and succinct? Did I learn anything from reading this? One question you should *not* ask yourself: Is this the way I would have written the article? The least fair, least useful reviews result from asking this question. One reason research is fun and exciting is that no two people approach a question in the same way. Perhaps you would have done it differently, and perhaps your way would have been better, but that is not the issue. You have been asked to evaluate an article as written, on its own terms. Do so.

Remember, too, that the manuscript you have been sent is a privileged communication. You must not cite it or use it in any way. You should not show it to others or discuss its contents. If you feel that a colleague or a graduate student might be a better referee, ask the editor's permission before passing the manuscript on. Communicate with the author only through the editor.

It is possible – and in some fields even probable – that a second journal will send an article to the same referee that the first journal used. If you are asked to referee an article that you have previously advised be rejected, you should behave in a civilized, ethical manner. It is not acceptable to blight anonymously and eternally another person's career. The solution least prejudicial to the author, yet helpful to the editor, is to decline without giving a reason and suggest another referee. There is an exception to this rule: an article that you felt was inappropriate for journal A but all right for journal B. It is of course reasonable to referee an article for journal B that you recommended for publication to journal A but that its editor nevertheless declined. (Do not be outraged if this happens. The journal editor or another referee may have disagreed, or perhaps the author declined to make changes required by the editor.)

Now, back to the author's hat. While one or more referees are reading your manuscript, what are you doing? Not sitting at home chewing your nails, I hope. You already have a second journal in mind for your article in case the first one rejects it. (In an article offering suggestions on journal writing, Richard Penaskovic recommends using the term *returned* rather than *rejected*. You, too, may find this comforting.) You are launched on a new project. But you have not forgotten about your article. On your calendar, about three months after the date you submitted your article, you have written a note reminding yourself to send the editor a polite note or e-mail:

"On 5 September I sent you my article on the Bermuda Triangle. When may I expect a response?" Mark a date three or four weeks ahead for another inquiry if you have not received an answer by then. If you still have no answer five months after your initial submission, telephone. Then, if the response is inadequate, write to the editor withdrawing your article from consideration (a letter is preferable to e-mail in this instance), and send it elsewhere. You need not wait for the physical return of your manuscript to do this. For articles in the sciences, or in any case where timely publication is vital because of the article's subject, this timetable should be speeded up considerably.

You've Got Mail

When a journal accepts your article, the editor may publish it as is or ask for revisions. If revisions are required, make sure you understand exactly what is wanted. For example, if the article is to be shortened, by how much? If you are to shorten the article, yet include additional material, how is this miracle to be accomplished? Find out when the revised manuscript is due. Make sure, too, that the article will definitely be published if you make the revisions. Sometimes an editor hedges, and you may not want to revise extensively to someone's specifications if the article may still be rejected despite your additional efforts. A "revise and resubmit" decision means that, after your revised article arrives, it will be sent out to referees again and may be rejected. At a minimum, seek the editor's assurance that if the article is to be re-reviewed, the same referees will be consulted. If you are not satisfied with the editor's answers, you might prefer to make only the revisions that are clearly necessary and then send it to another journal.

If you have quoted extensively from other people's work or if you are reprinting tables or illustrations from other sources, you must get written permission from the copyright holder.

Do this the minute the article is accepted. Chapter 10 provides information on acquiring such permission.

You may be asked to review a copy editor's work on your article, or you may merely receive proof to be read (see Chapter 10 for instructions). In either case, read carefully. When you receive an edited manuscript, you may still make changes and ask for clarification of editorial changes you do not like or understand. In proof, you must restrict yourself to changes that are absolutely necessary unless the editor permits more extensive alterations. Return manuscript and proofs on time.

Although it is certainly better to have an article accepted, you should not be disheartened by two or three rejections. The rejections in fact may have nothing to do with the quality of your work. That particular journal may have a backlog of articles in the same field, or the editor may feel that your article is – in the publisher's vague jargon – "not quite right for us." It may easily be "quite right" for another journal. If your article is returned, try to answer the referees' objections (if they are valid) and then send the article on to another journal. When articles are returned without comment, write a polite letter or e-mail to the editor asking whether you might see some of the referees' criticism. You may not get a response, but it can't hurt to ask. Also, be sure to incorporate any new information or citations that have appeared while your work was under consideration. Even if you do not change a word of the article, print out a fresh copy if the copy you sent to the first journal comes back dog eared and shopworn. There is no reason to make your second-choice journal aware of its status.

Some journal editors make a special effort to be helpful to authors who submit their work. They will send referees' comments and their own suggestions and sometimes even recommend other journals that might be more appropriate. Unfortunately, most editors do not have the time to do this. When you are given such generous help, write a note to thank the editor. Perhaps your next encounter with the journal will have a happier ending.

Revising Oral Presentations

Many journal articles begin as talks presented at professional meetings. Not every oral presentation can become an article. For example, a report on a work in progress is not ready for publication, and a paper that is part of a panel may not survive out of context. Many conference papers, however, can be revised for publication.

Before undertaking revision, check with the conference sponsors. Some groups publish proceedings of their meetings, and they may want to include your paper. Others ask that you give their own journal the right of first refusal. You should, of course, honor those expectations.

There are many differences between oral and written presentations. If you have ever sat through someone's reading of an article (after a banquet, in the worst case), you have some clues to the differences viewed from that angle. The talk was probably too long, too dense to follow easily, and devoid of enlivening spontaneous remarks. Reading an article instead of presenting a paper is a mistake. But submitting an unrevised talk to a journal is also a mistake. Shifting from the oral form to the written requires some work.

The most important consideration when revising a talk for publication is the audience for the article. The audience for your oral presentation may have been only a handful of specialists; perhaps it was a roomful of amateur enthusiasts. In any case, it is not the same group as the one your article will reach. Revise with your readers in mind and alter the level of detail, the background information, the tone, the tables and illustrations, and the documentation accordingly.

In some cases, revision will require substantive changes. It is always wise to incorporate changes based on your audience's reaction. Any doubts, misunderstandings, or questions your hearers expressed will occur to readers as well, and you should deal with those problems when you revise. If your talk was a brief summary of your work, you will probably want to flesh it out with examples and details when you prepare it for publication. The article may also offer opportunities to review background and earlier work, to discuss possible limitations or qualifications of your conclusions, and to expand on opportunities for further research. If, by contrast, your talk was discursive and chatty, you will have to tighten it up.

A speech generally contains references to the occasion of its presentation. In an article, an initial note can tell the reader where and when the material was first presented; references within the text should be eliminated. The obvious ones are easy to omit ("It is a pleasure to be here in Punxsutawney on Groundhog Day"), but be on the lookout for subtler references, such as those that refer to the nature of the audience, the interests of the group, or an earlier paper or other event at the conference. These, too, must be omitted or altered. Similarly, references to time should be adjusted.

If you have used visual aids, these must be adapted for publication. This is not simply a matter of preparing your slides in a different medium. Readers of journal articles have more time to look at tables or graphs and to relate them to the text. Speakers who have selected or compiled their tables somewhat hastily must make up for those lapses as they revise. Make sure that the table actually says what you have claimed, that it is accurate and succinct, and that you have documented the sources. If you have simply copied a table, graph, or drawing from someone else's work, you will have to get permission for publication. Also make sure that the illustrations are really needed. Speakers often use slides and overhead transparencies to liven things up and to keep the audience's attention. In the written incarnation, however, illustrations should be kept only if they are vital to the argument.

An article requires more rigorous documentation than a speech, which does not come with footnotes. In a speech you may get away with something like "As Lobachevsky has pointed out . . ." In an article you must add first name, article title, journal name, date, volume, and page number. You must also check to see that you have quoted accurately. Speakers occasionally indulge in such statements as "Someone once claimed that" or "At a conference I attended a few years ago, a speaker argued that . . ." Some of these quotations, I suspect, are fictional. In any case, they must be omitted or documented when revising for publication.

The tone of an article is generally more formal than that of a talk. You may wish to shift from the first or second person to the third, in addition to removing or formalizing jokes, anecdotes, and other casual features. You may have to find an appropriate punctuation mark or phrase to substitute for the raised eyebrow, hard stare, or eloquent gesture that you relied on when speaking.

When you are writing, you may want to provide more structure for your argument, and the medium of print allows you to use headings and subheadings. Some speakers display or circulate outlines of their talks, and these can be transformed into headings.

Although some speakers expend as much effort on an oral presentation as on a written one, they are the exceptions. Most academics regard such presentations as trial runs. Journal editors have learned this, and they do not look favorably on unrevised speeches. On the other hand, a speech that has been presented to a critical audience and then properly revised has received a sort of preliminary referee's report and can be a valuable contribution.

Money

Scholarly journals rarely pay contributors or referees. At most, authors receive a few extra copies of the journal or some offprints. Some journals – generally those in disciplines such as literature where amateurs frequently venture – even charge submission fees that you must pay before they will consider your article. These fees are meant to defray the cost of mailing articles to referees and to discourage frivolous submissions. In the physical and life sciences it is accepted practice to bill authors a "page charge" for publishing their work. This does not mean that enclosing a check with your manuscript guarantees publication. Rather, once the article is accepted on its merits, through the usual review procedure, you are informed that you must pay x dollars (anywhere from $10 to $100) per page. (In fact, some journals that impose page charges may waive them, but they generally limit the number of free articles per issue. This means that your article will probably be published, but not for quite a while.) Journals in the physical sciences have charged these fees since about 1930, and fees are common in the natural and medical sciences. Some journals in other fields are considering their adoption as well. Because there is a good deal of misunderstanding about them, they merit some discussion.

It costs money to publish a journal. Staff must be paid, as must typesetters and printers. Paper and ink cost money. The postal service charges for delivering mail. Journals are housed in buildings that charge rent, and they use utilities that charge fees. Computers and copying machines cost money. All of this must come from some combination of five main sources: subscriptions, advertising fees, page charges, offprint charges, and contributions from a university or a professional association (e.g., cash, release time for an editor, or subsidized rent). Subscriptions and advertising fees go hand in hand: The more subscriptions you have, the more advertising you can get and the more you can charge for it. This is why popular magazines can pay their contributors: More readers mean more advertisers paying more money, so even if the charge per subscription is not particularly high, the magazine is profitable. A specialized journal cannot do much to increase the number of subscribers (especially when academic hiring and library budgets are declining) or to increase subsidies from a university or an association. Although some journals could attract more advertising than they do, there are definite limits on what they can charge. Some journals, for ethical reasons, limit the sorts of advertising they accept or accept none at all; some have too few subscribers to appeal to advertisers. So that leaves only three sources of money to meet rising costs: subscription rates, offprint fees, and page charges. Page charges cover between a quarter and three-quarters of the costs of journals that impose them.[3] A journal without page charges must ask readers to pay higher subscription rates and must charge contributors more for offprints. If you belong to a professional organization that publishes a journal or if you subscribe to a journal, you are helping to underwrite publication. Paying a page charge is just another form of subsidy.

Some journals that do not ordinarily impose page charges may charge for publishing photographs (especially in color) or complex tables. These fees are meant not to discourage the use of such material but to cover the additional cost of preparing and reproducing it.

If page charges are common in your field, you should be prepared to pay them. Universities sometimes provide funds for this purpose. If your research is supported by grants from a federal agency or a private foundation, you should write publication costs into the proposal. (Federal agencies will pay page charges to nonprofit publishers.) These are legitimate costs, and your research is of little value if others cannot read about it.

Electronic Journals

When an author has prepared a manuscript electronically, and when the potential readers have computers, it may be possible to save a great deal of time and some money by skipping the paper-and-ink stage of publishing altogether. This is the rationale for electronic journals – journals that exist on paper only if the reader prints them out from a computer terminal. An electronic journal can work as an advanced electronic bulletin board, with writers sending their work directly to the members of a network. This is certainly quick, but it provides no quality control – no editor

---

[3] Marjorie Scal, "The Page Charge," *Scholarly Publishing* 3, no. 1 (October 1971): 64; National Science Foundation, "Federal Support of Scientific and Technical Publication" (1976), reprinted in *Publishing Research Quarterly* 14, 4 (Winter 1998/99): 9–23.

and no referees. The usefulness of such materials to readers is consequently limited, and the value of these publications to authors at the time of tenure decisions is doubtful. However, for speedy communication – perhaps with the goal of acquiring broad-based criticism and information – such journals are useful.

Alternatively, electronic journals can be edited and refereed. In this case, the electronic manuscript goes directly to an editor, via a modem or the Ethernet. The editor sends it electronically to referees, who return it electronically with comments. The editor can reject the manuscript electronically (there are no data on whether this is more or less traumatic than traditional rejection), send requests for revision, or accept the manuscript. When the manuscript is ready for publication, it is sent out to subscribers on a network, either free or for a subscription fee.

The main advantage of electronic journals is the saving of time that is possible because both mailing time and the production stages of typesetting, proofreading, printing, and binding are eliminated. Also, the whole idea of an "issue" can be dispensed with: articles can be published as they are accepted, without waiting for enough articles to accumulate to put together an issue or for the next month or quarter to come along. Because space is not a consideration, there is no such thing as a backlog of articles in a purely electronic journal. This makes electronic journals especially attractive in fields in which practitioners such as doctors need timely information on new treatments.

The costs of traditional production are also eliminated, but certain costs remain. In addition to evaluation, editing, and design, publishers of e-journals must pay people to maintain the site, format material, notify readers of new articles, maintain subscription lists, and market the publication. (Even if it is sent out free or posted free on the World Wide Web, you must let the market know it is there.) Nor is it possible to include advertising or charge for offprints. (One exception to the advertising limitation is journals whose websites are located on servers that permit advertising.)

When choosing an electronic journal, the same advice applies as for print journals: discuss the journal's reputation with colleagues, choose a refereed journal over one that is not refereed, and make sure you understand the editor's expectations.

Book Reviews

Most academics enjoy reviewing books in their fields. It is a way to make sure that you keep up with the current literature or, to put it bluntly, that you actually read the things you mean to read. You will not be paid for your review, but you will get a free book. Reviewing is also a relatively quick and painless way to publish. Although book reviews do not count with tenure committees nearly so much as refereed articles do, they are worth something. They also offer you a chance to express your opinion on subjects of interest to you.

If you want to review books for a journal, write to the editor or to the book review editor, if such a person is listed on the masthead. You should state your interest in reviewing, the fields in which you wish to review, and your qualifications. Many journals are eager to expand their stable of reviewers. Do not, however, submit unsolicited reviews. The editor has probably already assigned the book to another reviewer, and yours will not be published.

There are occasions when you should decline to review a book. If you have written a book that competes with the volume to be reviewed, you should decline. Arguably, you know the most about the subject, but you are unlikely to be objective. Nor should you review a book that you evaluated for the publisher or author before publication, or that you are reviewing for another publication. Close personal or professional ties to the author (especially if you are mentioned in the acknowledgments) are another reason to decline the assignment. If, after receiving a book for review, you feel that it is not worth reviewing, let the editor know. You may be asked to return the book so that it can be sent to another reviewer, or the editor may agree with you.

A book review is supposed to help readers decide whether to invest their time and money in a book. For that reason, the review should be primarily an evaluation, rather than a summary or abstract. Certainly, you will have to tell what the book is about, but that is only the beginning. Your evaluation can include comparisons with similar books when appropriate, but lengthy comparisons should be reserved for review essays whose purpose is to discuss several current works on a subject. Similarly, although your opinion of the book is the heart of the review, you should reserve lengthy expositions of your own ideas for essays of the sort found in *The New York Review of Books*. The reader of scholarly journals generally expects a review focused on the volume in question.

You may find it useful to think about how a book review compares with a referee's report. An obvious difference is that a review is signed. A more important difference is the audience. When you referee, you are writing for the editor, who must decide whether to publish, and for the author, to whom you are offering suggestions for revision. When you review, you are writing for potential readers who want to know what the book is about, whether it presents information and ideas not available elsewhere, and whether it is well written and accurate. When you referee a work in progress, your comments on grammar and usage or suggestions that another document be consulted are useful. When you review a bound book that will not be altered, your reader will be interested in minor flaws only if they are so numerous that they detract from the work. Nitpicking to demonstrate your own superior knowledge is neither necessary nor appreciated. Finally, a referee's report is informal, whereas a review is written for publication. You will want to take more pains with your writing, and you must adhere to the journal's specifications about length.

Refereeing and reviewing do share some important features. Both require that you meet deadlines. If you cannot review a book on time, decline. Both also require that you be objective. You should not attempt to review a book whose author you loathe or whose approach is an anathema. Your review would not be credible and would be a disservice to yourself and the reader. If you find that in all fairness you cannot recommend a book, say so matter of factly and explain why. As in refereeing, vitriol and ad hominem arguments are out of order.

Chapter 3

Revising a Dissertation

There are men that will make you books, and turn 'em loose
into the world, with as much dispatch as they would do a
dish of fritters.

Miguel de Cervantes

Many junior faculty members feeling pressure to publish see
their dissertations as the most likely place to start. At first
glance, this seems to be sound reasoning. After all, the
research is done, your work has been thoroughly reviewed
and approved by experts, and you are the world's leading
authority in the field. Why not just change the title page and
ship it off to a university press, sit back, and wait for the
inevitable acceptance, glowing reviews, and swift tenure and
promotion? Not so fast. Thirty or forty years ago it was often
possible to do that. University presses were expanding and
prospering, and it was not difficult for new Ph.D.'s to get their
dissertations published, perhaps with minor revisions. Today,
however, presses' resources are much more restricted, and the
publication of unrevised dissertations is rarely a wise use of
their time or money. Also, students in many fields are turning
to narrow topics that are intrinsically less worthy of publication as books. (Besides, dissertations are now easily available
on microfilm, in photocopy, or online.) On the whole, this
change has been for the better. Most unrevised dissertations
are not worth publishing, and the quality of scholarly books
has improved as presses have become more selective.

The Differences between a Thesis and a Book

Why isn't your thesis a book just waiting to be published? A thesis differs from a book in many of the same ways a graduate student differs from a faculty member. You may have noticed that as soon as you got your degree your status rose inexplicably. No longer an ignorant youth, excluded from department meetings and (if you were lucky) paid a salary in four digits, you are suddenly a scholar and colleague, with (if you are lucky) a five-digit salary. Instead of spending your life convincing people that you know something, you are in front of a classroom filled with students who think you know everything. Once the trembling candidate quaking before a committee, you are now sitting sternly and confidently on the other side of the table. The change seems to be instant and magical: yesterday a frog, today a prince or princess. In fact, of course, a lot of work went into the transformation.

A thesis is much like a graduate student: It has a limited purpose and a small audience; it is often insecure and defensive, justifying itself with excessive documentation; it is too narrowly focused; and it has not yet developed a style of its own. Henri Peyre lists "the most common faults" of the dissertation as "excessive length, repetitiousness, exasperating slowness of pace, monotonous synopses of novels, of plays, or of earlier critical works" and then says that dissertations are too defensive, dogmatic, and inaccessible, containing too many footnotes and too much jargon.[1] Among "the dissertation's deadly sins," Robert Plant Armstrong counts "amateurism, redundancy, trivialization, specializationalism, reductionism, and arrogance."[2]

Before you abandon your dissertation in shame and despair, please remember that not all dissertations are this bad. But before deciding whether yours is one that can be saved, you

[1] Henry Peyre, "Random Notes on a Misunderstanding," in *The Thesis and the Book*, ed. Eleanor Harman and Ian Montagnes (Toronto: University of Toronto Press, 1976), 13.
[2] Robert Plant Armstrong, "The Dissertation's Deadly Sins," in *The Thesis and the Book*, 28.

should understand the aspects of the dissertation that must be evaluated before any attempt at revision.

Purpose. The purpose of a dissertation is to demonstrate your ability to formulate a question or problem, do the research needed to resolve it, and write up the results. You must show that you have read and taken into account all the relevant work done by others, and you must anticipate objections that your committee may raise. This leads to the repetition, slowness, monotony, defensiveness, and other faults enumerated by Peyre and Armstrong. A book's purpose is to communicate ideas. There is no need to rehash common knowledge or attack straw men. There is a need to organize relevant material in a way that supports a coherent, original argument in an interesting, attractive manner.

Audience. A dissertation is directed to a committee whose job is to educate you. You can assume that they know your field, no matter how narrow. They must read your dissertation, no matter how boring it is, because that is what they are paid to do. People who read books, however, pay for the privilege. Your book must attract their attention and hold it. And their backgrounds are more varied than those of your committee members, so you must assume less depth of knowledge.

Author. Dissertations are written by students who must convince their readers that they have done their homework. Books are written by scholars whose readers assume they are intelligent, well educated, and well read. Even though you are the same person, your new status imposes new responsibilities and extends new privileges.

Scope. A thesis is narrowly focused. The subject is rarely set in a broader context, but lavish attention is paid to sources, methodology, and theory. A book must provide a context for its subject and should not rehearse the history of previous scholarship. It should stand on its own.

35

Tone and style. A thesis sounds like a demonstration of knowledge. Students tend to write in the passive voice, and the reader senses an enormous effort at objectivity. A dissertation is mannered and often full of jargon. Its superstructure shows through (Here's what I'm going to say. . . . Look! I'm saying it. . . . Here's what I just said). A book is a more open, honest communication. The degree of formality is a matter of choice, but the work should demonstrate that an individual human being with a personality did the thinking and writing.

Documentation. Because the dissertation is a display of acquired knowledge, it bulges with quotations and footnotes. The bibliography is meant to show that no conceivable source has been neglected. In a book, quotation is used appropriately and for limited purposes, footnoting is simplified and reduced, and all items in the bibliography are directly relevant.

As you decide what to do with your dissertation, keep these distinctions in mind. Perhaps you were fortunate enough to have an advisor who teaches students to write books instead of dissertations. If so, you can probably revise easily. But most people are not so lucky.

Deciding What to Do

You can do three things with a dissertation: Forget about it, turn it into a book, or extract one or more articles from it. In many cases, the wisest course is to put the thesis on the shelf and leave it there. Many dissertations are designed and executed as straightforward, single-purpose exercises. Once they have served their purpose, they have no further value. This is a hard fact to accept, particularly if the dissertation has cost you a lot of time, effort, and anguish. For that reason, almost everyone who has written about revising theses offers the same advice: Don't do anything with your dissertation right away. Set it aside for several months and go back to it only when you think you may be able to regard it more objectively.

Some writers figure that, instead of letting their work lie fallow in this waiting period, they should send it off to a publisher. Usually, the press of the university that granted the doctorate is approached; often the student's advisor sends a letter of endorsement. As a courtesy, the press will at least look at the manuscript and will perhaps send it to a reader. This is a terrible waste of the press's time and money and an unwarranted imposition. Probably not one dissertation in a hundred submitted this way is accepted. What's more, it is a mistake from the author's point of view. If you are like most people, when you reexamine your dissertation in a year's time you will be at least mildly embarrassed. You will see mistakes, gaps, and ill-chosen rhetoric. You will want to change things. If you have sent your thesis in its original form to a press, you will have alienated one prospective publisher unnecessarily. If the press has sent it to a reader, there will be at least one person at professional meetings whose eyes you will want to avoid – and you won't even know who it is. Do not submit your dissertation anywhere until you have let it rest for at least six months and then reread it. If your rereading discloses perfection, then send it off to a publisher.

One very common result of rereading one's dissertation is to relive all the agony that went into the original work. If you were one of those who suffered great pain in writing a thesis, it is probably best not to do anything with the dissertation. Ask yourself whether you can face it again, and if your honest answer is no or maybe, just let it go. You should also abandon the dissertation if you are simply tired of it. Revision is rarely quick or easy, and if the subject bores you and you are eager to get on with something else, do so. You will gain nothing from bringing an already stale mind to a mound of overworked material. Someday you may regain your interest, and that will be the time to return to the project. Another possibility is that your topic did not work out very well and proved to be barely adequate to sustain a dissertation. If so, it will not be enough for a book.

Another signal to leave the thesis unrevised is the feeling that you know it is not publishable but you don't know how to fix it. If you still cannot fix it after reading this chapter, set the dissertation aside for another year or two. Then, when you have done some other writing and have more confidence in your judgment, you may want to try again.

If rereading your dissertation revives your interest in the subject and does not cause nightmares, then you are ready to decide whether the work is worth revising. First, and most important, does your thesis have something new and important to say to a significant number of people? It may be buried in formalities and jargon, and it may be only a small part of the dissertation, but if there is something in there worth communicating, then revision is probably justified. As William C. Dowling says, "The genuine book is an elaboration of a single significant idea, and the warmed-over dissertation isn't."[3] If there is no such idea – if the originality amounts to mere refocusing or embroidery or technique – then reworking will waste your time. One test is to try to write a one-paragraph summary of the major idea in clear, ordinary, nonspecialist English. Do not discuss sources, data, or structure of argument. Just tell us what you have to say that we do not already know – and that we will find interesting. If you cannot do this, put the dissertation back on the shelf.

If there is an idea there, how much needs to be said about it – twenty pages or two hundred? In other words, do you have an article to write, or a book? Once the dissertation hardware is removed – the review of the literature, the excessive quotation, the chapter that turned out to be irrelevant but was left in to show that you tried – what will be left? Perhaps you have two or three ideas to express. If so, are they related logically so that they can be joined together in a book? Or do you have two or three articles to write? Another possibility is that the really important concept that came out of the dissertation was actually of minor significance in the thesis itself. When this is the case, you are really starting all over again.

[3] William C. Dowling, "Avoiding the Warmed-Over Dissertation," in *The Thesis and the Book*, 49.

The Thesis–Book Continuum

A number of excellent articles have been written on how to revise a dissertation. The most practical is the series by Olive Holmes that first appeared in *Scholarly Publishing* and was reprinted in *The Thesis and the Book*.[4] This chapter agrees generally with Holmes's advice. A more extreme view is taken by Dowling, who in the same volume advocates taking the single idea that emerges from your dissertation and starting all over. This process may well produce better books, but most authors prefer revision to complete rewriting. It is much more difficult to rethink the organization and structure of your work than it is simply to take out the pruning shears (and, where necessary, the hatchet) to reshape what you have.

There is no single moment during revision when your dissertation becomes a book. The two items are rather on a continuum (see Figure 1), and it is possible to stop at various places en route to "book" and declare your revision complete. The first step in using this idea is to place your dissertation accurately on the continuum. A typical dissertation will be at or near the left end of the scale in most respects. If you are a more sensitive writer and have had good advice, your thesis may show some features closer to the middle. If you are a very good writer who chose a broad, generally interesting topic and got very good advice, your dissertation may be very close to the right of the chart, although specific items like footnotes and bibliography may be all the way back at the left. See where your own work falls in respect to each item listed at the left of the figure.

Next you must decide where you want to end up. Do you want to achieve a first-rate book that would register all the way at the right of the scale? Do you want merely to disguise the dissertation's origins? Or do you want to create something in between? Then take a good look at what you must do to get from here to there.

---

4 Olive Holmes, "Thesis to Book: What to Get Rid Of" and "Thesis to Book: What to Do with What Is Left," in *The Thesis and the Book*, 52–85.

THESIS	Cosmetic cover-up	Limited remodeling	Complete overhaul	BOOK
Narrowly focused				Broadly focused
Minimal context				Substantial context
Impersonal, passive tone				Personal, direct tone
Mannered, discursive style; jargon	delete jargon	tighten language		Personal, easy style
Attracting reader immaterial	attract reader in introduction			Writing tells story
Visible superstructure		delete blatant transitions	rework to minimize structure	Organization: subtle to invisible
Extensive repetition	delete summaries	delete obvious repetition	delete borderline repetition	
Exhaustive literature review	delete least-relevant literature		delete borderline literature	

THESIS				BOOK
Explicit, detailed methodology	summarize methodology	include methodology in appendix	include methodology in preface	Methodology not included
Multiple headings	reduce number of headings			
Extensive quotations	reduce number of quotations	abridge quotations		
Multiple plot summaries	reduce number of plot summaries		include only vital plot summaries	
Multiple lists	delete nonessential lists	rework to include lists in text		
Multiple tables	delete nonessential tables	simplify tables		
Exhaustive footnotes	delete nonessential footnotes	convert to endnotes		
Exhaustive bibliography	delete nonessential citations			Selective bibliography

Figure 1. The thesis–book continuum

In two cases doing the minimum is easily justified. On the one hand, you may have a very well written thesis on an interesting topic, placed in a context that makes it accessible to a broader academic audience. Because it is a thesis, however, you have fitted it out with the appropriate trappings: excessive headings, quotations, footnotes, and lists; an exhaustive literature review and bibliography; and perhaps an overly visible outline. You can easily reduce or eliminate these elements and come up with a publishable manuscript. On the other hand, the value of your thesis may lie solely in its presentation of important new information. The audience will be small, but their need for what you have to say is great and possibly urgent. The publisher will decide whether to accept your manuscript almost entirely on the basis of its content, with only minimal expectations for literary merit. In this case, again, it makes sense to clean up the details and put your thesis in the mail. Both these examples, as different as they are, are candidates for piecemeal cosmetic cover-up. You will end up with a manuscript that has lots of crossing out and occasional changes that you can easily patch up on the computer.

When we move on to "limited remodeling," we are talking about some rewriting. Instead of merely removing jargon and academic clichés, you must tighten up your language, making it more precise, descriptive, and lively. You should define terms for a more general audience. You must remove blatant "directional signals" and repetition that had provided transitions and replace them with less obvious structural elements. In addition to removing redundant quotations, you must reduce those that remain and paraphrase where appropriate. The basic organization and argument will remain, but the length will be reduced and the writing will be more straightforward. You will, in a sense, go inside the writing instead of just fixing up the surface.

The changes described so far are reasonably self-contained and can be made without much rethinking. Structural changes, however, involve reshaping the dissertation. You must add the setting or context that will make your work accessible and attractive to people outside your immediate specialization, though not necessarily to the general reader. You must reorganize to avoid repetition and the need for traffic signs. And all this is in addition to the cosmetic and limited remodeling work already described. As in fixing up your house, even if you knock out walls and replaster, you still have to paint. Making structural changes is a qualitative jump from merely revising. You will not just be crossing out and making minor alterations; you will be rewriting whole sections and chapters. Although you will not be starting from scratch, you will have to look at your material in a fresh way, to imagine it in a new form. If you do not think you can do this, do a limited remodeling and call it quits.

The "complete overhaul" approaches Dowling's notion of extracting the significant idea from your dissertation and starting afresh. He tells you to rewrite completely, "realigning your original insights with your major point, getting rid of smothering documentation and digressive or irrelevant material, and (one hopes) gracefully subordinating the particular to the general."[5] The result of this labor, according to Dowling, is a rough draft. Clearly this course is not for everyone, but it is good advice if your topic is worth the effort, you feel up to making it, and you have enough time before you come up for tenure.

To summarize, if you think you should turn your dissertation into a book, let it sit for a while and then make an honest appraisal of its merits and your ability and desire to work on it. Decide how much you want to revise. Reread Strunk and White, *The Elements of Style,* before beginning. It will clear your head and keep your language clean. Review the section on writing well in Chapter 2 of this book. Read Chapter 4 on finding a publisher, both for inspiration and to get an early start, and sections in Chapter 10 on preparing a manuscript.

[5] Dowling, "Avoiding," 51.

Mining for Articles

If you find a number of significant ideas in your dissertation but conclude that they are best treated separately, then you should consider writing an article or two. Chapter 2 goes into the art of writing for journals in more detail, but a few points need to be made specifically about articles that begin in dissertations.

The first thing to consider is whether you really need to wait until the dissertation is complete before publishing anything from it. In the natural and physical sciences, many dissertation-related research projects generate brief journal articles while they are under way. Writers in the social sciences and humanities, too, should consider whether some of their work might be published while they are still working on the dissertation. Certainly, prospective employers are impressed by those who publish in graduate school. In addition, publication may put you in touch with people whose work will be helpful to you (although the journals outside the sciences are generally so slow that this is unlikely). In any event, if discrete parts of your research can be written up for journal publication, you should develop these as articles. Doing this will help you to see your work more clearly and should make your final writing of the dissertation easier. Having such articles published is unlikely to reduce the possibility of book publication, should you decide to try that when the dissertation is finished. In fact, an article in a well-read journal may attract the attention of a diligent book editor and bring you an invitation to submit your work.

What sorts of material are candidates for journal articles? Preliminary surveys, case studies, a methodological or technical innovation, new biographical material, a manuscript find, a bibliographic note – anything that stands on its own. You may even discover, in the end, that the material does not belong in the dissertation, yet it is new and interesting and can be written up with little extra effort. The amount of effort is important. After all, you are supposed to be writing your dissertation. Nevertheless, at this stage in your career, a publication – no matter how brief – is worth a week or two. If you have such material and cannot spare the time now, set it aside for the weeks when your committee is reading the dissertation or the summer before you take a job.

When the dissertation is finished, it can generate articles of a different sort. For example, your dissertation, once stripped of the literature review, methodology, excessive annotation, and the like, may boil down to a single interesting point that can be stated, illustrated, and proved in twenty or thirty pages. That is something to turn into an article. Unfortunately, you usually cannot just take the dissertation and hack it into shape. You should probably start writing from scratch.

It is also possible that, with minor revision, a chapter can be turned into an article. Case studies, biographical studies, textual studies, and the like are good candidates. Sometimes a bit of extra research is needed to round out the article.

Perhaps nothing in your dissertation can easily be transformed into a publishable article. You may still have material that could be the basis of some good new work that could be completed differently. Perhaps the case study you did of a short-lived dot-com startup was not earthshaking, but suppose you combined it with some other published studies and some theoretical work on high-tech startups. Alternatively, you could compare it with a similar but successful startup. Perhaps you unearthed some correspondence that was mostly irrelevant to the dissertation but interesting nevertheless. Sometimes a bit of statistical analysis that you did not include in the dissertation can be combined with published findings to show a relationship that is worth pointing out. In other words, do not regard the search for articles as a mere cut-and-paste effort. Look at the dissertation as a source of ideas as well as words.[6]

To return to the mining metaphor, however, be sure to recognize when the seam is exhausted. A dissertation was never meant to be the lode from which a lifetime's treasure is dug.

---

[6] For more ideas on inspiration for articles, see Richard Penaskovic, "Facing Up to the Publication Gun," *Scholarly Publishing* 16, no. 2 (January 1985): 136–40.

Chapter 4

Finding a Publisher for the Scholarly Book

It circulated for five years, through the halls of fifteen publishers, and finally ended up with Vanguard Press, which, as you can see, is rather deep into the alphabet.

Patrick Dennis, on *Auntie Mame*

Types of Book Publishers

Scholarly books are issued by five types of publishers: university presses, profit-making scholarly publishers, trade publishers, university centers and learned societies, and vanity presses. These publishers differ in their refereeing procedures, to some extent in the kinds of works they publish, in their approaches to marketing, and in the contractual arrangements they make with authors. Despite some overlap, they serve different purposes, and authors should understand the differences before deciding where to seek publication.

University Presses

University presses are the main outlet for book-length scholarly work. They are nonprofit publishers. Most university presses are self-supporting or have a small part of their costs underwritten by the sponsoring institutions and by occasional grants from private foundations or government agencies. Some have raised general endowments or endowments for books in certain fields. About one hundred university presses in the United States and Canada belong to the Association of American University Presses (AAUP); a few small university presses are not members of the AAUP.

A university press disseminates knowledge by publishing books and journals. In its search for the best in new scholarship, a press encourages research and writing. Some presses initiate scholarly projects such as reference books and new editions of the Bible or of classic literary and historical works. University presses also seek to extend the audience for scholarship by acquiring and promoting works that make current research accessible to a general, popular audience. In addition to traditional monographs, therefore, university presses may publish poetry, fiction, translations, children's books, anthologies, and cookbooks. Increasingly, they are publishing works of scholarship addressed to nonspecialists. Many university presses, especially those at public institutions, publish books on their state or region for both scholars and general readers. These may include works of history, literature, anthropology, botany, zoology, and political science.

University presses vary greatly in size: Some publish fewer than ten books a year, whereas others publish close to a thousand. Some specialize in a few academic fields, whereas others publish in nearly every subject.

Like any other part of a university, a press must carry out its noble aims in the less lofty realms of limited budgets, limited space, and limited staffs. A press has many publics to please: the university administration, sometimes the state legislature, the faculty, its authors, librarians, bookstore owners, and its readers. It is a complex organization that often seems mysterious to would-be authors. Because its purpose is to find, recruit, and publish the works of promising scholars, however, a press's staff is generally happy to meet with faculty to discuss how they work and what they are looking for. Although I will not go so far as to urge you to take an editor to lunch, I do suggest that you attend a press's open house, invite an editor to meet with your department's faculty and graduate students, and generally take advantage of the staff's expertise and interest. Even if you do not want to publish with your own university's press, or if it is not active in your discipline, the staff can be helpful and informative. They also welcome queries and invitations from nearby colleges and universities that do not have their own presses. Journal and book editors sometimes organize panels at academic meetings to provide information and exchange ideas.

Academics hold many misconceptions about university presses. The first is that because presses do not need to make a profit they do not concern themselves with the salability of a book. This is not true. Most university presses may run in the red on some titles, but they mustn't drown in the ink. They must be responsible publishers, using limited resources wisely, and they must on balance earn more than they spend. Because they cannot offset their inevitable losses on some titles with the profits from romance novels, celebrity biographies, and other "commercial properties," they must be very careful about how they use their funds. No university press will turn down a book simply because it will not be a bestseller, but costs and salability are always important considerations. The lifetime sale a university press expects of a given book may be as few as five hundred copies. However, every university press must publish some books that will sell considerably more than this. Many university press books could be published equally well by commercial (trade) houses, and on such titles presses must offer competitive terms to authors.

Another misconception is that a university press exists to publish books by the faculty of its own university. Although most presses encourage home faculty to submit manuscripts and do try to publish their work when it is worthwhile, all manuscripts are subject to the same reasonably impartial refereeing process. Works from outside the university are treated the same way as are those from within. Because this misconception is so widely held, many authors avoid their home presses for fear that colleagues will regard the publication of their manuscript as a favor. If you are publishing for prestige or promotion, and if your colleagues are unsophisticated about publishing, you may want to avoid your home press. In fact, you need not fear (or hope) that your home university press will accept your book just because you are on the faculty. Besides, publishing locally may guarantee more intense, prompt attention and enable you to be on the spot throughout the consideration and production of your book. Even if your home press does not publish in your field, its editors should be willing to give you advice on which presses do.

Another misconception about university presses is that they are stuffy, unimaginative, and uninterested in promoting their books. Some are stuffy, and some do not make much effort at promotion for many of their books. Most, however, are staffed by bright, innovative people who want their books to be bought and read. Again, you should consider your own interests. If a book is of limited salability, it will not help if the publisher emblazons the title on the flank of an elephant and parades it down Fifth Avenue. You should choose a publisher whose strength is in the area where you need the most help.

University presses generally pay royalties, though not always. The decision is based on expected sales and profitability. Some even offer advances, at least on an author's second book and on books that other publishers are competing for. No one, however, should count on making a lot of money from a scholarly monograph. (Chapter 11 illustrates the monetary return to an author and a publisher from a typical monograph.) Some university presses have begun to request subventions from authors. This controversial practice is discussed in Chapter 5.

The main difference between a university press and a commercial scholarly publisher (other than profitability) is the process used to select manuscripts. University presses use a rather elaborate system involving in-house reading, expert referees, and a faculty review board. This procedure has two main advantages for the author. First, you get expert opinions and the opportunity to revise your work, anticipating and avoiding adverse comments and reviews of the finished book. Second, it reassures colleagues, administrators, and search committees that your book is truly worthy of publication, having met the standards of impartial reviewers. The disadvantage is the amount of time it takes. A manuscript of average length will take from one to eight weeks for in-house review (depending on how busy the staff is, how thorough the review is, and whether cost estimates are required), a month or two per outside reader (usually at least two readers, occasionally as many as five), a week or two for recommendations to the faculty committee, and two weeks to two months waiting for the faculty committee to meet. Add in mailing time, and you're up to a minimum of three months. If a summer intervenes, you're up to a minimum of five or six months. And that allows no time for reviewers' tardiness. Occasionally review takes more than a year. Later in the chapter I suggest ways to minimize this period of agony.

University presses are also distinguished by greater emphasis on substantive editing and copyediting and (often) by higher standards of design and production (e.g., better paper and sturdier bindings).

The people who work at university presses are known by a number of titles. Each press has a director or president who has overall responsibility for the operations of the press, but from there down you will find little consistency in nomenclature. The person who goes out looking for books and evaluates incoming manuscripts may be an acquiring editor, a sponsoring editor, a senior editor, a humanities (or economics or biology) editor, or just plain editor. An editor in chief or editorial director may oversee the work of the acquiring editors and possibly the manuscript editors as well. Manuscript editors – who go over manuscripts line by line correcting spelling and grammatical errors, improving the flow of ideas, and suggesting other changes – are also called copyeditors, line editors, and sometimes editors, associate editors, or assistant editors. The senior copyeditor may be called the managing editor.

Outside the editorial department, production of your book will be handled by a designer and a production editor (who often coordinates freelance manuscript editing as well), production manager, production director, or production assistant. Marketing is headed by a manager or director, sometimes with assistants for advertising, direct mail, and promotion. A rights and permissions or subsidiary rights manager may be in charge of selling paperback, translation, serial, book club, and other rights. The business office employs numerous people, sometimes including the enticingly titled fulfillment manager, whose job is not to cater to authors' emotional well-being but to get the books out of the warehouse and into the hands of customers. Throughout this book I have tried to be as specific as possible when designating the person you should write or call on various matters. However, because presses are organized differently, this is very difficult. Generally, the acquiring editor is the person to regard as your connection with the rest of the staff, but in a small press, the manuscript editor may fill this function. As a result, I will sometimes refer simply to "the editor."

Commercial Scholarly Publishers

The commercial scholarly or "professional" publisher issues books for scholars in certain disciplines or for specific professional groups, such as practitioners in the behavioral, medical, physical, and life sciences, in business, or in engineering. One subgroup is sometimes referred to as "STM publishers," an abbreviation for scientific, technical, and medical. They often publish books in series. Academic Press, Jossey-Bass, Greenwood, and Addison-Wesley are good examples, as are some of the European publishers, such as Elsevier, Methuen, and Springer-Verlag. Many of these European publishers have editorial offices in the United States as well as in Europe. Commercial scholarly publishers compete with university presses for some books, so it is important to understand the differences between the two groups.

The selection processes of these publishers are similar to those of university presses, except they do not have faculty committees. Instead, individual editors and editorial committees make decisions based on referees' reports. Their decisions can therefore be made more quickly, although this is not always the case.

The quality of editing and production among commercial scholarly publishers varies greatly. Some expend a great deal of effort on editing, while some do only the most cursory correction of punctuation. Some routinely win industry prizes for design and production, while others add minimal design to disks supplied by the author. One complaint more frequently lodged against some commercial scholarly publishers than against university presses is that production time (the activities between the completion of the editing and the appearance of the book) is excessive. This may occur because a publisher has a small staff and a large backlog of manuscripts or because of cash-flow problems. (These problems are not unknown among university presses, either.) On the other hand, some small, new publishers have such technologically advanced equipment and flexible procedures that they can produce books in record time. Overall, there is greater variation in quality among for-profit publishers than among university presses. This means simply that authors must do more research and ask harder questions when selecting a for-profit publisher.

Scholarly and professional publishers market their books through well-developed mailing lists, exhibits at professional meetings, and advertisements in relevant journals. Their marketing focuses on well-defined target groups, not the general reader. The European publishers are experienced in selling books outside the United States and are therefore especially attractive to authors whose books have an overseas market, as many books in the sciences do. Because they need to make a profit and are not subsidized, they often price their books higher than a university press might, particularly highly specialized books and those for professionals used to paying high prices, such as doctors and lawyers. They are also more likely to pay royalties. Consider commercial scholarly and professional publishers if they are active in your discipline, particularly for books of a practical or an applied nature. Their efficiency in decision making may also be useful if you are facing publication pressures for tenure or promotion. However, you should make sure that the publisher is well regarded in your discipline and among the senior colleagues who will be making decisions about your future.

Trade Publishers

Academic authors may wish to work with a trade publisher. Trade publishers issue nonfiction that is of interest to the general public. Their name comes from the fact that they sell their books "through the trade," that is, in retail outlets. If you have written a book that will appeal to a broader audience than do most monographs, because of either its subject or your approach, you may want to try your luck with such a trade house. The relevant publishers are most of the giants (HarperCollins, Simon & Schuster, and so forth) as well as some independent trade houses (e.g., W. W. Norton or John Wiley).

Trade publishers' reviewing procedures vary, but their decisions are usually more prompt than those of university presses. However, an unsolicited manuscript will often get short shrift from a trade house. It simply may be added to a stack of manuscripts to be read when and if someone has the time. Unless you have an agent, can get some sort of introduction to an editor, or make sure through correspondence that your manuscript is expected and desired, submission to a trade publisher may not be a good idea.

Prestigious trade houses generally carry the same clout with college administrators as does a university press. The dean may be less impressed by run-of-the mill publishers. If you are worried about promotion or tenure, check out the attitudes of the powers that be.

In marketing, trade publishers are likely to place magazine advertisements, and they employ salespeople to visit bookstores and libraries. They view bookstores and online booksellers as the main outlets for their publications. They are good at reaching the general public but do not generally target specific audiences. Large university presses with experience in marketing general interest or professional books are just as effective at marketing such books as are the trade houses.

Smaller university presses generally do not do as well, because they lack the experience, the contacts, and the budget. However, if a smaller press views your book as a potential best-seller (on a university press scale), it may go all out and make an exceptional marketing effort. This is particularly true for books with great local or regional sales potential.

Trade publishers pay royalties and sometimes offer cash advances. An "advance against royalties" is simply payment to the author of a specified amount that the publisher subsequently deducts from royalties. It is not money in addition to royalties. Only a handful of academic authors receive six-figure advances, but even a small advance may help defray research expenses. The amount depends on what the publisher expects the book to earn, and the timing will depend on the author's reputation and how badly the publisher wants the book. An established author with a salable idea may get an advance or a partial advance on the basis of an outline and a sample chapter. More commonly, the advance is paid on delivery of the completed manuscript. If you get an advance for an incomplete manuscript and do not finish the job (or do not finish it to the publisher's satisfaction), the publisher may ask you to return the advance, as your contract will state. In fact, however, publishers usually insist on this only if the amount is large, but it is unwise to count on their sympathy. Should the publisher misjudge your book's marketability and not sell enough copies to pay off your advance, that is the publisher's problem; you cannot be asked to return the advance for that reason.

You should approach a general trade publisher only if you honestly believe that your work is of interest to those outside academe. Otherwise, you are wasting both your time and the publisher's. Chapter 9 discusses trade books in more detail.

University Centers and Learned Societies

Often, university-affiliated institutes and centers publish books in their special fields, although sometimes their publishing is limited to research they have sponsored. This is a good way to publish your book for a small, specialized audience. The production varies in elaborateness from a photocopied typescript in a spiral binding to paperbacks typeset with a laser printer to regular typeset, casebound, jacketed books. Some series are refereed; others are not. Some of these groups have distribution arrangements with university presses. Some pay royalties. You should not neglect these organizations, particularly for specialized works. The most reputable ones will impress a dean as much as a university press will.

To get information about a center or institute, ask about its publishing program, refereeing procedures, and recent publications. The best way to evaluate a university center series is to find out how colleagues in your field regard it. Are the books reviewed in the best journals? Does the series have a few well-known authors? Just ask around.

Similarly, some learned societies, museums, libraries, and state historical societies publish monograph series that are suitable for a manuscript that will sell too few copies to interest a university press. These are all respectable, and many are extremely prestigious. Some publish books for general readers that sell very well and receive national attention. They range in scope from large international scientific organizations to local historical societies. Go to the library or the organization's website to see what sorts of things they are doing and the kinds of books they are interested in.

Vanity Presses, Self-publishing, and Cooperatives

Vanity presses, sometimes called subsidy publishers, charge authors money to publish their books. If the author is willing to pay, they are willing to publish. No editorial or expert judgment enters the picture. For this reason, publication by a vanity press carries no prestige and no clout with tenure committees. Nor does it bring riches, because you are paying all the production costs plus a profit to the publisher. Your book will not be reviewed in reputable publications. If you just want to see your work printed and bound and can afford to pay handsomely for it, there's no harm done. But there's no benefit, either.

How do you spot a vanity press? Anyone who advertises, "Writers! Publish your book in no time flat!!!" is a vanity publisher, and vanity presses are not listed in *Literary Market Place*, the annual directory of publishing houses and other literary services. If you do not detect the nature of the press earlier, it will certainly be clear in the contract.

Some publishers sit on the border between genuine scholarly publishing and vanity publishing. They claim to offer peer review, but in fact their review procedures are nominal and their editorial committees are rubber stamps. They require author subventions on virtually every title they publish. If you are in doubt about a publisher, either steer clear or ask hard questions. For example, what percentage of the manuscripts submitted to them do they publish? Will you receive referees' reports? On what financial assumptions are subventions based (see Chapter 5)? Also ask your department chair and dean whether publication by that press will count in your favor.

Self-publishing and publishing cooperatives are cheaper than vanity presses, but like vanity presses they offer no prestige and provide no independent review of the quality of your work. They are designed for people who are convinced they have written a best-seller and do not want to cut a publisher in on the profits. (In all fairness, a few have proved right on this score and have made a lot of money.) Again, in the unlikely case that you simply want your work in type and bound, these options will do just fine. Chapters 6 and 10 offer advice on the mechanics of self-publishing.

What about self-publishing on the Web? The same advantages and disadvantages apply: It is cheap and quick, but there is no review of the quality of your work and no prestige attached to the publication. Publishing on the Web is likely to attract more personal responses to your work than traditional publication. Whether this is good or bad depends on whom the responses come from. And, as many teaching faculty have learned, publication on the Web seems to invite plagiarism, so that your work may turn up in student papers, out of context and without attribution, much more often than it would have if published on paper. Organized publishing on the Web seems to work better and is discussed in Chapter 12.

Choosing a Publisher

The most important issue in choosing a publisher is whether the press publishes in your field. No matter how good your philosophy manuscript is, a press that has not published philosophy for a decade is a bad bet. Make a list of ten or twenty recent books in your field and look up the publishers. Also look through *Literary Market Place* and the *Directory* of the Association of American University Presses. If you have written an economics book, then a publisher that produces a series in economics or that lists a staff member whose title is "economics editor" is a likely prospect. The AAUP *Directory* includes a chart that lists subjects and the presses active in them. Talk to publishers' representatives at academic meetings and conventions. They will not have time then to look at a manuscript, but they can let you know whether the press is likely to be interested. Look at publishers' catalogues and check their websites. See which publishing houses are advertising in the journals you read, and evaluate the quality of their recent selections. Then compile a list of a dozen likely publishers from those who are currently active in your subject.

The next task – and it is a very important one – is to compose a letter and supporting documents to send to prospective publishers (this is sometimes called a prospectus). The letter, a page or two long, should provide a brief summary of your manuscript, the audiences to whom you expect it to appeal, and what is unique, important, and exciting about it. It should be written for an intelligent, critical, well-read lay reader (that's what a publisher is). This is a work of salesmanship and advocacy; the goal is to convince the editor to ask to see your manuscript. It should be honest and straightforward, but this is not the occasion to express lingering doubts or deep-seated misgivings. If a well-known scholar in your field, one of the press's authors, or an expert at the press's sponsoring university knows the manuscript, suggest that the press consult the scholar. *Spare no effort in writing this letter.* If it is muddled, boring, semiliterate, or just thrown together, the publisher may not even look at your manuscript, let alone publish it.

In addition to the letter, you should send the table of contents, lists (or just numbers) of tables and illustrations, a brief summary or narrative outline (sometimes the introduction will serve), a sample chapter, and a curriculum vitae if yours is impressive. The curriculum vitae is optional; skip it if you are unpublished and unknown. If you do not include it, however, use your letter to provide vital information such as where you did your graduate work. Do not send more than this unless you are asked.

Send the letter and documentation to the publishers on your list. In a field such as history, you may have a dozen prospects; in the sciences, perhaps half a dozen. Address your materials to a person, not a title. Get the appropriate name from a current directory or the website – either the director or the acquisitions (or executive) editor in your field. If your book would be part of a series, and if you know the series editor, you can send the prospectus directly to that person rather than to a member of the press's staff. Personalize each letter and print it out; never send a form letter. (Curricula vitae, tables of contents, and so forth can be photocopies.) You want to show that you would be a model author, so write carefully, type neatly, and proofread thoroughly.

It is not legitimate to submit a complete manuscript to more than one publisher at a time (unless both presses are aware of the dual submission and agree to it), but it is perfectly all right to solicit interest from several presses simultaneously. At this stage, presses are generally not investing in readers' reports, and they do not expect exclusive consideration.

Letters of introduction or endorsement can be useful when trying to interest publishers in your work. If a scholar who has published with the press or who is well known in your field writes such a letter, the acquiring editor will pay attention. For such a letter to be useful, however, the writer must be both familiar with your manuscript and able to endorse it sincerely. You will do more harm than good by forwarding a vague letter saying only that you are an awfully nice person who has undoubtedly done a good job.

Once you have gotten responses indicating interest in your manuscript, you need to decide where to send it first. You can judge publishers by the quality of what they publish and how well they market their products, so look closely at recent books they have issued. Are they well designed and readable? Are they well manufactured? Are they books that you would like to see on a shelf next to yours? Have you received mailings or seen advertisements for their books?

Ask people who have published with various presses about their experiences. Was the refereeing handled promptly and fairly? Did editing begin soon after acceptance? Were they pleased with the quality of the editing? Would they submit their next manuscript to the same publisher or go elsewhere? Ask more than one author per press, because authors and experiences vary. Weight the responses according to your needs. For example, if you know you are a careless writer, you want a publisher who will take the time to do a thorough job of copyediting.

Another consideration may be the press's ability to market your book abroad. Some scientific and technical books can be sold in considerable quantities in Europe and Asia without being translated. A study of German history or society may be a good candidate for translation into German. If your book has such prospects, be sure to select a press that has the ability to promote your book effectively in the relevant markets. Ask the acquiring editor how the press would handle this opportunity. In such cases, international commercial publishers may have a clear advantage.

After considering these factors, list the interested presses in the order of your preference and send your manuscript to the first one on the list. Ask the acquiring editor whether the press would like two copies of the manuscript. (This permits simultaneous review by either two referees or a referee and an in-house editor.) Do not tell the other publishers that you are sending it elsewhere first; knowing that a rival rejected your manuscript may color their decision.

Agents and Editorial Consultants

Academic writers often wonder whether literary agents can help place their manuscripts. Usually the answer is no. Literary agents receive a fee of 10 or 15 percent of the author's royalties. Because the royalties on most scholarly monographs barely keep their authors in toner cartridges, there is little reason for an agent to take them on. Textbook companies do not usually deal with agents either. The only time an agent is likely to be interested and useful is when you have written a trade book, one for a general audience that should be published by a commercial house. An agent who agrees with your assessment of the manuscript's potential may accept you as a client, particularly if you have published other books, and having an agent will certainly help you persuade trade houses to look at the manuscript. Chapter 9 provides more information about literary agents.

Editorial consultants, sometimes called author's editors, work directly with authors rather than exclusively for publishers. Some institutions, particularly hospitals and research institutes, employ such editors to work with staff authors. Most author's editors, though, are freelancers. They offer services ranging from manuscript evaluation (usually for a fixed fee) to copyediting (usually at an hourly rate). They can be helpful to first-time authors, revisers of dissertations, writers for whom English is a second language, or authors of manuscripts that present unusual problems. They can also help when a manuscript has been turned down two or three times and the author is unsure about how to revise. However, they vary greatly in their qualifications and experience. Many people who have never worked for a publisher and who in fact

60

have little editorial experience of any kind put themselves forward as editors. Should you decide to seek the help of an independent editor, find someone who has had at least three years of editorial experience with a university press (on staff or as a freelance editor) and who has worked in your field. There are many such people. Ask an editor at a nearby university press to recommend someone if you need help and be willing to pay for the author's editor's services. You should be aware, too, that your publisher will still copyedit your manuscript, even if your own editor has done an excellent job.

Sometimes publishers will accept a manuscript contingent on the author's hiring an author's editor to revise it. Presses do this when they believe that a manuscript's content is valuable but that the writing and organization need more editorial work than they are willing to contribute. This may be costly, but if it is the only way of securing acceptance it will be worth the expense. Ask the publisher to suggest two or three editors and call each one. Ask how soon they could get to your manuscript and what their fees are. (They will not be able to give you a firm estimate of total cost without seeing the manuscript.) Hire the one with whom you feel most comfortable. Make sure the publisher sends your editor the referees' reports and in-house editorial evaluations, as well as the name of an editor at the press to consult during the work.

Submitting the Manuscript

Before submitting your manuscript to a publisher, you must get it into the proper physical form. Chapter 10 explains the correct preparation of manuscripts. When you do submit your manuscript, you need to give the publisher some important information. First, you should explain that others have expressed interest in the manuscript and that you are therefore hoping for a prompt response. It never hurts to let them know they have competition. Second, if you want to suggest possible readers or warn them away from readers you expect would be hostile, now is the time. You should be honest about this. Do not recommend your dissertation advisor, best friend, or sister-in-law. Do recommend the best-qualified people in the field, particularly if they are known to be fair and open-minded. Publishers may not use your suggestions, but if the same names come up when they ask others, they will. Give complete names, current addresses, phone numbers, and e-mail addresses. Valid reasons for asking that they not use specific readers include personal animosity, professional rivalry, or ideological disagreements. Third, if there is anything peculiar about the manuscript that may raise eyebrows, mention and explain it. This shows that you are aware of the issue and prevents it from becoming a surprise stumbling block. Such oddities might range from an unusual notation system through the use of nonstandard editions to your denial of the law of gravity. Finally, if the publisher has sent forms to be filled out or has requested information, fill out the forms or answer the questions. Close the letter with a request that they let you know when you may expect a decision.

Keep at least one copy of the manuscript for yourself, even if you have it on disk and on your hard drive. Never send the only copy of a manuscript anywhere. Publishers are not responsible for things getting lost in the mail, and postal insurance will at most cover photocopying. Send the manuscript first class and certified or by a commercial delivery service. Certification makes a package easier to trace. Wrap the manuscript carefully and seal it well in a sturdy box or a padded book-mailing bag.

Refereeing

University presses and other scholarly publishers base their publishing decisions largely on the opinions of consulting scholars, and trade houses often consult outside experts. Although the following discussion refers mainly to university presses, it applies as well to other publishers.

When a publisher receives a manuscript, an editor reads it to see whether it seems suitable for the press, to judge the quality of the writing and the amount of editing likely to be required, and to decide what sort of expert reader is needed. A manuscript may be rejected on the basis of this reading, usually because it will not fit into the press's publishing program. (The submission of a prospectus, recommended earlier, may enable the editor to make this decision before seeing the whole manuscript, thus saving you some time and pain.) A manuscript that requires more extensive editing than the press is prepared to do may also receive an early rejection. Some presses work up a financial analysis of the book. They estimate production costs and likely sales and see what the likely investment and return will be. Other presses wait until they have made a tentative or firm positive decision before doing this analysis. A financial analysis can result in rejection, particularly if your book is full of tables or illustrations and is likely to have very limited sales. That is one reason to alert the publisher to these features – and to your willingness to reduce the number of tables – in your initial letter of inquiry.

If the manuscript survives the in-house reading and financial analysis, it is sent to a specialist in the field, known as a reader or referee. The selection of the first referee often determines the press's final decision: A convincing, well-stated argument for rejection usually carries the day. A positive review will generally lead to a second reading. (Some presses will ask for two copies of your manuscript so that they can send it to two readers at once.) If the readers disagree, the press will either seek a third opinion (sometimes sending along the two conflicting reports) or else resolve the matter by making its own evaluation of the two reports. Excessive, undocumented praise or condemnation is suspect. A publisher wants a careful, rational reading rather than a gut reaction.

Publishers often ask readers to fill out questionnaires. Figure 2 is a list of questions often found on such forms. If you can be sufficiently detached, try to give the answers you would expect from a reader of your manuscript. This may help you to anticipate criticism and revise your work accordingly.

1 Originality and value: Is the manuscript a contribution to the field? Is it original? Is it important? Did you learn something from reading it?

2 Scholarship: Is the scholarship sound? Was the research well planned? Was it well executed? Have any major sources been neglected? Is the documentation adequate? Are the notes and bibliography in an appropriate, usable format? Is the information the manuscript provides, to the best of your knowledge, accurate?

3 Purpose: What is the purpose of the book? How well does the author accomplish this purpose?

4 Market: Is this work vital to specialists in the field? Does it have any value as a textbook? Will it be of interest to readers outside the immediate field?

5 Competing works: Are there any other books published on this subject? How does this work compare with them? What does it add to their coverage of the subject?

6 Style: Is the manuscript clearly written and readable? Is the length appropriate? Did you find the style appealing?

7 Organization: Is the book well organized? Is there any repetition? Is the argument easy to follow?

8 Special features: If the manuscript contains tables, figures, or other illustrations, are they adequate? Are they necessary? Are they easy to understand?

9 Do you have any suggestions for improving the manuscript?

10 Do you recommend that the manuscript be published?

Figure 2. Typical questions for manuscript readers.

Whether your work is accepted or rejected, you can expect to get at least excerpts or paraphrases from the readers' reports. You will not be told the name of the reader unless the report was positive and the reader has given permission. Nor should you insist on getting the entire report. Contrary to popular opinion, editors are basically kindhearted people. If criticism seems excessively harsh, undiplomatic, or irrelevant, they may withhold it. They will usually send anything they think may be helpful to you. If you do not understand a comment, feel free to ask for clarification.

Sometimes an editor will send referees' negative comments and ask the author to respond. This is generally a signal that the press remains interested in your work but is reluctant to forward the recommendation to the editorial committee until it can reassure them about the reviewers' misgivings. They are giving you an opportunity to clarify misunderstandings and correct errors. It is also an opportunity to point out, diplomatically, where the reviewer is wrong and explain why. You should frame a very careful response, because the tone of your letter is as important as the content. You should convey understanding of the issues raised, confidence in your own judgment, and willingness to make changes where appropriate. Although you may think the reader is an ill-informed dullard, you must take all comments seriously and not display your impatience (no matter how well justified it may be). If you are able to remove the doubts raised by the referee, your manuscript will probably be accepted.

Please note that rarely, if ever, does it do any good to protest a rejection. Read the comments as calmly and objectively as possible, make any changes you think are appropriate, and send the manuscript off to the next publisher on your list. Rejections are never heartening, but they can be useful if you get good advice. You should not be unduly discouraged until the number of rejections hits two digits. Think of rejections as criticism or advice and do not take them personally. It is hard to detach yourself from something to which you have devoted so much time, but make the effort. You can learn from the experience if you view it objectively. And always remember that few books are published by the first or second publisher that looks at them; one publisher's meat is another's poison.

Getting a Prompt Answer

Whether your work is going to be rejected or accepted, you want a prompt decision. Screening prospective publishers to make sure they are active in your field, sending out prospectuses, and carefully choosing where to submit first will help prevent time-consuming, unnecessary rejections. Once you have submitted your manuscript to a publisher, the best way to prevent delays is to speak up. If you have not heard from a press within three months, write a polite letter or e-mail asking when you may expect a decision. If your letter is not answered within two weeks, write again or call. You may be told, "We expect to reach a decision by June 15." When June 20 arrives with no word, write or call again. Keep after them. Do not be obnoxious, just firm. A polite letter or moderately worded phone call will do. But do not be afraid to be persistent. No publisher will reject your manuscript just because you are assertive. Threats, nagging, and tears, however, are counterproductive.

Should things get out of hand – your letters go unanswered, your phone calls are not returned, and months slip by – take firm action. Set a date by which you expect a response and inform the publisher. If you do not hear by then, write a letter withdrawing the manuscript from consideration and send it elsewhere. Send postage and ask that the manuscript be returned. If you like, you can write a letter of complaint to the president of the university. This will not get your manuscript accepted (and by now you probably don't want to work with that press anyway), but it will get a response and may prevent future abuse of authors.

Authors have been known to submit a manuscript, hear nothing for a year, and then meekly accept a form rejection letter. Don't do it! Be reasonable in your demands, but expect responsive, responsible behavior in return.

Revisions

A publisher may accept your manuscript but ask that you make certain revisions. Sometimes you will not get a contract until the revisions are made. If you do get a contract, it will have a clause about the acceptability of the final manuscript. Make sure that you and the acquiring editor agree on precisely what revisions are required. "Please shorten the manuscript" is inadequate; get the number of pages to be cut, or a percentage, and specific suggestions for cutting. "Fix up your notation system" requires elaboration: Exactly how should the notes be done? What style guide should you follow? "Clean up the tables" should be accompanied by a sample of the proper format. If you are asked to revise according to the suggestions of a referee, make a list of the expected changes as you understand them and ask your editor to confirm its accuracy and completeness. This is especially important if acceptance of the manuscript is contingent on revision, but it is worth doing even if the changes are merely suggested. Agree in writing on a realistic date for completion of the revisions.

You may find some of the requested revisions to be unacceptable. You may feel that they threaten the integrity of your work, that they are ill advised or irresponsible. If so, explain your objections. Both your needs and the publisher's can probably be accommodated. If not, you may have to find another publisher. The only guideline here is to make sure that the fuss you raise is commensurate with the importance of the issue. It is not worth going to the mat over footnote style or whether the book will have five illustrations or eight. Do insist that your ideas and argument remain intact.

If your publisher has not asked for revisions, but you feel some are needed, discuss this with the acquiring editor. Explain what changes you have in mind and how long it will take you to make them. The manuscript editor will want to postpone work until your changes are complete.

Chapter 5

Working with Your Publisher

I have dealt with a good many publishers, and while I have found some few of them arrogant, discourteous, oppressive, and generally abominable in both personal and business intercourse, I desire to record my testimony that as a class they are courteous and honorable gentlemen; fair and liberal in views, intentions, and actions, and pleasant and intelligent in mind and intercourse.

Frederick B. Perkins

When a publisher accepts your book, you are beginning a relationship that will last for years. Both of you will be happier if you understand clearly what the publisher expects and what you can reasonably expect of the publisher. The basic responsibilities of both author and publisher are set out in the publishing contract, and you must read and understand that document. You should also know how to work with the press's staff throughout the various stages of editing and production. Finally, you should think about how you can help the publisher promote your book.

The Contract

You will receive a contract when a publisher decides to publish your book. Most publishers send two copies, both signed, with the request that you sign and return one copy. Others will send a draft contract for your review. Even in the former case, you should never sign a contract until you have read and understood it. Nor, in the former case, should you conclude, as many authors do, that the contract is nonnegotiable, that you must simply take it or leave it. Within limits, contract provisions can be altered, and you should not hesitate to discuss your concerns with the publisher. This is now easier than it once was, because contracts are often written in plain English rather than in legal jargon. They are less mysterious, and it is easier to see how their provisions affect you.

This section explains what you can expect from a contract with a publisher. Although it will help you to interpret the terms of a contract offered to you, it is not meant as a substitute for a lawyer's advice. If your book has unusual complications, if it has movie or TV possibilities, or if you are simply uneasy about the whole process, find a lawyer who specializes in the law of intellectual property (copyright and patents) or communications law. Your state bar association or a law school faculty member can provide a referral. The sections that follow describe the main elements of a publishing contract and some typical provisions. Publishing contracts, of course, may vary in format and organization; see *One Book/Five Ways*, listed in the bibliography, for examples.

Timing

A publisher may offer you a contract at any time from receipt of your prospectus to acceptance of the finished, revised manuscript. A first-time author is unlikely to be offered a contract for a mere prospectus, although this does happen occasionally. Established authors may get contracts on the basis of a prospectus alone, although publishers usually want to see a chapter or two. As scholarly publishers have become more aggressive and competitive in acquiring books, the advance contract has become more common.

Publishers feel safe in offering contracts for unwritten books because all publishing contracts contain an escape clause. They usually say something like "The author agrees to deliver to the publisher a manuscript acceptable in form, style, and content." In other words, even though you have a contract, your manuscript is still subject to internal editorial review, review by expert referees, and – in the case of a university press – approval by the press's faculty board. This clause is very broad and, as a result, has been the subject of litigation between trade publishers and authors. It is not a license for publishers to change their minds arbitrarily but a way for them to ensure that the product they ultimately acquire is of the quality they expected when they made the offer. Imagine the publisher as someone who has bought a house on the basis of an architect's plans. A buyer who approves plans for a house with four bedrooms, three baths, and 3,000 square feet of livable space will not happily pay for and take possession of one with three bedrooms, one bath, and 2,000 square feet. This clause allows the publisher to demand revisions, additions, excisions, and so forth. If such clauses did not exist, it is unlikely that any but best-selling authors would ever receive contracts for unfinished books.

A contract for an unfinished book – just like a contract for a finished one – binds the author to sending the completed manuscript to that publisher and bars negotiations with other publishers. In that sense, it is unequal: The author has no escape clause. However, an advance contract does offer certain advantages for the author. It permits early and continuing collaboration, so that you get an editor's advice as you are writing, perhaps avoiding massive revision. It may include a cash advance, which always comes in handy. It may be helpful in securing tenure, promotion, or research grants. By relieving you of the worry of finding a publisher, it may enable you to work better. As a practical consideration, an advance contract reached at an early stage may make it easier to produce the book from your electronic files. Finally, although the contract does have an escape clause, it is an expression of the publisher's commitment to your book. Some university presses do not offer advance contracts without approval from their faculty boards; clearly such a contract is a serious undertaking. Others make the offer more casually.

In either case, however, I believe that publishers put more effort into helping an author revise a manuscript that is not quite satisfactory if it is under contract than they do if they are seeing it for the first time.

Advance contracts do carry some disadvantages. The publisher you would most like to work with may not offer a contract whereas another does. Then you will have to accept the security of your second choice if you want a contract in hand. Contracts always specify a delivery date, and if you do not manage deadlines well, this can be a source of unwanted pressure and anxiety. Publishers are almost always willing to allow extra time, but contracts are sometimes canceled when a manuscript is long overdue. (This is particularly true of books that are marketable because of timeliness, such as those to be published in connection with a centennial or other commemorative event.) Contracts also generally specify maximum or minimum length, as well as a maximum number of tables, illustrations, or maps. If you have not yet started the book, or are not very far along, it may be difficult to evaluate the reasonableness of these limits. Again, no publisher will back out of a contract because a manuscript has one extra table, but if you promise a 300-page manuscript and deliver 700 pages, you may be in trouble.

The best time to sign a contract is when you know with a fair degree of certainty both what the book is going to be like and when you can finish it – and when the contract is offered by a publisher you think you will be happy with. Be wary of offers from presses that you know little about and that have seen little of your work. The possibilities of misunderstanding, conflict, and disappointment are too great.

Purpose

The purpose of a publishing contract is to transfer some of your rights as an author to the publisher in exchange for publication and, generally, payment. When you write a book you own it, just as you own any other sort of property. And what you own is not merely the manuscript as a physical object (which, indeed, you can sell or give away separately) but the right to copy it, distribute it, translate it, film it – to exploit it in a great variety of ways. As an individual, you are not in a very good position to take advantage of your book's potential, so you reach an agreement with a publisher to develop it.

Your rights to the book will last seventy years past your death, according to current U.S. copyright law, a period during which your publisher may also become defunct or possibly be reincarnated as a subsidiary of a video game and fast food conglomerate. A well-drawn contract will protect your interests, and those of your heirs, far into the future, when no person now living will be around to recall what happened.

A contract, even when written in the stuffiest legal prose, is a living document. Before it is signed, it is the subject of negotiation, of give and take, of bargaining. After the contract is signed its full possibilities come to life. What looked like a boilerplate clause about translation rights comes to life when a French publisher wants to issue a French edition. Perhaps the provision for a paperback edition that you ignored as unlikely suddenly becomes crucial ten years later when your book unpredictably becomes a standard text in undergraduate courses. The provisions for electronic rights become reality when a chapter of your book is included in a CD-ROM or your publisher issues it as an e-book. A contract is designed to provide for all contingencies, no matter how remote. As you read it, make sure you understand what each clause means and what it implies for possible future events.

To make sure that you and the publisher work together amicably and efficiently throughout the book's publication and subsequent life, the contract spells out the rights and responsibilities of both publisher and author. It provides remedies for each party should the other fail to meet some requirement. The purpose is not to enable the publisher to steal the profits, make you do all the work, or weasel out at the last minute. Nor should the contract allow you to receive royalties when the publisher is losing vast sums on your book, to avoid doing jobs that are best done by the author, or to run off to another publisher in the middle of production.

To some extent, as noted, the terms of a contract are negotiable. Negotiations should be undertaken in a calm and objective frame of mind. Avoid paranoia. Explain why you want to change something and be prepared to offer a concession in return. This chapter will help you know what is usual and reasonable, giving you a realistic view of which contract provisions matter most, which you can expect to alter, and how much change you can hope to negotiate.

Transfer of Copyright

As the author of your work, you own the copyright. Most publishing contracts require that the author transfer, or assign, the copyright to the publisher. This means that all rights that were yours become the publisher's. These include, but are not limited to, the rights to publish the book in English and all other languages, to publish excerpts or condensations in magazines, and to adapt it for film or television. It is not legally necessary to transfer the copyright; you can instead grant only certain rights to the publisher and reserve the rest. For example, you might grant the publisher only the right to publish the book in a hardbound edition in the English language. Some specialized publishers do ask only for cloth and paper publishing rights because they assume that the books they publish have no further commercial possibilities, and they have no interest in pursuing the sale of translation, serial, and other rights. Most publishers, however, will not accept such a limited grant.

It is not generally to the author's advantage to retain rights because such an arrangement would require the author to sell all the other rights (paperback, translation, movie, and so forth) separately. Aside from the fact that few of these rights are valuable for most scholarly books, authors are rarely equipped to negotiate with paperback houses, foreign publishers, and movie moguls. Publishers can do this better, and the share they take of the profits is generally well earned. Authors of best-sellers, along with their agents, may try to reserve various rights, but even they rarely succeed. For bestsellers, much of the publisher's profit comes from the sale of foreign, paperback, serial, movie, or TV rights rather than from sales of the hardback book. They are unlikely to give up these profits.

By transferring the copyright, you do not give up your share of profits from nonbook rights. As we shall see, the contract spells out how the proceeds from the sale or licensing of each right are divided, and the percentages are negotiable.

Transfers of copyright are not eternal. They can be terminated in two ways. First, the contract may provide for termination after a specified period or if the publisher allows the book to go out of print (i.e., if the publisher no longer has copies available for sale and declines to reprint). Second, even if the contract does not mention termination, the copyright law allows authors (or their surviving spouses, children, or grandchildren) to terminate the transfer during the five years beginning thirty-five years after the date of the transfer and ending forty years after that date (for publication rights, the five-year period can begin either forty years after the date of the transfer or thirty-five years after first publication, whichever is earlier). After thirty-five or forty years, however, most of the damage is done, so including a termination clause in the contract is much to your benefit. Termination returns to you only the basic publication right plus any others not yet sold or licensed. For example, if your publisher has sold the Italian publishing rights, that contract continues in force for its full term, despite your termination of the assignment of copyright from which it was derived.

Technology has complicated the termination clause, because the meaning of "out of print" has become unclear. Until recently, a book was out of print when the publisher had no actual copies left to sell. Now, however, when a book is physically out of print, the publisher may license a company to print copies from their electronic files when a bookstore or individual places an order. These copies are often physically indistinguishable from the original edition. Such "on-demand" publishing renders the notion of out-of-print books obsolete. Indeed, it might make sense to publish some books only on demand. Some books may be published only electronically, so that all copies (unless printed out by the purchaser) are virtual rather than actual. These are never really "in print." If this issue concerns you, you might ask your editor for written clarification. There seems to be no standard way of dealing with this question just yet.

Specific Rights

The most basic right involved in a book contract is the right of publication, of offering copies to the public. The contract will grant the publisher the exclusive right to publish your work in book form; in return, the publisher will (usually) pay you a royalty, as I explain shortly. Generally, contracts will include under this right book publication in all languages throughout the world. You must understand that by granting the publisher this exclusive right you are promising not to allow anyone else to publish your work as a book in any language anywhere in the world.

How publishers exploit this right will depend on their view of the book's market abroad and on their usual marketing arrangements. For example, a large Anglo-American press is in an excellent position to sell your book in English in the United States, Canada, the United Kingdom, Australia – throughout the English-speaking world. American publishers are likely to seek British co-publishers if they foresee the possibility of sales in the United Kingdom. To exploit a non-English market, presses sell translation rights. Some publishers are more diligent about such activities than others, and some books are more salable abroad than others. If you have ideas about translations, share them with your acquisitions editor or the subsidiary rights manager. More important, if a foreign press or scholar approaches you about translation rights, respond by explaining that the rights are held by your publisher and that you will pass on the inquiry. The proceeds from such sales will be divided between you and the publisher, as I explain shortly.

Some contracts specify that the publisher will consult the author before selling foreign rights. If your book has potential for translation, and if you are knowledgeable about the publishers in the relevant countries, such a clause is valuable. Similarly, if you are fluent in a language, you may want to ask for the right to review and approve any translation into that language.

A closely related right that is sometimes listed separately is that of publishing the book in paperback. The paperback rights to best-sellers are generally sold (sometimes at auction) to paperback houses for large sums. With rare exceptions, however, publishers of scholarly books retain these rights and publish the paperback edition (if there is one) themselves. Authors are paid a royalty.

Rights other than publication and translation rights are sometimes called subsidiary rights. One group of such rights that the contract will specify is serial rights – the right to publish portions of your book in magazines, journals, or newspapers. "First serial" rights refer to such publication before the book appears; "second serial" rights apply to such publication after book publication. You need not worry if some of the material in your book, or even a whole chapter, has appeared in a journal, although you should certainly let the publisher know. Once you have signed a contract, however, you should not attempt to publish portions of your manuscript elsewhere without consulting the book publisher.

Serial rights can be important in generating income, especially if they are sold to a periodical with a large general circulation (e.g., *The New Yorker* or *Scientific American*). More often their importance lies in their ability to generate sales by calling attention to the book, even if the direct payment by the periodical is small. As in the sale of foreign rights, proceeds of such sales are divided between author and publisher, and the contract may require the publisher to seek the author's consent before granting such rights.

The right to sell abridged, "digest," or condensed versions of your work may also be specified. Scholarly books are rarely of interest to *Reader's Digest*, but abridgments may be anthologized, and condensations of multivolume works are not unheard of, especially when such condensation makes them attractive as textbooks. You will probably want to ask for the right to review and approve abridgments and condensations; in fact, you may want to specify that you be asked first to do any condensation the publisher itself issues or licenses to another publisher.

Excerpts from scholarly works are sometimes published in readers or anthologies (print or electronic), and your contract will mention such uses specifically. Usually the compiler will want to use a chapter of your book, although sometimes an abridged version is used. You are granting the publisher the right to review such requests, to specify the conditions under which the material can be used, and to set and collect a fee. You may also want to review such requests, and the contract will specify your share in the fee. Like you, the publisher will be concerned about the way your material is treated in the anthology; permission probably would be denied if your work was to be used as a bad example or if the abridgment distorted your argument. The publisher also will be concerned about the effect of the compilation on the commercial value of your work. For example, the inclusion of one chapter in an anthology might increase interest in your book and enhance sales, whereas publication of another chapter (say, the conclusion) might actually reduce sales of your book. Any requests you receive for reprinting part of your work in an anthology must be referred to the publisher. You or your publisher may also receive requests to include part of your book in an electronic database or other nonprint medium. These requests should be handled in the same way.

Similarly the contract will specify that the publisher has the right to grant permission to quote from your work. "Permissions" are discussed briefly later in this chapter and at length in Chapter 10. When other writers want to publish portions of your work that fall somewhere between a few words and an anthology selection, they must ask permission. These requests are a real nuisance, and you should be delighted that your publisher is taking them on. If any fee is collected, it will be shared according to the contract provision.

Book club rights increase circulation and sales of your book. Although few scholarly books are candidates for the Literary Guild or Book-of-the-Month Club, some may interest more specialized groups. It is probably worth your while to look through the book club listings in *Literary Market Place* to see whether any group looks promising. If you find one or two, send the suggestion to your publisher. Authors generally receive less money per copy on books sold through book clubs (contracts generally share the proceeds of book club sales equally between author and publisher, but book clubs receive large discounts). Nevertheless, sales to book clubs permit publishers to take advantage of the economies of larger print runs (see Chapter 11), and they do enhance the visibility and sales of books.

The contract will also list specifically some rights that are more exotic – and less likely to be sold. Even though your monograph is unlike to appear on *Masterpiece Theater* or to be animated by the Walt Disney Studios, read the provisions and check on the division of revenues.

Electronic and multimedia rights are currently the subject of dispute between authors' groups and publishers. Some publishers are issuing contracts that require the author to assign all electronic rights; authors' groups and agents argue that authors should retain such rights. The discussion is important because no one knows how extensive electronic and multimedia exploitation will be, what forms it will take, or how much revenue these uses will generate. Publishers want to know that authors will not take a profitable use of their work elsewhere; authors want to ensure that they are not giving away something of value – especially if they fear that the publisher will not know how to exploit electronic rights.

There are no norms to follow on electronic rights, so you will have to negotiate this on your own. You may wish to grant the publisher some rights (e.g., the right to sell portions of the work for use in electronic anthologies) but not others (e.g., the right to put the full text online). For any rights that you do assign, the contract should specify the royalty rate you will receive for electronic products issued by your own publisher and the percentage of revenues you will receive from the sale or licensing of electronic rights to others. These percentages should be comparable to those offered for print rights. If your contract does not specifically assign electronic rights to the publisher or contain a clause that says all rights not specifically assigned belong to the publisher, then you have retained these rights. The publisher may add a clause forbidding you to use electronic rights in a way that would reduce revenues from the print edition.

Despite the great variety of rights, their transfer to the publisher involves only a few important ideas that you need to understand. First, the publisher will exploit only some of these rights directly, selling or licensing most of them to others. For example, an American publisher will sell to a French publisher the right to translate the book into French and sell it in the French market; grant a movie producer an option to produce a film version; and sell an excerpt to *Vanity Fair*. These arrangements may be exclusive or nonexclusive (perhaps *Elle* will buy another excerpt, or two different anthologies might include the same chapter); indefinite or for a specific period (movie options expire and can then be sold to another would-be producer); and worldwide or geographically limited (Spanish-language rights throughout the world, for example, as opposed to English-language rights outside North America). Also, although few books can be fully exploited, every contract provides for all rights just in case. Do not ignore these provisions, even though they seem remote. Finally, even if you have assigned all rights to the publisher, you retain a financial and professional stake in them. Pass along all inquiries about translations, anthologies, and so forth, as well as any ideas you have about possible buyers of various rights, to your acquiring editor or to the manager of subsidiary rights.

The Publisher's Duties

As explained earlier, you assign the copyright of your book to a publisher in exchange for publication and payment. The publisher's most important obligation is to publish your book – that is, to edit, design, produce, market, and distribute it. The contract will make this clear, but it will not usually state how quickly the publisher must do all of this. You may ask that the publisher agree to publish the book within a certain time after you submit a complete, revised manuscript; two years would certainly be adequate. Most publishers would prefer not to include such a clause, and they often have good reasons. But if you are concerned about excessive delay, either because your book is on a current topic or because the press has a reputation for tardiness, you can ask. (Remember, however, that should the deadline pass, you would have to start all over again to find another publisher. This is unlikely to get the book out faster.)

The contract will require that the publisher copyright your book and make sure that it is published in conformity with copyright regulations. This is very simple for publishers to do. Most publishers will print the standard copyright notice in an appropriate place in the book, although the law no longer requires this. Most will also file a form, send two copies of the work (for deposit in the Library of Congress), and pay a small fee to the U.S. Register of Copyrights. Although your rights are protected without registration (i.e., your failure to register the copyright does not make it legal for others to steal your work), you cannot sue for copyright infringement until the book is registered. Because registration is simple and inexpensive, most publishers consider it a wise precaution.

Upon publication of your book, the publisher will give you a specified number of free copies (usually five or ten). Most contracts also permit you to buy additional copies for your own use (not for resale) at a discount of 40 to 50 percent. Many publishers also offer authors smaller discounts on all the books they publish.

Royalties and Other Payments

The royalty system is a financial expression of the idea that the fates of author and publisher are inextricable. If a book succeeds, both parties share in the rewards. If it fails, neither party makes any money. Why, you may ask, is the author's share a measly 5 to 10 percent? Chapter 11 illustrates how that percentage compares with the publisher's profit and, in fact, demonstrates that it is usually a pretty fair share. For now, it is probably adequate to understand that the publisher does not get the other 90 to 95 percent; most of it goes to typesetters, printers, binders, paper manufacturers, wholesale jobbers, and retail stores. The publisher's share must also pay salaries, rent, utilities, and other expenses.

Royalties, generally paid once or twice a year, begin sometime after publication, depending on the publisher's accounting year. The check is preceded or accompanied by a statement of sales or revenues. The contract will spell out when royalties are to be paid and should give you permission to inspect the publisher's records insofar as they relate to your book.

Some contracts provide for an advance to be paid on royalties. As noted in Chapter 4, an advance is a cash payment made to the author on signing the contract, on delivering an acceptable manuscript, or at some other specified moment. It is not money paid in addition to royalties or instead of them; it is simply a sum paid in advance and subsequently deducted from the royalties the book earns. Obviously, publishers will not offer advances of more than they expect a book to earn. Authors of scholarly monographs can expect only small advances, if any. Publishers may offer an advance to help you finish your book more quickly (e.g., money for a research trip), to help you pay for illustrations or other costs, or just to compete successfully with another publisher. You can ask for an advance, but do not expect a large sum. For example, suppose the publisher expects to sell 2,000 copies of your book (an optimistic estimate for many a monograph) at $30.00 a copy, paying you 6 percent of the retail price in royalties. The most you can expect to earn over the book's lifetime would be

$3,600, and the publisher would probably balk at advancing more than half of that.

Royalty rates vary and are negotiable. They are calculated as a percentage either of retail price or of net revenues (the publisher's receipts) of your book. It is easy to estimate royalties calculated on retail price: If a book sells for $30.00 and royalty is 10 percent, you will receive $3.00 for each copy sold. When royalties are paid on net revenues, the calculation is more difficult. Some books are sold directly to readers for the full $30.00; others are sold to retailers and wholesalers at discounts ranging from 20 to 40 percent or more (netting $24.00 to $18.00 or less). Your 10 percent, then, is $3.00, $2.40, or $1.80. Generally, royalties based on retail price will be paid at a lower percentage than those based on net revenue. As a rule of thumb, 10 percent of net is roughly equal to 6 or 7 percent of retail. The percentages are negotiable, though the base usually is not: Publishers prefer uniform accounting procedures. This means if you are offered a royalty of 8 percent of net revenue, you may succeed at bargaining for 9 or 10 percent of net, but you will not get 8 (or even 6) percent of retail.

Regardless of the base on which royalties are calculated, the range of royalties begins at zero. Some publishers simply do not pay royalties on some books. Some pay royalties but only after a certain number of books (usually 500 or 1,000) have been sold; this practice has become increasingly common. Some offer an escalating royalty schedule: As sales reach certain specified levels, the percentage increases (say 5 percent for the first 2,500; 7.5 percent for the next 2,500; and 10 percent thereafter). Most offer one schedule for casebound (hardback) books and another for paperbacks. The top of the scale for scholarly books is probably 10 percent of retail; for textbooks, it is 15 percent. Feel free to bargain within this range, but do not expect to raise an offer by more than a percentage point or two.

One case in which it is appropriate to ask for higher royalties is that in which you do work that is traditionally the publisher's. If, for example, you enter the manuscript editor's changes and the typesetting codes onto your computer disks so that the book can be set directly from those disks, you are entitled to higher royalties than if you had merely provided hard copy or an electronic typescript. Some publishers automatically write this differential into their contracts, giving an extra percentage point or two to the harder-working author. Others might simply pay the author an amount based on the typesetting charges saved. Alternatively, the savings can be used to keep the price of the book down.

Most contracts list the types of transactions for which royalties are not paid. These include books given away free as a courtesy or for review, books that are returned by booksellers, and books sold at or below cost. The first category is obvious, but the others require a brief explanation. Unlike most retailers, booksellers have the privilege of returning merchandise that they cannot sell. Thus, what registers on the publisher's ledger as a sale in January may appear as a return in June. Alfred Knopf referred to this phenomenon as "Gone today, here tomorrow." Because returned books are never actually sold, no royalties are paid on them. This may be reflected in royalty statements, with an amount deducted from second-year royalties for books that appeared to be sold – and on which royalties were paid – in the first year but that were subsequently returned. Trade publishers may also deduct a certain amount from royalties as a reserve against expected returns. Books may be sold below the publisher's manufacturing cost when they are "remaindered." If, after a few years (or a shorter time, for trade publishers), a book is selling very slowly or not at all, the publisher may offer it at a sale price. If it still does not sell, the publisher may sell the remaining copies to a company that pays very little and then sells them for somewhat more. (The obvious example is the giant coffee-table book on the bargain table for $4.95.) Unsold hardcover books are often remaindered when a trade book is issued in paperback. If the book is sold to the remainder house at a price below the publisher's cost, the author receives no royalty. After all, the royalty is a share in the book's success.

Many contracts provide that the publisher need not pay royalties when the total due is less than a specified amount or when fewer than a certain number of books are sold. This is done because of the bookkeeping costs involved. Generally the sum is held over until the next year, although sometimes it is not paid at all. This is a reasonable provision if the amount specified is reasonable – say, $25.00 or the sales needed to generate that amount in royalties. Sums beyond that should be paid out. After all, it doesn't cost that much to write a check.

Although royalty contracts are the most common, publishers sometimes pay authors a fee, either at one time or in installments (say, one-third on signing the contract, one-third on submitting the manuscript, and one-third on final acceptance). The advantage for the author is getting cash up front; the disadvantage is that in the end the author will get less than royalties would have provided if the book does well. The fee arrangement is most common for contributors to a collection of articles or essays, where it is a practical and generally fair way of doing business. However, a contract of this sort for a complete volume should provide for unanticipated success. For example, the author should get an additional payment if the book is reprinted, or a supplementary royalty schedule might kick in after a certain (large) number of copies have been sold.

In addition to royalties or fees, an author may receive payments from a publisher that represent the author's share of rights sold or licensed to others. The contract will state what percentage of the proceeds the author gets from the sale of such rights. The variations are endless, but 50 percent is common. For serial and movie rights, the author's share may rise to 75 or even 90 percent. These shares are paid either when the publisher collects them or in the annual royalty accounting.

In sum, the publisher's job is to publish your book, exploit its possibilities, and collect and share the proceeds of all sales. What is the author's job?

The Author's Duties

The contract will tell you when you have to deliver the completed manuscript (if you have not already done so) and in how many copies. It may specify a minimum or maximum length and the number of tables, maps, photographs, and other illustrations that will be expected. It may be very specific about the physical condition of the manuscript. Most scholarly publishers now require that you submit your manuscript on computer disks or electronically as well as in hard copy. This provision may be very specific about the software to be used and other details. Still other contracts will require that you submit "camera-ready copy" (pages that can be photographed as is, for printing). This is most common for books containing material that cannot easily be typeset, such as Chinese characters. If you are unable or unwilling to do this kind of work, you must negotiate these provisions with the publisher. The contract will also enumerate the tasks you must do during production: reviewing the copyediting, proofreading, and preparing an index. Chapter 10 discusses these processes in detail. What you need to understand as you read the contract is the financial implications of these provisions.

The publishing contract specifies at what stages in the production process you will be allowed to make changes and how extensive those changes can be. In reviewing the edited manuscript, you are free to make changes quite liberally. In fact, you should regard this as the last opportunity to make changes. When you are reading proof, the number of changes you can make is greatly restricted. Some contracts permit no changes in proof beyond correcting the typesetter's errors. Others allow a small number, which is expressed as a percentage of the total typesetting cost. This is a very difficult number for authors to interpret. Say the contract provides that you will be charged for all changes that cost more than 5 percent of typesetting costs. If the typesetting bill is $3,000, then you will be allowed to chalk up $150 worth of changes without charge. Changes made to proof are far more expensive than the original typesetting, so that the $150 gets eaten up very quickly. In fact, 5 percent barely allows for normal human error. It would be very unusual for a publisher to allow the author more extensive free changes in proof. The only time this possibility would be worth raising is the case in which a book is very timely and last-minute changes in, say, election statistics are expected. In most cases, the best way to avoid disagreements and expense is to review the edited manuscript very carefully and make all your changes then.

If you are submitting your manuscript on disk or electronically and are responsible for entering editorial and authorial changes, this clause is rendered meaningless: The typesetter's bill will be reduced (or even eliminated if the publisher uses its own laser printer), and the cost of making changes falls on you anyway. What is important in these cases is that you not make changes without the publisher's knowledge. Although I have not seen an appropriate substitute clause, publishers should soon think of a way to limit the timing and extent of changes that does not relate to typesetting charges. Unfortunately, some publishers have thrown up their hands and offer contracts that simply permit no changes. This does not allow for correcting the errors that creep into all books.

The standard contract provides for the author's reading of galley and page proof only, or only page proof if the galley stage is omitted. If you wish to see later stages of proof, you will have to negotiate such a provision with your publisher. This is necessary only in the case of an unusually complex or demanding work, such as a critical or documentary edition, or a work with many illustrations or an elaborate layout; such a request is unlikely to be granted in other cases.

Another duty that may fall to the author is to provide artwork. This means that you must locate or create the art, get written permission to use it, provide acceptable copies, and pay reproduction charges and permissions fees. Chapter 10 provides detailed information on procuring illustrations. For now, you should understand that, except for some textbooks, the contract places this responsibility clearly with you. In the case of a heavily illustrated book, you may be able to get the publisher to pay such costs out of royalties so that you do not have to come up with large amounts of cash. All these possibilities should be raised and negotiated.

Most contracts stipulate that the author must provide an index or pay to have it done. Chapter 10 provides advice on preparing indexes. At the contract stage, however, if you think you will want to hire a professional indexer, ask the publisher to find one and, if possible, advance the fee from your royalties.

The clause that imposes a duty on almost every academic author is the one that gives the author the responsibility for getting permission to reprint other people's work. This is an obvious task in the case of anthologies and for illustrated books, but it occurs in dealing with unillustrated monographs as well. Whenever you use someone else's tables, figures, or words at significant length, you must get written permission and, if requested, pay a fee. Chapter 10 provides guidelines, and your publisher may have some suggestions as well.

You may be asked to give the publisher the "right of first refusal" on your next book. This means you must submit it to the publisher first, to accept or not. Most publishers will give up this right if you ask them to do so. If the relationship works out well, you will come back anyway; and if it doesn't, they will not want a hostile author. Some contracts simply stipulate that you not publish any competing book as long as this one is in print. This provision is relevant mostly to textbook publishing.

Important Legal Considerations

In signing your contract, you represent that the work is your own, that it is not libelous, and that you have not promised it to anyone else. Sometimes you must agree to pay any expenses arising out of litigation involving claims of libel, copyright infringement, or plagiarism. These representations are a combination of ethical commitments that we all hope are universally understood and of legal considerations that require some explanation.

Of course, if we all obeyed the ethical canons of our professions automatically, they would not need to be written into contracts. Rather than moralize, let me remind you very simply that you have an obligation to credit others accurately and fully for their work. "Others" include colleagues whose work you have used, students who have assisted with research, and friends or informants who have provided information. "Work" includes words, ideas, drawings, memories, data – all the raw material of scholarship. All original work is built on the contributions of others, and these contributions must be acknowledged. I must remind you also that what you write should be true – no falsified data, no fictional notes, no creative quotations. Also, do not sign more than one contract for the same book.

Using someone else's work without giving credit may go beyond plagiarism into copyright infringement. As a responsible author, you should understand the fundamentals of copyright law. Under U.S. copyright law, all works of an author – whether published or not – are protected against unauthorized use from the moment of their creation until seventy years after the author's death. (There are some variations on this for older U.S. works because the current law went into effect in 1978.) "Works" include fiction, nonfiction, poetry, letters, tables, graphs, paintings, sculpture, drawings, photographs, music, and song lyrics. Works never before published are protected until December 31, 2002, even if the author has been dead more than seventy years. The law is designed to protect authors' rights, not to restrict unnecessarily the legitimate use of their works by others. Under the doctrine of fair use, you can quote a reasonable (though unspecified) amount from protected published works without permission. If you wish to use more than that, or if you wish to quote from unpublished works that remain under copyright, you must get written permission from the copyright holder and, if asked, pay a fee. Although this may seem a nuisance when you are the quoter, you can appreciate its importance when you are a potential quotee. Chapter 10 provides a summary of when you need permission to quote and how to go about obtaining it. The bibliography includes books that provide more detailed information about copyright.

Libel is a legal problem that academic authors tend to ignore, believing that it is something only journalists have to worry about. Unfortunately, it is quite possible for a scholarly writer to libel someone. You commit libel when you write something about a living person that is both untrue and harmful. In libel law, harmful statements are those that damage a person's reputation, business or profession, or social life. They include statements or suggestions that someone is a criminal, communist, Nazi, or bankrupt; suffers from a feared disease; or has behaved unethically. There are of course many other possibilities. Libelous statements need not be blatant. They can be as subtle as the classic entry in a ship's log, "Captain was sober today."

Libel law is complex and changing. For example, the standards applied vary depending on whether the subject is an ordinary person or a public official. Libel law is also much stricter outside the United States, most relevantly in the United Kingdom and Canada. If you are writing about controversial events or subjects, you need to be sure that what you say about living people could be proved in court. If you are not sure, you need to write very carefully. Though you need not resort to the journalist's "alleged perpetrator," you can avoid difficulty. For example, instead of claiming that "Alderman X accepted bribes from numerous contractors," you may need to write, "Good government groups have repeatedly charged Alderman X with accepting bribes, but he has denied the charges. He has been tried twice for bribery, but both trials ended with hung juries." You may also want to have a lawyer review your manuscript for libel. Your state bar association will refer you to lawyers experienced in the field.

Even scholars writing about events that occurred hundreds of years ago can commit libel by making careless accusations against fellow scholars. In commenting on the work of others, you should avoid hyperbole. If you consider a theory far-fetched, limit yourself to a reasoned assessment of the theory and do not call its originator a fool, an incompetent, or a lunatic. Do not accuse your colleagues of plagiarism, shoddy research, or unethical conduct unless you can prove the charges. And even if you think you can, is it really worth the expense and delay of a lawsuit? Litigation can keep your book in limbo for years and cost thousands of dollars. It is best to avoid the problem with careful research and writing.

Like copyright law, libel law is not meant to limit freedom of expression. It is designed to protect against unwarranted embarrassment and harm to one's professional or personal reputation. On the whole, compliance with the law benefits writing by making it more careful, accurate, and precise.

Signature

If there is anything in the contract that you do not understand, ask the publisher to explain it. If some provision is extremely important to you and is not spelled out, explain this to the publisher and ask for a rider on the contract or a letter of understanding. For example, you may wish to review translations, excerpts, or condensations for accuracy. Do not rely on oral agreements or casual reassurances. When you understand everything in the contract and are satisfied with it, sign one copy and return it. Keep the other copy in a safe place.

If you are working with a coauthor or coeditor, both of you will sign a contract with the publisher as "the authors." The publisher will hold you jointly responsible for reviewing the editing, getting permissions, indexing, and so forth. You and your coauthor may reach a separate understanding about who will do what, but the publisher will not enforce it. In other words, if your coauthor fails to live up to his or her side of the bargain, you must do it. It is generally wise to draw up an agreement in writing with your coauthor about who will do what, with a provision for failure. For example, the coauthor who decides not to read proof as promised might be obliged to pay for the services of a professional proofreader.

Subventions

Many university presses receive subsidies from private foundations or government agencies. For a long time, some presses hesitated to seek outside money with strings attached, fearing a loss of control or integrity. For example, if a foundation or government agency offered a press $50,000 to publish books in economics, might the publisher not select more economics books than otherwise? Or even accept inferior works to avoid losing the gift? This hesitation has largely been overcome as the fears associated with limited-purpose grants have proved unfounded.

Author Subventions

A more controversial form of subsidy is the author subvention – a grant of money from the author to defray the costs of publication. Because this practice raises the specter of vanity publishing, it is controversial among publishers. In fact, it is not the same as vanity publishing, but the differences can become blurred. Remember that a vanity press will publish anything, as long as the author pays for it. The author's money is both necessary and sufficient for a positive editorial decision. University presses that request author subventions separate the decision to publish from the author's willingness to pay. If the manuscript does not meet their standards, they will not publish it, even if the author offers money. In other words, the subvention may be necessary, but it is not sufficient. Sometimes it isn't even necessary: The press may request a subvention but publish even if the money is not forthcoming.

Another difference is the amount of money requested. A vanity press requires the author to pay all costs plus a profit to the publisher. A university press will ask only that the author share costs. According to a 1977 survey, the average subvention requested by university presses was between $2,000 and $5,000, with the range covering $1,000 or less through $15,000 (although it can go as high as $100,000 for books with color plates).[1] Despite overall inflation, these numbers have not

---

[1] John Hazel Smith, "Subventions of Scholarly Publishing," *Scholarly Publishing* 9, no. 1 (October 1977): 19–29, provides details on amounts and conditions of subventions. In a more recent discussion, Fred Kameny suggests that the amounts of subsidies have not changed and discusses ethical issues: "Authors with Deep Pockets: The Ethics of Subsidies," *Journal of Scholarly Publishing* 29, no. 2 (January 1998): 65–70.

changed very much. Finally, university presses ask for subventions not to enhance their profits but to enable them to publish books that otherwise would not make economic sense. You may have written a book that will be of immense value to a few hundred people. If it is to be published in an edition of a few hundred copies at a reasonable price, a subvention will be needed. A book of wider appeal – with potential sales of, say, a thousand copies – that is expensive to produce because of elaborate tables, many photographs, or difficult typesetting may also require a subvention. Presses do not routinely request subventions, but many will ask for them when a good manuscript cannot otherwise pay its way.

Having authors provide electronic manuscripts or camera-ready copy is an indirect subvention in that it shifts costs that have traditionally been the publisher's to the authors. Providing an index, proofreading, and paying permissions fees are also subsidies, although they are hallowed by tradition.

Some publishers, in lieu of a cash subvention, ask for a commitment on the part of the author's university bookstore to purchase a certain number of copies, presumably for sale as textbooks. This seems to me more problematic than a cash subvention. If the book really is a textbook it should be published as such and should be used in courses other than the author's. Many universities require faculty members to get a dean's permission to use their own books as texts, to avoid abuse. Subventions can legitimately come from authors, their institutions, or foundations but not, I think, from students.

What should you do if a reputable press accepts your manuscript but asks for a subvention? You can, of course, refuse. They may agree to publish the book anyway, or you can go to another publisher. But if the publisher is the one you know you want to work with, if you are under pressure to publish quickly, or if you have been turned down by several other presses – and if you can come up with the money – you may well agree to pay the subvention.

The subvention need not come from your own pocket. Some universities are willing to pay subventions for faculty members and have special funds for the purpose. Others are willing but have to label the grant something else – research assistance, faculty grants-in-aid, or some other blanket category. Still others cannot give money for faculty publication but can provide services, including production of artwork and photographs, proofreading, keyboarding, preparation of an index, mailing of advertising flyers, and so forth. In specialized fields, a publisher may require you to provide camera-ready copy rather than typesetting the book (this practice is more common among commercial scholarly publishers and university research centers than among university presses). Your university may be willing to provide this service. Explore these possibilities with your publisher and your dean.

If you do agree to pay a subvention, there are four issues to raise before signing a contract. First, make sure the amount is reasonable. You can ask how it was computed, and look again at the range of subventions given earlier. If your manuscript is a fairly ordinary scholarly work – up to 500 manuscript pages, without many tables or illustrations, and using no foreign alphabets – anything over $5,000 is probably excessive. If it is illustrated, especially with color plates, if it has a lot of tables or requires complex typesetting, the amount requested may reasonably be much higher. Do not hesitate to bargain over the amount. Remember, the publisher does want your book.

Second, the contract should provide for royalties to return the subvention if the book miraculously sells enough copies to repay the publisher's investment. Publishers are not infallible, and their pessimism about sales may be excessive.

Third, ask the publisher to cooperate with you in seeking outside money. Publishers should be aware of funding sources in fields in which they are active, and they should be willing to spend some time looking for help. The next section provides an introduction to this process.

Last, if your department or administration suggests that it regards the subvention as a form of vanity publishing, the press director should write a letter explaining that the decision to publish was made on the basis of the manuscript's quality, without regard to the availability of a subvention, that it was subjected to normal refereeing procedures, and that the subvention is requested only because of the work's limited salability. If you cannot raise the money and do not have it yourself, say so. The press may well go ahead anyway.

Author subventions present publishers with a difficult problem. On the one hand, they invite accusations of vanity publishing and the possibility of undue outside influence; on the other hand, they make possible the publication of much valuable but unprofitable scholarship and make it less necessary for presses to seek out semicommerical manuscripts. They also make it possible to keep the price of a book low enough to maximize sales and readership. I cannot see any ethical problems from the author's point of view – although raising the money is a practical problem. The book has been accepted on its merits, and the subvention in no way detracts from its quality. Of course, anyone would rather not pay a subvention, but it may be a wise investment. If, for example, being promoted to associate professor requires having a book published and brings a pay increase, the average subvention pays for itself pretty quickly.

Seeking Grants

Much academic research is supported by grants from government agencies or private foundations. Some of these same agencies and foundations also provide grants for publication costs, but most do not have special grant programs for this purpose. Others do have subvention programs but limit their grants to translations, critical editions, or other specific sorts of publications. The same agencies that supported your research may also provide a subvention for publication costs if they are approached properly. It is worth reminding grantors that the research they have supported is far more valuable if it is widely disseminated through publication, even if such dissemination is not likely to pay for itself.

The best time to approach a foundation or agency about funding publication is when you apply for the research grant. Depending on the regulations of the grantor, you may be able to apply in your original proposal for such publication costs as preparing illustrations; paying permissions fees; paying page charges; hiring an editor, indexer, proofreader, or word processor; or preparing camera-ready copy. You may also be able to request funds for a direct subvention to a publisher. But you must anticipate and estimate all of these costs at the time of the proposal.

If you do not ask for such funds along with your application for research support, it may be possible to go back to the foundation or agency with a later request. Even if they do not list such expenses among those they will support, they may do so if asked, particularly because the subvention is generally far smaller than the research grant. When making such a request after the research is completed, you would do well to have a publisher lined up who is willing to provide financial estimates justifying the subvention; most will do this happily. Of course, if you are fortunate enough to have some money left over from the original grant, you may be able to use that for the subvention. Do not do so, however, without asking permission.

It is also possible to find support for publication costs from fresh sources. If you are working with your home university press, you can jointly investigate local foundations, corporations, or institutions that might provide support. At some universities, as surprising a source as the alumni foundation has funds for such projects. Otherwise, you can seek help from groups in your area, while the publisher looks for support in theirs. Your university's office of grants and contracts can provide assistance in this task. A publisher who is active in your field should be aware of any national foundations that support work in that field. The publisher should also know about national programs that support scholarly publication. In any case, it is important for you and the publisher to work together, or at least to keep one another informed of fund-raising activities. It is embarrassing to the author and publisher, and extremely annoying to foundations, when separate applications come from a publisher and an author seeking support for the same book.

Working with an Editor

When your manuscript is accepted, with final revisions completed, the acquiring editor and managing editor will review
it and decide whether it is ready to go into production. At this
stage, the manuscript must contain all your revisions and
responses to readers' and editors' comments. It must also be
in acceptable physical condition so that the manuscript editor
and designer can work with it.

Once your manuscript is judged ready for production, it
will be assigned to a manuscript or copy editor and possibly
to a production editor. The manuscript editor's job is to help
you get the book into the most readable form possible.
Depending on the state of your manuscript, this work will
range from very minor corrections to extensive changes. You
will have a chance to review these changes and, if necessary,
discuss them with your editor. Throughout the editing
process, keep four things in mind: (1) This is your book, and
the ideas and general style should remain yours; (2) the editor
is not an expert in your field, but that editor is an expert in
scholarly publishing, and you should listen to advice of that
sort offered; (3) editorial changes should not be taken as personal insults; and (4) you and the editor are on the same side,
and both of you want the book to be as good as possible.

What sorts of changes will a manuscript editor suggest (or
insist on)? All editing, no matter how slight, attends to details of
grammar, usage, punctuation, capitalization, and spelling.
Chances are that the editor knows a good deal more about these
subjects than you do, but if you see an error or do not understand a change, point it out and ask for an explanation. If your
field has stylistic peculiarities (like the philosopher's eccentric
spelling of *premiss*), let the editor know ahead of time.

Many words are spelled differently in the United States,
Canada, and Great Britain, and there is some variation in
usage and punctuation among these English-speaking countries. Publishers generally insist on the spelling and punctuation accepted in their own country, although they sometimes
decide it is not worth the trouble to alter the author's work.

No publisher, in any country, will allow a mixture of spelling systems. Books that are published in both the United States and Great Britain will almost always use one system or the other for both editions; rarely do publishers reset a book merely to alter spelling.

You should also know about "house style." This is a reference not to writing style but to such details as what nouns should be capitalized, whether terms should be in quotes or italicized, how to arrange notes, how to deal with foreign words, when to spell out numerals, and so forth. It is the kind of style referred to in the *The Chicago Manual of Style*, which is the bible of scholarly publishing. An editor will make your book conform to house style, to the style of your discipline, or to some consistent version of your own style. If, under the shelter of house style, the editor makes changes that conflict with the canons of your discipline, you should raise the issue. For example, political scientists like to refer to Representative Smith, whereas *Chicago* prefers Congressman. Another possible problem with house style arises through misunderstanding of special terms. In *Paradise Lost*, for example, Sin and Death are characters, so their names must be capitalized in a book analyzing the epic. An editor who does not know this may lowercase them. Fix them and explain why, lest they get changed back again. At some presses, the copy editor sends a style sheet to the author before beginning work, so that difficulties can be ironed out in advance. Some presses also send one or two edited chapters to the author for review before proceeding. British and U.S. styles differ, so if you work with a transatlantic publisher, you may find editorial changes of this sort more obtrusive.

Your own style is another matter. Wolcott Gibbs, an editor at *The New Yorker*, once instructed his editors to "try to preserve an author's style if he is an author and has a style."[2] You may or may not have a style in this grander sense of the word. If your style includes verbosity, pomposity, or pedantry, be

---

[2] Quoted in James Thurber, *The Years with Ross* (Boston: Little, Brown, 1959; rept. ed., New York: Ballantine, 1972), 117.

grateful to the editor who refuses to preserve it. If you take justifiable pride in your writing, then you probably will not be subjected to excessive tampering. If you feel your work is being overedited, say so.

Humor is a matter of style that deserves special comment. If your editor tells you that a joke or pun is in bad taste, not funny, or inappropriate, do not argue. Ninety-nine percent of the time, the editor is right.

Do not fight changes designed to make your manuscript more accessible. It may be true that everyone interested in corporatism in Brazil reads Portuguese, but if they are the only ones who buy your book, you are in trouble. Readers interested in corporatism outside Brazil may buy it if you make it possible for them to read it. So when your editor asks you to translate your Portuguese quotations, do so. Define terms when asked, and change jargon to English. Plain speaking never detracts from scholarly value.

You and your manuscript editor should deal diplomatically with each other. A good editor will ask polite questions and suggest changes without comment or with tactful comments. If you have written a book about twentieth-century France and misspelled de Gaulle, or called him Alfred, the editor will fix your gaffe silently, without pointing out what a dumb mistake it is. You should also be polite in answering queries. Do not write, "No!!! You moron!!! Don't you know that cooking inactivates the avidin not the biotin????" Just answer, "No, avidin is right."

Remember, too, that editors do not change things randomly. They have reasons. Perhaps your sentence was awkward, ambiguous, or just too long. When you do not like a change, or the change has altered your meaning, try to locate the original problem and offer an alternative solution. If you cannot figure it out, explain what is wrong with the editor's change and work it out together.

Occasionally authors feel they have been saddled with an incompetent editor. If you are having real problems, call or write to the copy editor, express your misgivings, and explain your reasons. If this does not work, get in touch with the acquisitions editor who accepted your manuscript, who can then act as a mediator.

You will get the copyedited manuscript back for review. The physical form of this manuscript will depend on the publisher's procedures and on whether your computer disks will be used for typesetting. You may receive ordinary hard copy, with the editor's changes written on it; this is the traditional process. Alternatively, you may receive "red-lined" hard copy: a printout of the edited manuscript with alterations, deletions, and queries printed out like text, but distinguished typographically by certain symbols (for example, angle brackets). Each word-processing program uses different symbols, but they are not difficult to decipher. You may also be sent a disk. This enables you to view, at your option, the edited electronic copy with the red-lining either visible so that you can track the editor's changes, or suppressed so that you see clean copy. The queries may be embedded in the disk so that they become visible on screen. You may – though this is unlikely – receive a clean, edited copy that shows only queries, not editorial changes. Although some journals handle electronic manuscripts this way, most book publishers would not do so without consulting the author in advance. In any case, you will probably be asked to make changes and respond to queries on hard copy, rather than electronically, unless you are also entering typesetting codes or providing camera-ready pages. (Chapter 10 provides further details about handling electronic manuscripts.) After answering queries and reviewing the editing, give the manuscript one final, very careful reading. This is really your last chance to make changes. In proof, changes – if permitted at all – are costly, time consuming, and risky. (The advent of desktop typesetting has reduced the cost and the risks, but they still exist.)

Some publishers employ production editors who oversee manuscript editing, design, and manufacture. The production editor is your liaison with the copy editor, the designer, and manufacturers. The production editor is particularly important to authors when the press uses freelance copy editors. Most presses use freelancers occasionally, and some use them for nearly all copyediting. This enables the publisher to maintain a smaller staff and to use editors who specialize in certain fields. For example, a press may not publish enough books in biology to employ full-time a first-rate life sciences editor; a freelancer fills this need. Freelancers are essential in textbook publishing, which is seasonal. If all copy editors and production people were employed full-time, they would spend several months a year twiddling their thumbs. Some authors are insulted when their books are assigned to freelancers, believing that they are not as good as in-house editors and their own book must have been relegated to second-class citizenship. This is completely erroneous.

One of the production editor's main functions is to keep your book on schedule. To cooperate, you must be honest about deadlines. If you are asked to review the edited manuscript in two weeks, try to do so. But if you know this is impossible, warn the manuscript or production editor immediately, so that the editor can plan accordingly. Once the manuscript has been sent to the typesetter, meeting deadlines is crucial. The typesetter's schedule is fairly inflexible, and if you are late in returning proof, publication of your book may be considerably delayed. For example, returning galleys a week late may delay page proof a month or more, causing the typesetter to miss the printer's and binder's deadlines and thereby adding at least another month to the schedule. Take deadlines very seriously.

Manuscript to Bound Book

Once the edited manuscript goes off to the typesetter, you have two responsibilities: proofreading and indexing. Chapter 10 explains when and how to do both. In the meantime, your publisher's staff is tending to production and marketing.

Typesetting, the first stage of production, includes proofreading and corrections. With traditional typesetting, these processes take three to four months. If the type is set directly from the author's computer disks, several weeks may be saved, but proofreading will still be necessary. Strange things can happen between disk and proof. While final proofs are being prepared, the author must create the index. It is obviously important for the author to keep to the schedule in proofreading and indexing. Most authors, on completing the index, expect their book to appear in a matter of days. Unfortunately, although the author's work is done, the publisher's is far from over. The printer has to make plates and print the books; the publisher must check final proofs and folded and gathered pages; the same printer or another must print the jackets; both pages and jackets must be delivered to the bindery. The binder must manufacture a die, stamp the binding, and bind the books. The quality of manufacturing is just as important as the quality of the writing, editing, and design, and all of these jobs must be done right.

The process involves a lot of suppliers and manufacturers, so there are many possible sources of delay. For example, paper may not be delivered on time, or shipping to the bindery may be slowed, or the publisher may discover an error that necessitates reprinting all or part of the book. The well-organized publisher will minimize the chance of delays and will allow for some slippage in the schedule. Nevertheless, if you do not receive a copy of your book within a couple of weeks of the date you have been given, call your editor to see what has happened. Publishers do not make a penny until the volume goes on sale, so they are as eager as you are to get finished books. You are suffering together.

The Ad in *The New York Times*

Published authors' most frequent complaint is that their books are not advertised enough. It is true that books do not sell if they are not promoted, but it is not true that advertising in the major media – or even in scholarly journals – automatically increases sales. When did you last buy a scholarly book just because you saw an ad? If you are like most academic readers, you buy books after reading reviews or hearing about them from colleagues. It is gratifying to see your book advertised, but it is not necessarily cost effective. Every scholarly book has a finite sales potential, because the number of experts in the field is not large and because the number of research libraries is small. The publisher's goal is to make sure that every person who is likely to want your book is aware that it exists. Usually, the best way to inform the readers of scholarly books is to ensure that the book is widely reviewed and that the people and libraries most concerned with the subject of the book receive an announcement. Thus, university presses spend their marketing budgets on sending out review copies and doing mailings to appropriate lists. An ad in *The New York Times Book Review* may sell a collection of essays by Stephen Jay Gould; it will not sell a monograph on archeological analysis or quantum mechanics. (Textbooks and trade books are marketed differently; see Chapters 7 and 9.)

Authors can do a great deal to help publishers promote their books. You are most likely to know which journals will review your book, at which meetings it should be exhibited, and which organizations have mailing lists that might be appropriate. You can also suggest names of people who will offer enthusiastic praise that can be printed on the dust jacket and in mailing pieces. If your publisher (usually in the person of a marketing manager or director) does not ask your advice on these matters, give it anyway – preferably early, around the time you return the edited manuscript. The marketing manager or your acquiring editor may ask you to write a brief description of the book and may send a detailed questionnaire. Write the description and answer the questions, following the instructions provided. Ask to see dust jacket, catalogue, and advertising copy before it is printed, and review it for accuracy. But try to be realistic in assessing the breadth of readership.

You can also send your editor a list of prizes for which your book is eligible. *Literary Market Place* lists the major prizes, and your publisher probably knows about those. But there are often less well known prizes specific to your field that offer small cash awards, prestige for you and your publisher, and some free publicity. Be sure to decline membership on prize committees for the years in which your book may be nominated.

You will have to be realistic about how much the publisher can spend on marketing your book. A monograph that is expected to sell a thousand copies simply does not warrant a major campaign. In the case of trade books, for which demand is far more elastic, this prophecy may be self-fulfilling. A novelist may be right in claiming that more money spent on advertising or on a nationwide tour would have generated more sales. Scholarly publishers, though, cannot expect to sell to readers outside a small group that is usually easy to define – and to reach – without using expensive campaigns. Your efforts are best directed toward defining the audience and suggesting ways to reach it.

Keep your acquiring editor or the marketing department informed well in advance of any activities such as speaking engagements or participation in symposia that might generate interest in your book. If you are speaking on another campus – a lecture tour soon after publication may be worth arranging – the marketing department will try to get copies of your book into the campus bookstore. When you speak, mention your book by title and publisher, whenever relevant, and display it if possible. If you are unsure of the technique, watch a few best-selling authors on TV talk shows.

Use your campus news office to publicize your book. If the book has any link to your region, local newspapers may do an interview or feature story. Alumni magazines are another source of publicity.

In matters of promotion, you and the publisher have the same goal: to sell as many books as possible. The more help you can offer, the better. But when the marketing manager tells you that *Oprah* is out, believe it.

After Publication

Even after your book is published and being sold, your relationship with the publisher continues. Journals will send copies of reviews to the publisher, who will forward them to you. You will get annual sales figures and royalty reports. You probably will have some new ideas about marketing to pass along.

Some of the reviews your publisher forwards to you will be unfavorable, less favorable than you would have liked, or at least unperceptive. Some may even seem extremely unfair. What should you do when this happens? In 99 cases out of 100, the wisest course is to do nothing. Authors frequently overreact to criticism and feel the need to respond even to minor negative points in an otherwise positive review. It rarely does any good to object to a review. Even if the journal prints your objections (which it need not do unless they are substantial or the review was libelous), your response generally makes readers who may not have read the review assume that it was worse than it was. If you feel you must respond to a review, limit yourself to a straightforward correction of errors. You may instead enlist a colleague to respond in a measured way.

You may also discover errors in the book, either in your own reading or through the keen observation of friends and colleagues. Keep a record of these, on the chance that your book will be reprinted, and send them to your publisher from time to time. Many scholarly books are reprinted, and if yours is among them it may be possible to make minor corrections. For textbooks, which are more likely to be reprinted than are monographs, students are good detectors of error. Faculty members sometimes send students' comments and corrections to publishers. Some publishers even include tear-out postcards for students to use when they find mistakes or wish to make suggestions. If you write a revised edition of a textbook, such comments can help you correct errors and clarify misunderstandings.

Revised editions are less common than reprintings. A reprinting is simply a restocking, the printing of additional copies of the same book. A new edition incorporates major changes – an added chapter, a revised conclusion, overall updating, or the like. Only if your book is selling continuously in significant quantities, usually as a result of textbook adoptions, will a revised edition make sense.

The possibility of increased sales may also motivate your publisher to issue your book in paperback. Among publishers there is a great deal of debate and very little information about the advisability of issuing hardback and paper editions simultaneously, waiting six months to publish the paperback, or waiting longer. For most scholarly books, there is no justification for a paperback edition: Everyone who wants the book has bought the hardback edition. If your book comes out in paper, the price will be lower, and both the percentage and the actual dollars per book paid in royalties will be smaller (7.5 percent of list price is a common paperback royalty). If you think there is justification for a paperback edition of your book, take the evidence to your acquiring editor. Market research can determine whether the edition is worthwhile.

Your publisher will notify you if your book is being remaindered. This means that sales have diminished to the point that it is not worth keeping the book in stock. The publisher will try to sell the unsold copies to a remainder house that in turn sells them at a large discount. Failing this, the publisher will sell your book for pulp. Authors are understandably horrified at such euthanasia. You can take some comfort in knowing that university presses postpone this moment of truth for quite a while (much longer than trade houses), and they will probably offer you the chance to buy the remaining copies at or near cost.

Sometimes authors feel that a publisher has not given their books a fair chance. If your book goes out of print and the publisher does not want to reprint it, you can have the rights revert to you (provided your contract contains such a clause, as explained earlier). At that point, you can try to convince another publisher to give it a second chance, either as a high-priced, small-edition reprint or as a paperback.

When you have completed the research and writing of a book, you are about two-thirds finished. You still must do a lot of planning and negotiating, and you must be prepared to work effectively with a publisher. Once your manuscript has been accepted, you and the publisher become partners. You both want the book to read well, look good, sell abundantly, and attract favorable reviews and publicity. In addition to cooperating with the manuscript editor, therefore, you should provide information and suggestions for promotion and advertising. You should contribute your own abilities and expertise, and your publisher's staff should contribute theirs. A book may be written and printed, but if it is not also distributed and read, your efforts become a pointless exercise. If you and your publisher do your jobs in a spirit of cooperation, the relationship will be rewarding for both of you.

Chapter 6

Multiauthor Books and Anthologies

I never could understand how two men can write a book together; to me that's like three people getting together to have a baby.

Evelyn Waugh

Multiauthor books are of two sorts: collections of original essays and anthologies of previously published material. The first sort of collection is usually published by a university press or other scholarly publisher; it includes festschrifts, symposium proceedings, and commissioned volumes on current topics. The specialized encyclopedia is an especially complex variant. Although such books may occasionally include one or two articles that have been published elsewhere, most of the material must be original. The second sort of collection is most often prepared for use as a required or supplementary text for a course and is usually published by a textbook publisher. Some such anthologies, however – especially of literature and translations – are published by scholarly publishers. Because each sort of volume is prepared very differently, this chapter discusses them separately. In each case, the compiler must deal with legal or contractual problems, editorial problems, and mechanical problems. The chapter is written mainly for the volume editor or compiler, but contributors to such volumes will also find it useful.

Collections of Original Essays

Compiling and editing a collection of scholarly articles can be one of the most nerve-racking experiences of a lifetime. You are dealing with multiple egos, multiple addresses, multiple problems, multiple missed deadlines, and multiple tempers. You must negotiate between the publisher and the contributors, and that can be very difficult. In this chapter I discuss the various problems that can arise and offer alternative solutions. When possible, I suggest ways to prevent the problems from arising in the first place. Certain procedures can make publication quicker and relatively painless. No matter how careful you are, however, the book will take longer to compile and produce than you think. If you picture yourself as an amateur general contractor building a large house in an out-of-the way place with the help of plumbers, carpenters, electricians, plasterers, painters, and others from around the country, you may be able to imagine the difficulties and delays that lie ahead.

If all the contributors to a volume have access to computers, the process can be speeded up considerably: Contributors can send drafts to the editor on disk or electronically; the editor can easily make suggestions and revisions; and the completed electronic manuscript can be sent to the publisher. When you approach potential contributors, ask them whether they can prepare their work on a computer and, if so, what kind of hardware and software they use. Most programs allow for easy convertibility, at least for text, with only minor adjustments. If one or two contributors cannot produce electronic manuscripts, you may want to have them keyboarded yourself. This allows you more easily to make such features as footnote style consistent and gives you greater control over the project. As early as possible, consult with your acquiring editor about how such a manuscript should be handled; also see Chapter 10 for information on preparing electronic manuscripts.

Collections of articles generally do not sell as well as monographs, and to keep costs down, publishers may ask volume editors to supply camera-ready copy or formatted electronic manuscripts. Chapter 10 provides instructions for preparing such material. A special difficulty arises in the case of multiauthor volumes, however. Contributors can prepare the copy of their chapter, but unless they all use the same fonts and printers and follow directions carefully the result may be very unattractive. If the volume editor prepares the final pages, the result will be more consistent and pleasing to the eye, but this takes a lot of work.

Problems

Collections of scholarly articles are usually generated by inviting certain authors to contribute papers on designated topics. They are frequently invited to present the articles orally at a symposium or conference, with publication to follow, although sometimes no oral presentation is contemplated. Sometimes contributors circulate drafts within the group and comment on one another's work, either at a meeting or long distance. Such collections may be initiated by publishers who will contract with an editor to assemble the volume. At other times the editor, as an individual or as the representative of an association, will have to put together a proposal and find a publisher.

In the latter case, the first problem that arises is to interest a publisher. Because of the difficulties discussed shortly, publishers rarely commit themselves to an idea for a multiauthor book before seeing at least a complete table of contents and some of the articles. Even if the topic is current and the contributors are well known, the book remains a pig in a poke. Ask your prospective contributors for suggestions about publishers; they can sometimes provide useful contacts.

Whether you or the publisher initiates the project, the contract will be contingent on receipt of a manuscript satisfactory in form, content, and style. In addition, an author-initiated project will have to survive the normal refereeing process. A publisher may provide a list of topics to be covered and may even suggest specific authors. Make sure you understand what is expected in length, coverage, audience, and so forth. A misunderstanding at this point may catch up with you when it is too late to do anything about it.

You must also select contributors. You probably know who is doing what in your field and what their general reputations are. That is a good starting point, but it is not enough. Read prospective contributors' recent publications and inquire discreetly among colleagues about contributors' reputations for promptness and cooperativeness. When you write to the proposed contributors describing the project, make it clear that you are merely exploring possibilities.

Ask whether potential contributors would be willing to *submit* an article of *n* words on specific topic *x* within *t* months. If they write back, "I have a marvelous article that's tangentially about *x* lying around; would you take that?" decline politely. If the response says, "Your project sounds really fascinating, but I'm terribly overcommitted and couldn't get to it for at least a year. Can you wait that long?" say no. If the answer is, "Well, I'm not really doing anything along these lines, but I probably could come up with something if you can't find anyone else," find someone else. The lack of enthusiasm will show up as a lack of quality.

If you are editing a specialized encyclopedia, you will also need to select an editorial board. The board serves two purposes: to add prestige and credibility to the enterprise and to give you help in defining topics and selecting contributors. Ideally, each member should provide both prestige and advice; if not, you need a larger board. Encyclopedias are longer (sometimes multivolume), contain more (usually shorter) articles, and involve more contributors. Simply keeping track of such a project can be difficult, but the real problems are the intellectual ones of setting the limits of the subject and dividing it into manageable topics, with nothing superfluous included and nothing necessary left out.

An encyclopedia is such a large undertaking that it is vital to involve a publisher with reference book experience from the outset. Indeed, most such projects are initiated by publishers. If you have an idea for an encyclopedia or similar reference work, you should seek a publisher very early on. You might want to form a small editorial board and draw up a partial list of topics and possible contributors, but it is unwise to invest more time than that without a publisher's commitment.

For any multiauthor book, once you have contributors lined up, send each of them a letter of intent. Your publisher should provide these, or you can draw them up yourself. The letter should state the topic to be covered, the length of the article, and the date it is due. It should make clear that you can demand revisions or reject an unsuitable or unworthy submission. The letter should also point out that the publisher may also reject a submission or ask for revisions. In other words, publication is not guaranteed. The letter should include an agreement by the contributors not to publish their work elsewhere before the volume appears (and after it appears only with permission). The letter should also state whether the contributors are responsible for reviewing the editing of their manuscripts and for proofreading galleys and pages. Finally, if a contributor is to be paid, the amount should be stated and it should be clear when payment will be made (on signature of the letter? after final acceptance? on publication?). The letter of intent should also grant book publication rights to the publisher or to you as volume editor. For an encyclopedia, the publisher will probably insist on electronic rights. If so, this provision should be included in the letter to contributors.

When your list of contributors is complete, you may want to set up an electronic discussion list to share information, answer questions, and develop a sense of camaraderie. At a minimum, set up an electronic mailing list in your own address book so that you can correspond easily with the entire group.

Just because you have contributors and a publisher, don't think your worries are over. What happens when a contributor fails to write a chapter? If a contributor backs out early enough, you can look for a substitute. Unfortunately, what usually happens is that the deadline arrives, the paper doesn't, and you are left holding the bag. After all, you cannot force anyone to write. The best thing to do is to notify the tardy scholar that the agreement between you is canceled because the deadline has been missed and then forget about that article. If the omission of the topic is glaring, then you can use your introduction to cover it as best you can. Let your publisher know that the essay will not be forthcoming. You might be able to find someone else to write on short notice, but it is not very likely.

To prevent this disaster, keep in regular contact with your contributors, remind them of approaching deadlines, and ask how things are going. They may not tell you the truth, but they will at least have the task in mind. Periodic e-mails, letters, and calls may give you enough notice of impending failure to find a substitute. In any case, make sure deadlines are explicit, and make it clear that you intend to enforce them.

A more depressing problem is what to do with the article that is delivered on time but isn't any good. If the manuscript is not salvageable, you should admit this and return it diplomatically to the author. Never a pleasant task, it is better done early and mercifully than dragged out in the unrealistic expectation of a miracle. If the manuscript has some redeeming scholarly value but needs work, tell the author specifically and clearly what needs to be done and set a deadline for the work. Offer consultation and assistance. In this case, you should make a firm decision on the minimum quality you can accept and stick to it. Do not let time pressures force you into accepting garbage. The publisher's reviewers will catch the lapse anyway, and you will come in for a share of their criticism. The only way to prevent this problem is to choose your contributors carefully, as described earlier.

Unevenness in the volume often plagues multiauthor works – unequal quality among the articles, contributors writing for different audiences, overlapping coverage of topics, or gaps in coverage. These problems arise quite naturally, because contributors are concerned exclusively with their individual pieces. It is your job, as volume editor, to see the big picture, to keep it in mind, and to convey it to the contributors. You must decide the central theme of the volume and how each article will contribute to it. You will probably write an introduction that sets this out for the readers. At the outset, you should write an overview that does the same for the contributors. Describe the prospective audience and define the level of sophistication and specificity it demands. Tell each contributor what the other articles do and who is writing them. Try to anticipate areas of overlap or conflict and settle border disputes in advance. Encourage authors to keep in touch with you and with one another (this is where the online discussion list can help). Send regular progress reports and suggestions. Periodically ask for outlines or preliminary drafts from each author and ask permission to circulate these when appropriate. Try to make the venture a cooperative effort rather than a gathering of discrete projects.

If English is not a contributor's first language, you may need to polish the article a bit (or a lot) before submitting it to the publisher. Make sure the author understands and accepts your editing and be prepared to do the work. If you yourself are not that good a writer, find someone else to do it. If the author's English borders on the nonexistent, you may want to have the article submitted in the author's first language and hire a professional translator. (Always give credit to the translator, whether professional or amateur.)

When the entire volume is complete, read it and edit it. It is very tempting at this point to rush it off to the publisher. Despite my admonitions and your efforts, the deadline has probably passed. You have seen outlines and drafts and made suggestions. Now read and edit again. This extra effort can make the difference between a jumbled set of essays and a coherent collection of well-written chapters.

Read each contribution separately and make editorial changes and suggestions. Then read through the volume as a whole. Does it hold together? Does the theme emerge logically and consistently? Does it seem reasonably even in tone and sophistication, or do certain essays leap out as extraordinarily difficult or insultingly superficial? Is there too much overlap? Make further revisions in each article to solve these problems.

Next, do what you can to weave the volume together. Make sure your introduction sets out the theme of the volume, explains how each article contributes to the whole, and covers any remaining gaps. If cross-references from one article to another would be helpful, add them. Consider writing brief introductions to each section of the book or to each essay.

If your review results in significant changes to any article, send it back to the author for approval. Only when this is done should you declare the book ready for publication.

Contributor impatience can be a headache. An author who submits a good manuscript on time wants a prompt publication decision and prompt publication. If the process is delayed through the fault of others, the model author grows impatient. The problem is that the impatience is justified. Your job is to minimize the delay. First, make it clear from the outset that the publisher's evaluation will take time. Second – repeating myself, as you will have to do – establish deadlines and enforce them. It is not fair that the cooperative author has to wait around for the dawdlers. The author left out in the cold because of missing the deadline may also be angry, but with much less justification.

You bear the responsibility for dealing with authors who object to the publisher's copyediting, who are out of the country when proof is to be read, and who forgot that they had to supply camera-ready artwork. Your initial letter should have spelled out these duties, but chances are your contributors will forget. Remind them in your regular communications. Whatever decisions you make about editing and proofreading, you must keep reminding contributors of their responsibilities and give them enough advance warning to save time for their chores.

Money is the last of your worries. A collection of essays probably will not make much money, and the royalty rate offered may be low. Because you will bear most of the responsibility and do most of the work, the royalties (if any) should go to you. Books that will generate more income may carry an advance large enough to make payment to contributors possible. If you do receive more than a token payment, you may want to offer contributors a small honorarium. In no case, however, should you pay some contributors and not others. You should not pay contributors unequally unless they are making very different contributions. For example, if you have some very long articles and some shorter ones, you may want to pay the authors of the long pieces more. Some publishers will offer a single payment, in lieu of royalties, either to the compiler or to the compiler and the contributors.

Encyclopedias are priced to make a profit, and the typical financial arrangements reflect this. The author is generally paid an advance to cover the costs of compiling the volume (postage, phone calls, secretarial help, etc.), as well as royalties. Members of the editorial board usually receive a small fee, and contributors are usually paid. The amounts depend on the length of the articles and range from a free copy of the book to perhaps two or three hundred dollars. The timing of any cash payment is important. Publishers prefer to pay contributors on publication. From the editor's point of view, it is better to pay contributors when their articles are accepted. This arrangement motivates contributors to meet their deadlines and makes them less likely to complain about publication delays. However, these payments add up to a substantial sum, and your publisher may not be willing to change their policy. (It is also much easier to write all the checks at once, rather than piecemeal.)

To summarize, here is a suggested procedure for working with contributors to multiauthor volumes before the publishing process begins. The next section outlines a procedure to make things run smoothly during production. For an encyclopedia, steps 2 and 3 should be reversed.

1. Define the topic of the book and draw up a list of chapters needed.
2. Select potential contributors carefully and solicit their participation in a letter that describes the volume and their individual contributions in detail.
3. Seek a publisher for the volume.
4. Once contributors are chosen, send out letters of intent. Include a more detailed description of the book, the expected

contributors and their topics, and what is expected of each author. Provide instructions on manuscript and artwork preparation, reference and note style, permissions, and other details. Tell contributors what sorts of software you can accept.

5. When signed letters of intent are returned to you, send all contributors the other contributors' names, addresses, phone numbers, and e-mail addresses and remind them of deadlines. (This step is not necessary for an encyclopedia.)

6. Regularly circulate progress reports on publishers' interest, articles (or outlines) received, and deadlines approaching.

7. Telephone or e-mail contributors periodically to check on progress and to remind them that you are there.

8. When you receive outlines, drafts, queries, or finished articles, read them carefully and respond promptly. Make your suggestions as specific as possible and do not hesitate to reject the unsalvageable.

9. Be diplomatic in dealing with contributors, answer all correspondence promptly, and keep them informed of progress. The more closely involved they are in the book's creation, the more productive and cooperative they will be.

10. Do your own careful reading, review, and revision, including the composition of introductory and transitional material.

11. Once the manuscript is complete, notify all contributors that it is going to a publisher and keep them informed of the publisher's response. Final acceptance of the manuscript calls for a celebratory letter, phone call, or e-mail announcement.

Production

Once a publisher accepts the final version of a multiauthor book for production, the press will send it through the usual sequence of editing, design, typesetting, proofreading, printing, and binding. You and the publisher should decide jointly who will perform the chores of obtaining permission to quote copyrighted material, reviewing copyediting, gathering illustrations, and reading proof – you or the contributors. Usually the publisher regards you as the author, so that any failure of the contributors to perform their jobs becomes your problem. The following division of labor makes sense in that the person who can do each job most efficiently is assigned the task. However, your book may be different, or special circumstances (a contributor on sabbatical in Tibet) may dictate changes.

You should write for permission to reprint copyrighted material. The limit imposed on quotation under the "fair use" clause of the copyright act is cumulative for your entire book. Thus, if several contributors each quote a relatively small amount from the same book, you may need permission even though no single contributor would. You are the only person in a position to sort out permissions problems, and your contract with the publisher makes you responsible, so you should do it. (See Chapter 10 for details on permissions.)

You should ask contributors to sign letters of agreement or contracts with the publisher. These provide for the assignment of copyright (see Chapter 5) and set out other conditions. Usually the publisher will provide you with such a letter, with enough copies for each contributor. Alternatively, the sample letter in *The Chicago Manual of Style* can be modified to make it suitable for your volume.

Contributors should generally review the copyediting of their own articles. However, because they have already reviewed your changes, this is not crucial, particularly if the copyediting is light. Especially when time is pressing (as it usually is), you might ask contributors to waive this right. If you do have contributors review the editing, those who cannot do so should designate a trusted colleague (preferably you) as a substitute, in writing. Notify contributors of changes in style that you have accepted, lest they change everything back. You should be prepared to mediate disagreements between the copyeditor and contributors if disputes arise and to enforce deadlines. A contributor overly sensitive to your suggestions is likely to take umbrage at a copyeditor's changes, so warn the editor ahead of time. Similarly, the editor may want to work first on the contributions of the most dilatory, so that the contributors will have more time for review without holding up the volume. It is a good idea for contributors to return their manuscripts to you. Then you can review them, handle queries from the authors, prod the tardy, and make final changes before returning them to the manuscript editor. Schedule time for this in your planning.

Contributors must provide drafts of their own artwork, but you and the publisher must decide whether it is necessary for all final drawing to be done by the same artist. If not, the publisher should provide specifications and directions and let the contributors fend for themselves. If the art is to be uniform, then hire an artist. Whether the contributors will take on the cost will depend on the usual practice in your field and on the letters of intent you signed with them. In the sciences, for example, where authors customarily pay journals page charges plus art fees, contributors will probably not balk at paying. You will have to negotiate such arrangements as early as possible.

You should generally take responsibility for proofreading. Although there is some value in having contributors proofread their own work, this is time-consuming and risky in that the contributors may want to start rewriting when it is too late. Let them know that the review of the copyediting (or of your editing) marks their last chance to make changes and that they will not see proof. If you are not a good proofreader, hire someone to do the work for you (the publisher can recommend a proofreader). You should still read the proof for sense, but you can rely on the proofreader for details. If your proofreading raises questions that only the contributor can answer, a phone call or e-mail should resolve the problem. For highly technical manuscripts, however, the contributor may be the best proofreader. In this case, send contributors a copy of their individual proof and keep a copy yourself. Set a firm deadline, and if a contributor does not return proof on time, rely on your own reading. If contributors make excessive changes or argue about the style adopted throughout the volume, it is your job to tell them that the changes they want will not be made.

You are responsible for the index (see Chapter 10) as well as for providing a glossary or bibliography if the publisher requires it. In addition, you must gather biographical material on the contributors to be included in the volume. You must keep an up-to-date list of contributors' addresses and academic affiliations.

One final note: If you are sharing the volume editor's responsibilities with a colleague, divide up the chores sensibly and keep in touch. There is no point in wasting time and creating confusion by duplicating effort.

Anthologies and Readers

Anthologies and readers may be produced in traditional print formats, as online publications, or both. Although the tasks involved in compiling them are similar regardless of format, the technical chores of production are different. As long as you are working with a publisher, you should not have to perform these tasks. For a print anthology, the publisher is responsible for typesetting, printing, and binding. Similarly, for an electronic anthology, the publisher should code and format the material, put it up on a server, and maintain the site. The intellectual and clerical tasks remain the responsibility of the author.

The intellectual tasks to be performed in compiling an anthology are selection and presentation. The clerical tasks are permissions and physical preparation.

Before you can select materials for an anthology, you must have a clear idea of your purpose and audience. In what courses will the book be used? What time period should be covered? What topics must be included? Are you presenting one consistent view of an issue or illustrating conflicting opinions? Is your book meant to supplement a text or stand on its own? Is its purpose to provide information or stimulate debate? What reading level and previous knowledge can you assume on the part of your readers? How is your anthology going to differ from existing ones? If you are preparing an electronic anthology, you may also need to think about how extensively it should be illustrated, how elaborate a system of links should be incorporated, and how it should be navigated.

You should think through all these questions and prepare a prospectus to send to potential publishers (see Chapter 7). First, formulate criteria for selections to be included. The criteria should reflect the goals you have set out. As you review material for inclusion, check it against the criteria you have set. With any luck, you will have more material than you need. You can rank competing articles according to how well they meet your criteria and also on their secondary qualities. For example, perhaps two essays fill the same spot and are of roughly equal quality, but one is half as long as the other. Come up with a list of first choices and back it up with some alternatives. (Your list of alternatives can double as a list of supplementary reading.) For your benefit and that of an acquiring editor, you should write a brief description of each article (author, title, date, length, subject) and an explanation of its appropriateness for your collection. A prospectus that includes your understanding of the book's purpose and audience, your selection criteria, and this descriptive list should be all you need to sell the book.

You also need to decide how to present the selections. Will your written contribution be limited to a brief preface? Or will you provide a lengthy introduction to the volume plus headnotes for each selection? Will you write study or discussion questions? Will you annotate selections? Does the book need a bibliography? An index (for print) or a search mechanism other than a simple word search (for electronic texts)? Get all these issues worked out as soon as possible. When you do find a publisher, your editor will want to review your selections and your decisions about such matters as annotation and may suggest a number of changes. Your list of alternative selections will be particularly useful at this point.

As soon as you find a publisher and have decided which selections to include, you must begin to write for permission to reprint. Your letters must state that you want to reprint the selection in its entirety in an anthology and should explain the book's nature, whether it is print or electronic, and anticipated market. If the book is not intended for classroom use and will have a small circulation, make this clear so that the copyright holder will charge less. You will probably be charged more for an electronic publication. Some publishers may not be able to give permission for electronic publication but will refer you to the author.

You must expect to pay a fee, but your letter need not mention this; let the copyright holder ask for the fee. In most cases, your contract will provide for your publisher's payment of this fee as an advance against royalties. If you are being paid a lump sum in lieu of royalties, the publisher generally will pay permissions fees outright, up to a specified total. This arrangement is more common when the publisher initiates the project.

To determine who holds the rights to a selection, either look at the original publication or see where someone else got permission to reprint by checking the copyright page, acknowledgments, or credit line in another anthology. Do not assume that material is in the public domain simply because you found it on the Web. Reputable sites will provide credit lines for artwork, quotations, and reprinted material. Others reproduce copyrighted material without permission, either deliberately or through ignorance. Your publisher will need to know that you have been diligent.

Your text should be drawn from the original source, preferably in print. Texts on the Web are less reliable than those in print. Frequently they have been scanned and inadequately proofread. At other times, coding problems introduce inaccuracies. Also, even many websites that take pains to reproduce texts accurately use inferior editions because they are in the public domain. Always work from the best available printed text or a recent text on an authoritative website, such as those of documentary or textual editing projects.

If you are abridging an article, specify what you are omitting. You may need separate permission for illustrations in an article; check the credit lines in each selection. As explained in Chapter 10, prepare each letter in triplicate and send two copies to the publisher who holds rights. If permission is denied or the fee is too high, substitute another article and write promptly for permission. It is possible to bargain on permissions fees, and if you really want the original article you should try to get the fee reduced.

Occasionally the restrictions placed on electronic use of artwork makes its use impractical. For example, a museum may require poor resolution so that works cannot be printed out. Others may wish to give permission only for a limited term, which may not be practical for your purposes.

To prepare a print anthology, you will need reprints or high-quality photocopies of each page to be included. You may have to copy from a bound volume, and in these cases be careful to get the whole page copied without losing either edge. Each page of your manuscript should be an 8½- by 11-inch sheet, either a photocopy or a cutout page pasted or taped to the sheet. Use one side of the page only; if you have only one reprint you will have to photocopy the backs of pages. If the material was originally set in columns, cut the columns apart and paste one column to each 8½- by 11-inch sheet. Add your introductions, annotations, study questions, and credit lines where they belong and prepare a title page and table of contents.

For an electronic anthology, you must provide electronic files or links to acceptable online texts. If you scan a printed text to create a file, you must proofread it carefully. The same is true if you rekeyboard it.

If the articles you are going to reprint contain figures or photographs, you will have to get original art or glossy prints for print publication. Electronic publication requires that you use an existing electronic image or scan a high-quality print. You can ask for prints or electronic images in your request for permission. If prints of graphs or cartoons are not available, you may have to have them redrawn; check with your editor about the possibility of duplicating the art from reprints before going to such expense.

You must read through your manuscript to see whether mechanical alterations are needed. For example, you should eliminate cross-references to material that appeared in the original but is not included in your anthology and change cross-references to material that is in your anthology but on a different page. For electronic anthologies, you may wish to change cross-references to links. You may have to renumber tables and figures and alter the text references to them; in electronic works, "see table 4" should be replaced by a link to the table. Footnotes may need renumbering; these too can be linked in an electronic publication. You can correct obvious typographical errors in the original, but you should not make any other changes without the owner's written permission. You should make only the deletions that you specified in your permissions letter, and you must mark these with ellipses. (See *The Chicago Manual of Style* for the proper use of ellipses.)

Before sending the manuscript to your publisher, check the table of contents against the manuscript for the correct spelling of the authors' names and the correct and complete titles of the selections. Check credit lines against permissions letters to make sure you have all permissions and that you have placed and worded the credits as required. Make these two checks again in proof.

Self-publishing

If you are planning an anthology for an advanced course with a small enrollment, you may find it difficult to interest a publisher. Publishers may also turn up their noses at an anthology you are contemplating for use in your own introductory course if they think it is unlikely to be adopted elsewhere. Or you may decide to replace the photocopied course pack you use for your class with an online publication. In these cases, you may want to publish the book yourself.

After selecting the articles you wish to include, obtaining permission, and writing introductory material, you must decide how elaborately to produce the book. If it is just for your own classes, you can paste up the original articles for inexpensive photocopying, shop around for the best price, and have them bound (looseleaf and comb, or plastic-spiral, bindings are not expensive). Some printers near college campuses offer this service regularly. A 200-page book can be produced for about $6.00 a copy, and you can sell it through your bookstore or the printer at cost or at a profit. (Your university may regulate such sales; check with your department chair.)

Even if the anthology is exclusively for the use of your own students, and even if you sell it at cost, you must get written permission from copyright holders. Failure to do so is a violation of the copyright law, and one that publishers are taking seriously. A reputable copy shop will refuse to print the book for you unless you either show them the permissions you have received or ask them to do this for you. The permissions letter should explain the limited use you plan and the number of copies you will print. The fees that publishers charge should be included in your computation of costs and in the price you charge.

It may be easier for you, and more convenient for your students, to put such material online. This works best if most of your selections are available on the Web, so that your "course pack" can simply provide a link to the document, article, or painting students are to study. For other elements, you will have to keyboard or scan the material and proofread. You will also need to get permission for material that you put on the Web yourself. In your letters, be sure to specify that the copyrighted items will be used only for your class, give the approximate enrollment, and specify the way you will protect the material (usually by requiring a password or by limiting access to users with a university account).

If you hope to sell your book or Web compilation beyond your own campus, you will have to write appropriate permissions letters to copyright holders and, if you are printing it, produce something more attractive. Read the section in Chapter 10 on preparing camera-ready copy. Before beginning production, consult some local printers on the most practical page size and get estimates for printing and binding. You will probably not want to undertake a large-scale marketing effort, but sending a form letter and order blank to colleagues teaching in the same field is practical and effective. Be sure to do the mailing in time for them to adopt the book for the following semester. Keep good records of your costs and sales both for your tax returns and to help you decide whether to continue your new venture.

Selling an electronic anthology is much trickier. Most publishers are not sure how to do this; even Stephen King decided that online self-publishing was not worth the effort. You need a way to control access and collect revenues, and you cannot use your university's site or server for commercial ventures.

In any self-publishing effort, there is an element of financial risk. Do not print more copies than you think you can sell in a year, and be sure to make this estimate on a day when you're feeling pessimistic. It is not difficult to reprint if you need to, and small printings require less storage space. They also allow for correcting mistakes and making worthwhile additions. Be realistic about the costs in time and money that you are expending.

Should your book succeed beyond your own campus, you may be able to interest a publisher in it. You can submit a copy of your book along with sales figures. Be sure to insist on a respectable royalty, because you will have done much of the publisher's work. You may, of course, decide to continue on your own. Before you invest large sums, however, be sure you want to spend time and money on a greater marketing effort, on maintaining a larger inventory, and on shipping and billing. The experience will give you a practical appreciation of what publishers do, but you may well be happier with a theoretical understanding.

Chapter 7

Finding a Publisher for the College Textbook

The book originated in the suggestion of a publisher, as many more good books have done than the arrogance of the man of letters is commonly inclined to admit.

G. K. Chesterton, on *The Pickwick Papers*

The College Textbook

A textbook is designed specifically to help an instructor teach a subject and students learn it. Although scholarly monographs and collections of articles are sometimes used as supplementary or even main texts in a college course, their primary purpose is to disseminate new thought or research findings. Textbooks, by contrast, rarely represent the culmination of research or what is traditionally considered "scholarly" activity. Instead, they summarize, organize, and analyze the accumulated wisdom of an area of knowledge, presenting it in a way that is comprehensible to students at a specific level of competence.

The writers of the most successful textbooks in a field are not necessarily – or even usually – at the cutting edge of research. They are more often, though not always, extremely good teachers. The skills required to write a good textbook are those of organization, synthesis, explication, and communication. However, the ability to communicate orally in a lecture class or seminar does not automatically translate into the ability to write effectively. As you write a textbook, you do not get instant student responses of understanding or befuddlement. You cannot carry on a conversation or discussion. You must decide, on the basis of logic, instinct, and experience, what requires extensive explanation and what will be grasped quickly.

In writing a textbook, you must consider not only the student but also the teacher. After all, the teacher will decide whether to adopt your text or a competing volume. This means that your book must be easy to use as the foundation of a course. To satisfy instructors, you must cover all the basic ground, the core material of the discipline. If using your text would force teachers to find supplementary materials for important subjects, teachers are not likely to adopt it.

At the same time, college faculty members are an independent lot, and they do not like to be dictated to. Your book should not, therefore, require a rigid course structure – particularly if it will mean that many teachers must radically revise lecture notes. In organizing your book, you should keep this in mind and, if possible, arrange the text in a way that permits it to be used flexibly. For example, it might be divided into units that can be taught in different order and that can be presented independently of one another. Your publisher will offer advice on such matters.

Teachers also adopt books for less rational reasons. They may like the way a book feels in their hands or lies on a lectern, or they may prefer a fat, impressive volume to a thinner book that uses less bulky paper and larger pages. They may prefer brightly colored, illustrated bindings to plain bindings with dust jackets. Publishers know about this sort of thing, and you should not be surprised when they raise such seemingly superficial issues.

Another general point about textbooks must be noted, too: The amounts of money involved in textbook publishing are far greater than those related to scholarly books. Textbook publishers must make a profit, and although they take risks, they do not publish books that are likely to lose money. Even textbooks for unusual or advanced courses are published in larger editions, with more elaborate design and larger marketing budgets, than are most monographs. Books for popular introductory courses are large-scale undertakings. Textbook publishers may invest a half-million dollars in launching a basic text, and they expect to sell many hundreds of thousands of copies over the years. This naturally means that authors can expect to earn far larger royalties from basic textbooks than from monographs. It also means that publishers must consider very carefully where they are going to invest their resources.

Because textbooks with large anticipated sales demand large investments of money and effort, publishers usually conduct extensive market surveys and consultations with potential users. Textbook publishers know the market, and their decisions are based on economic considerations. A scholarly publisher may take a chance on an innovative bit of scholarship, a well-written biography of an obscure figure, or an intriguing but off-the-wall philosophical treatise. Textbook publishers cannot afford to take risks on excitement, experimentation, or artistry.

Finally, the timing of publication is crucial in textbook publishing. It may not matter whether your monograph hits the bookstores in July or November, but it certainly does matter that faculty members see a textbook early enough to make an adoption decision and that they can count on the books being on the shelf in time for classes. Deadlines are important in any kind of publishing, but they are doubly important for textbooks. The schedule for publishing a textbook may become very rushed, and there may not be time to dot all the scholarly *i*'s and cross all the academic *t*'s.

One result of the primacy of financial considerations is that textbook acquiring editors tend to be different sorts of people than university press editors. Usually they have arrived in the acquisitions department via sales and marketing rather than manuscript editing or academia. If all publishers are on a continuum between the worlds of scholarship and business, textbook editors are closer to the business end. A psychologist talking to the psychology editor of a university press will find the conversation running toward psychology; the same person talking to a textbook editor will end up discussing the market and rival texts. There are exceptions, of course, and some editors move between the two worlds. But on the whole, you will find that textbook publishing has an aura far removed from that of academe.

Textbooks for advanced or specialized courses, particularly those that represent one particular methodological or theoretical approach, may be more attractive to a university press or commercial scholarly publisher than to a textbook house. On such projects, you would do well to approach both sorts of publishers to see where the interest is greater.

Choosing a Publisher

The textbook industry has undergone a great deal of consolidation over the past twenty years. Many houses that were once independent are now owned by large publishing groups, and some of the larger companies have been bought by still larger news or entertainment conglomerates. Although this has reduced authors' choices somewhat, the effect has not been as drastic as expected. Many imprints remain editorially independent, and different divisions of large conglomerates still find themselves competing against one another in some fields. Overall, authors' opportunities do not seem to have diminished.

Many of the rules about finding a scholarly publisher also apply to selecting a textbook publisher, but there are some major differences. The most important is that textbook publishers rarely base their decisions on a completed manuscript. They prefer to begin working with an author at the earliest possible stage of the book's development. You are free to shop around and let publishers compete for your book; it is not like scholarly publishing, with its expectation of exclusive review. (Of course, once you have a contract, that's it.) Because you are not close to having a finished manuscript while you are seeking a publisher, the prospectus for the college textbook is far more important.

The Prospectus

The textbook prospectus is a more complicated document than the query letter for a monograph, but it has the same purpose. As you write it, remember that you are trying to sell an idea – and your ability to carry it out – to the publisher. You begin with broad descriptive material. First, you must explain the topic of your book and its theme or approach. Even an introductory survey text has a theme that differentiates it from other texts. A second important topic is coverage – which topics will be discussed and which omitted. You should provide a rationale for any unusual inclusions or omissions. Third, what educational approach does your manuscript incorporate? For example, do you begin each section with an illustrative case study and then go on to discuss the theories and process it illustrates?

Next, you can cover market considerations such as the courses for which the book is suitable, how commonly such courses are offered, with what enrollments, and at what level; the kinds of students the book is written for (community college, freshman nonmajors, junior majors); and how the book differs from existing texts. This is the place to show your familiarity with what is available and to explain how you can do better. Some publishers expect a detailed comparison of your proposed book with all existing texts. I think that is their job – and one that they entrust to prospective authors at their peril – but gaining a variety of perspectives can be of value to you as you develop your own ideas. A general comparison with major texts should be adequate, along with a demonstration of differences in significant details.

You can also include any special features you plan, such as biographical sketches of notable figures in the field or brief first-person accounts of famous discoveries.

You must also convince the publisher that you are qualified to write the book. Do you have a record of publication? What courses have you taught, and for how long? Have you received teaching awards? Have you used any of the proposed material in class, and with what results? If you can provide duplicated class material and written student evaluations, these will be helpful.

Finally, estimate the length of your manuscript and the number of illustrations you expect to use, and explain the status of your manuscript: How much is written, and when can you finish it?

All of this material can be presented as a prospectus or as a letter. If you write it as a prospectus, include a brief cover letter as well. In addition to the prospectus or letter, enclose a curriculum vitae, a detailed table of contents, chapter outlines or summaries, and at least one sample chapter (the introduction plus two substantive chapters is ideal). You can send the prospectus to as many publishers as you like, but it saves time and money to select the ones most likely to be interested and to do a good job.

Shopping Around

You must find out which textbook publishers are active in your field. You can do this by looking at the texts you and your colleagues are using, by surveying the textbook ads you get in the mail, and by looking through the business cards of the college representatives who visit you each semester. Do not rule out publishers just because they already have a text in your field. Larger companies may publish several books in one area, especially for courses with large enrollments. Perhaps the current text is selling poorly or the publisher needs a text at a different ability level or with an innovative approach. Any company that publishes in your subject is a possibility.

College representatives (salespeople) for textbook publishers are valuable contacts. Part of their job is to sniff out new manuscripts. If you have a good idea for a textbook, they will be delighted to take it back to an acquisitions editor. But you do not need to wait for the college rep to appear at your door. Write a note, send an e-mail, or make a phone call. If you have been consistently unimpressed by a publisher's sales force, you may want to cross the publisher off your list. After all, they are the ones who will be selling (or failing to sell) your book. However, there are other important considerations in choosing a textbook publisher as well.

Money may be a major factor for you. Larger publishers can offer larger advances, and that can certainly make a difference. Remember, though, that the advance is not in addition to royalties, just an early payment. Publishers will not advance you more than they think the book will earn, so the larger advance just means you get the money now instead of later. Royalties on textbooks are generally at least 10 to 12 percent of list or net. If you are not pressed for cash, you should evaluate the potential income from each publisher according to the royalty rate and how well and how long they will produce and promote the book. Read the textbooks the publishers have on their lists. Are they good? Would you use them? Do other people use them? Publishers will tell you how well their texts are doing, but you should look at those numbers critically and compare statistics. How many copies were sold in the first year? In the second year? What share of the market does that represent? If the sales drop off dramatically in the second year and disappear in the third, that tells you something important about the quality of the book and the publisher's sales effort. There will always be some reduction in sales owing to the circulation of used books, but a good basic text that is well promoted and kept up-to-date with revised editions should continue to sell year after year.

Just as textbook publishing is expensive for the publisher, it can also be expensive for the author. If you must pay for permissions, illustrations, and indexing out of pocket, you will have to come up with a considerable amount of cash. See whether the publisher will pay permissions fees for quotations and illustrations. Will they pay an artist to draw special art for the book and a photo researcher to find existing photographs? Some may offer to pay part or all of these fees, and you should factor that into your calculations. For many textbooks, these costs can mount up to thousands of dollars. If they will not pay or share any of these costs, ask them to advance the fees out of royalties so that you don't have to pay cash. (Chapter 10 provides further information on illustrations and permissions.)

Most textbook publishers employ developmental editors to help authors turn ideas into finished manuscripts. They fill in the gap between acquisitions and manuscript or production editors. Ask the acquiring editor how the developmental editors work. How much support will they provide? Will they read and comment on each chapter as it is finished? Will they send chapters out for specialists' suggestions? Can the developmental editor help with illustrations? Will the publisher arrange classroom testing of material? Will they help you to do so, or expect you to do it without help?

You also need to know whether the publisher's marketing department can provide you with research reports on competing texts. If so, you and the developmental editor can decide how to use the information to best advantage. Market research can also help you determine the scope and level of the text you write by telling you what prerequisites most students will have had, what material they have generally covered in earlier courses, and how advanced they are in basic skills and in your academic field.

Determine, too, what each publisher will expect in the way of supplementary materials, and whether you are required to supply them. For example, will you have to write a lab manual, instructor's guide, sample exams, a study guide? Will someone else write them, for your review? Will your textbook be sold with computer software, such as self-paced exercises? Does the publisher want to offer a slide collection, or a CD-ROM with art reproductions? How much technical help will you get in preparing such sophisticated materials? Sometimes a collection of readings is considered supplementary to a text, although it requires enough work to be considered a book on its own. (See Chapter 6 on anthologies.) Introductory texts are increasingly being viewed as packages, and you need to know just how much work you are letting yourself in for.

You cannot always judge the quality of manuscript editing by reading a finished book. A good editor's work is invisible, and if a book is well written you cannot tell whether the credit should go to the author or the editor. However, a poorly edited book is the publisher's fault. If you can spot grammatical errors, stylistic inconsistencies, excessive repetition, and similar problems, then the book was badly edited. If the quality of your writing is important to you, find a publisher whose books are consistently well edited. Often a smaller publisher will devote more effort to editing, but size is not an infallible guide. Ask the acquisitions editor how copyediting is handled. Make sure the publisher takes it seriously, allows sufficient time, expects you to review the editing, and provides advice on writing (and, if possible, written guidelines) to its authors. If the acquisitions editor promises not to touch a word of your golden prose, go elsewhere. No one's textbook prose is that golden. How high is the turnover in editorial staff? If editors keep quitting, there may be something wrong, and the production of your book is likely to be delayed. In addition, you may become frustrated as each new editor thinks of new revisions for you to make, or reinterprets previous understandings. Ask colleagues who have published with a firm about their experience.

Look at the design and special features of a publisher's books. Are the books easy to read and use? Are they attractive? Do they demonstrate innovative thinking in study aids and other pedagogic features? Are there enough illustrations? Are the illustrations well drawn or reproduced haphazardly from aging sources? Are elements like the glossary and index of good quality? See whether the book is well made. Is the paper of good quality? Is the printing clear, crisp, and even? Are photographs clearly printed? Is the binding likely to survive a year of transportation in a backpack?

Ask the publisher how your book will be promoted. Do they have an adequate sales staff? Are they good at their job? What about mailings and convention booths? If you have never seen a sales rep from a given company, probably other faculty haven't either.

Ask how soon the publisher would expect a first draft and when publication is anticipated. They may be in too much of a hurry for you. Finally, ask how long the publisher keeps books in print and how often revised editions will be issued. The need for frequent revision varies from field to field – astronomy changes faster than metaphysics – but you should be sure that the publisher is willing to revise as necessary. The loss of sales due to resale of used books is another motivation to revise. Remember, of course, that if the book does not succeed on the first try, the question will become moot. You will not get any guarantees on this point, but make sure the firm's general practice is not to let reasonably successful books die prematurely.

If you get more than one offer of publication, weigh all these elements – money (advance, royalty rates, and sharing of expenses), editorial support and capabilities, design talent, production quality, sales record and potential – and choose the publisher you would most like to work with. You will receive a contract, which you should read very carefully (see the section on contracts in Chapter 5). Given the amounts of money at stake, you may want a lawyer to review it for you. Your state bar association or a law school faculty member can refer you to an expert in communications law or in the law of intellectual property. As mentioned earlier, pay special attention to provisions about illustrations and permissions, which are an important part of textbook authorship. Whenever possible, have the contract permit prepublication costs such as permissions fees, artists' fees, and indexing to be paid for by the publisher or deducted from royalties rather than paid out of your pocket. Now all you have to do is write the book.

Chapter 8

Working with Your Textbook Publisher

> ... As we were leaving he hinted
> That a student could hardly do less
> Than see how the volumes were printed
> At the time-honoured Clarendon Press.
> So I went there with scholarly yearning,
> And I gathered from kind Mr. Gell,
> Some books were to stimulate learning,
> And some were intended to sell.
>
> *Oxford Magazine*, 1892

Writing, reviewing, and revising a textbook manuscript are very different from the parallel processes in scholarly publishing. As noted in Chapter 7, the purpose and contents of a textbook are not those of the scholarly monograph. Textbooks also differ in the level of difficulty, in format, and in the degree of illustration. And as I also noted earlier, textbooks must please your colleagues or they will not use them. A monograph presents a unique viewpoint. If it is well documented and convincingly written, it will be read (and sometimes appreciated) even by those who disagree with its conclusions and approach. But a textbook must try to be all things to all teachers, and this necessitates a different review process and the consideration of a new range of writing issues.

Writing a Textbook

A textbook must be credible and authoritative. The key element in conveying credibility is, of course, your competence to write the book. You must know your subject thoroughly. The basic sources in your field, as well as the current literature, must be at your fingertips. Let us assume, though, that you would not attempt to write about a subject you do not know. Let us also assume that you can write clearly, at least with the help of an editor. What pitfalls must you avoid that can detract from the authority you should be able to convey?

The first is exaggeration. Do not say *all* when you mean *most*, or *most* when you mean *many*, or *many* when you mean *some*, or *some* when you mean *a few*.[1] If you must assign the status of "most exciting discovery of the decade," limit it to one discovery – and make it a good one. In describing research, you will often have to simplify conclusions, but do not exaggerate the implications of a study or gloss over any significant limitations on its applicability.

A second threat to credibility is obvious bias, especially if it is unacknowledged. Students may not notice this, but instructors will. If your text is designed specifically to represent one school of thought, that should be explicit. It should probably even be part of the title: *Economics: A Supply-Side Analysis; Psychology: A Behaviorist Approach.* But in a general, all-purpose text, all schools should be represented evenhandedly. This does not mean one school, one paragraph. It does mean that your explications of various arguments should be objective and fair, and that respectable points of view are not neglected. Be careful not to overrepresent theories simply because their bizarre nature makes them more entertaining.

A third way to lose credibility is to make dogmatic and arbitrary statements. This is largely a matter of tone. You can say that there is only one right way to do something without ridi-

---

[1] Robert Graves and Alan Hodge offer a concise guide to such expressions on p. 140 of *The Reader Over Your Shoulder: A Handbook for Writers of English Prose* (New York: Macmillan, 1944).

culing the alternatives or those who believe them, which might get you into libel trouble anyway. If you need to resort to "this is so because I say so," there is something wrong with your argument. Students respond better if they feel that they have discovered the truth themselves, and they resist having conclusions forced on them.

In addition to credibility, you must strive for general acceptability. Your book will be considered for adoption and will be read by men, women, African Americans, Whites, American Indians, Hispanics, Asian Americans, older people, teenagers, Republicans, Democrats, Libertarians, Socialists, fundamentalists of all faiths, and atheists – among others. It cannot be all things to all people, and you do not want to be so fearful of offending that you become tongue-tied. You can, however, make an effort to be fair and to avoid such blatant offenses as stereotyping or ignoring minorities, ridiculing religious or political opinions, or misrepresenting arguments.

Many of these issues are much easier to handle than people believe. A great deal of fuss has been raised about sexist language, more specifically the incorrect use of the generic *he*. Words such as *he, man, mankind,* and *salesman* do not include women. *Man* and *mankind* can be replaced by *human being, humanity,* or *civilization; salesmen* can be called *salespeople, sales agents,* or *sales representatives.* To avoid the he/she construction, sentences can be cast in the plural, or you can use the second-person *you*. A little imagination makes the problem go away. Many publishers and professional organizations offer guidelines on avoiding sexist language, and you can consult a useful book by Marilyn Schwartz called *Guidelines for Bias-Free Writing* or Rosalie Maggio's *Talking About People*. If you do not avoid sexist language, your copyeditor will remove it for you.

Beyond the problem of language, you should avoid sexism in your examples, case histories, and illustrations. If you feel that making these elements gender-neutral renders them too vague or even inaccurate, you can divide them roughly equally by gender. When you do this, be sure that positive and negative examples are equally distributed between the sexes, unless of course the apparent inequities reflect genuine gender differences.

Avoiding racist language is not difficult, but there are more subtle issues to watch for. White authors tend to assume unconsciously that everyone is White. Remarks such as "Our ancestors came to America in search of freedom" become absurd when you remember that ancestors were of several colors besides white. You must, of course, avoid stereotyped images, examples, and illustrations.

It is no longer safe to assume that your readers are all between the ages of seventeen and twenty-two. Many older people are returning to college, and you cannot take for granted that they share the vocabulary and experiences of the current generation of adolescents. Of course, you may not share these either, and it is a mistake to try to write as if you do. Any teenager will tell you that no one over thirty can aspire to coolness.

In some fields, religion is an issue. How and when the world was created and the status of evolution are again matters of dispute. These questions can be handled briefly, but they should not be ignored, dismissed, or ridiculed. On questions where religious belief is a major factor and passions are strong – abortion, for example – you must be extremely careful to present opposing points of view fairly. Choose the strongest arguments on each side and try to write matter-of-factly and without emotion. This helps the instructor conduct a discussion that is based on information and reason, rather than feelings and faith.

Politics, the other issue we do not discuss in polite company, arises in many fields. You need not be bland, but you should present at least two sides to every issue and not hold any respectable argument up to ridicule. In textbook writing, it may be difficult to draw the line between fairness and "political correctness." Some elementary and high school texts have been criticized for blandness and ridiculed for picturing not only the right ethnic mix in a classroom but the right vegetables in a salad. Although the pressure is less intense at the college level, authors need to be alert to editorial suggestions that are well meant but incorrect. For example, gender-neutral language may distort the account of a historical event or medical experiment, and attempts to include people of color when none were present will lead to justified criticism. Be fair, and be accurate.

On all of these issues writing a textbook can be an opportunity for you to learn – to reexamine prejudices, to read authors you have dismissed out of hand, and to rethink your position on a number of substantial intellectual issues. If you regard the problems of racial, sexual, religious, and political bias in writing as a genuine challenge rather than as a series of minor obstacles, you may find yourself enjoying the task and growing in its performance.

Reviews and Rewriting

Before you begin writing, you and your editor should work out a schedule and a plan for review. You should agree on a detailed outline and on a timetable for submitting chapters. Make sure you understand the reviewing process to be used and the kinds of revision you may have to undertake. Textbook publishers use a very different system of review from the one university presses employ, and the revisions they anticipate are far more extensive.

It is also at this stage that you and your publisher, usually in the person of a developmental editor, will set out the special features and organizational details that will make your book more useful and salable. As I noted in Chapter 7, the instructors who will decide whether to adopt your book have a limited amount of flexibility. The published description of their courses and the conventions of their disciplines determine what must be covered, and their own energy limits how much they are willing to revise a course from year to year. Usually, a textbook should be organized to follow the order in which most instructors teach the subject. A convenient way to find out how your colleagues teach their courses is to look at syllabi on the Web. Many instructors have Web pages for their courses, and these can be a very useful source of information on coverage, texts used, supplementary materials expected, and so forth. It is often possible, too, to organize a text so that it can be used in various ways. This possibility can be explained to the instructor in the preface or the instructor's manual, with alternative tables of contents spelling out the details. The more flexible the text, the more it may be adopted.

Almost every textbook includes some sort of special material: glossaries, suggested readings, problems (both worked-out and unsolved), answers to problems, chapter summaries and reviews, inspirational essays by prominent figures in the field, brief biographies, brief essays to highlight controversial or current issues – the possibilities are endless. You may already have discussed these matters with your acquiring editor, but now is the time to determine the nature, number, and length of these features. You and your developmental editor can use market research results and reviewers' comments to come up with an appropriate group of supplementary features. These details help attract students and instructors to the text, increase the students' interest, help them learn the material, and occasionally inspire a few students to further study. They are important selling points and also important learning aids. Consider their use carefully and do them well.

It is also possible to use extra features to expand the market for the book. For example, by providing exercises at different levels of difficulty, you can make the book useful for classes of varying abilities. Supplementary materials can also provide ideas and challenges for more able or advanced students. Discuss all of these possibilities with your editor.

Although details may vary, the basic textbook editorial process includes three types of review: market, content, and editorial. The market evaluation is used first to determine whether a new textbook can be expected to sell. The publisher surveys existing texts and tries to learn how well they are doing, what faculty members think of them, which features make them appealing, and where they are vulnerable. The results of this research are then applied to your project, as the publisher determines the appropriate length, subject coverage, extent and type of illustration, level of difficulty, price range, and so forth. Many of these questions are interrelated. For example, a book for students who are not good readers may require heavier illustration, and a long book of complex design cannot sell for $12.95. Obviously, the market review must be done very early in the game, and the basic nature of the book must be decided before you have done much writing. Authors can contribute to this process, but the publisher is the real expert here. If you and your publisher disagree seriously at this stage, you should find another publisher.

Content reviews take place when the text is finished. (Sometimes various sections of a manuscript will be sent off earlier to experts in specific fields.) The reviewers are your academic colleagues, and they are asked whether your manuscript is accurate, balanced, up-to-date, authoritative, and complete. They will be asked to offer suggestions for additions and deletions, expansion and tightening, and other alterations. They may point out some recent research that would enhance your presentation or claim that you have spent too much time on one topic and too little on another. If you have your facts wrong, they will correct them (if you're lucky). They may detect errors in logic or confusion in arguments. The reviewers will be asked whether they would use the book in their courses and, if not, what is wrong.

Remember that the publisher will not take content reviews as gospel. The reviewers are experts, but they are not infallible. In fact, they will often disagree among themselves. If ten reviewers unanimously suggest the same change, your developmental editor (after recovering from the shock) will probably insist on it. More likely, however, suggestions will be weighed and evaluated, and some will be followed, while others are discarded.

You are an expert, too, and you must participate actively in this stage of the review. Your publisher has not solicited and paid for reviews to show you up or embarrass you. The purpose is to give you some advice, to anticipate criticism, and to improve your book. And it is still your book. If you think a reviewer is dead wrong, say so. You may agree with a reader's criticism but offer a different solution. The most important and difficult task at this stage is to consider the reviews objectively and use them wisely. You cannot do this if you are too easily insulted, too stubborn, not stubborn enough, or lazy. Ask yourself why you are resisting a suggestion. Is it because you know it is wrong or unworkable? Because you worked really hard on that section and – even though the change would be helpful – you cannot face it again? Because you do not like the tone of the criticism? Your developmental editor has tried to get you the best advice available, but your reaction will determine whether the advice will be put to good use. Remember, too, that the editor is on your side. You are in a hurry to get the book into production, but so are the acquisitions and developmental editors, production manager, and sales director. They are offering suggestions not to put obstacles in your path but to improve the final product. Even if a reviewer's comments are sarcastic or belittling (and they rarely are), your editor is not offering them in that spirit. Try to detach your ego from the process, and it will go a lot easier.

Finally, the outside reviews are no substitute for your own careful reading. Reviewers will catch some factual and logical errors, but they will not catch them all. Your name is on the book, and it is, in the end, your responsibility to ensure its accuracy. If fatigue or haste led you to leave a quote or reference unchecked, an allusion vague, or a statement unverified, go back to the library and get it right. Someone will catch the mistake, and it is best if you do.

The editorial review is concerned with issues of style, tone, organization, and comprehensibility. The reviewer may be a member of the publisher's staff or an outside expert. Details and specific changes will be taken care of in copyediting, but alterations that require extensive reorganization or major writing problems that recur throughout the manuscript are best taken care of now.

Let me offer some examples of the kinds of problems that may be detected at this stage. In style, a reviewer may note that you are inconsistent in your point of view, sometimes referring to yourself as "the author," sometimes resorting to an editorial "we," occasionally lapsing into a chatty "I remember ..." You may refer to your readers as "you" in one chapter and "the student" in another, and include them in the "we" in still other places. This problem is easily corrected, but it is best handled as a conscious decision made jointly by author and editor.

A problem in tone might be a feeling on the part of the reviewer that you are being authoritarian rather than authoritative, that you are talking down to your readers by offering dogmatic statements rather than reasoned arguments. Or a reviewer might feel that your tone is too familiar and chatty, that you are inserting your personality into places where it does not belong. The reviewer will offer examples of these problems. Now, perhaps you have chosen the familiar tone deliberately and believe strongly that it makes your writing and teaching more effective. If so, you will want to discuss this with your editor. Chances are the editor will agree with your general tack but suggest that you may have gone overboard occasionally.

You are familiar with many kinds of general organizational problems in writing, but one or two are specific to textbooks. Here the reviewer may point out that students cannot understand Chapter 5 until they have read the first half of Chapter 12, or that a figure in Chapter 7 uses terms not introduced until Chapter 9. You will have to correct such problems. Similarly, the reviewer may point out the difficulty of teaching a topic (say, photosynthesis) before you have introduced certain concepts (in this case, perhaps molecular and cellular structure). Again, you will have to rethink your organization.

Comprehensibility includes the question of how easy it is to understand various explanations in the text, but at this point the reviewer is more concerned with the general level of your writing and the adequacy of supplementary illustrative material. If you are writing a book aimed at first-year community college students, your vocabulary and sentence structure must be less sophisticated than those you would use in a book for junior or senior majors in the field. It is easy to lose sight of this as you write. On these questions, you should take the reviewer's advice very seriously. Of course you have no trouble understanding the material. The class you tested it on did just fine, too, because they listened to your lectures and asked questions. But you are not a good judge of how easy it is to understand your own writing.

The reviewer may also point out places where you need an extended example, a graph, or a diagram, or suggest that certain material be treated as optional detail and placed in boxes or appendices. You and your developmental editor should consider these suggestions and incorporate them when appropriate.

With all these suggestions flying around, it is important to decide exactly how you will go about revising your work. First, make sure that you and your developmental editor have the same understanding about what is to be done. Unless the revisions are extremely limited, it is a good idea to put in writing exactly what you are going to do – which suggestions you will incorporate, which you will ignore, what you will rewrite, what you will add, and so on. This ensures that you and your editor agree, and it also gives you a set of goals and a plan of attack.

Then do the revision. Tackle the major changes first – the additions, reorganization, and rewriting. Next make the minor, specific changes that are needed. When this is finished, if you have time, leave the manuscript alone for a week or two. Finally, sit down, reread the whole thing from beginning to end, and make sure you are satisfied with it. Then prepare a final manuscript, either according to the publisher's instructions or following the general instructions in Chapter 10.

Working with Your Editors

After all the reviews and revisions you have completed, you may be surprised to learn that yet another person is about to have a go at your manuscript, but here comes the copyeditor. The earlier editorial review was designed to pick up general or recurring problems. The copyeditor, however, goes over your work word by word, sentence by sentence. Grammatical and spelling errors, awkward phrasing, and poor diction must be corrected, and stylistic consistency will be imposed. Logical inconsistencies will be eliminated and ambiguities clarified. If an example does not make sense, or a process is poorly explained, or chronology is unclear, the copyeditor will catch your lapse.

Copyeditors sometimes ask what seem to be stupid questions. The copyeditor working on a scholarly book tries to view the work through a scholar's eyes, but a textbook editor views your work through the eyes of a student. If your textbook is for first-year chemistry, an effective copyeditor will try to read your explanations as a freshman would. If the editor cannot understand something, students will not be able to either.

Review the edited manuscript carefully, checking changes and answering all queries. Return the manuscript promptly, so that production can begin.

In textbook publishing, the roles of author and editor overlap in many places, and the relationship lasts for months or even years. There are a number of ways to make communication between you and your editors more effective and pleasant, beyond observing the normal, everyday rules of civility and decency.

As I have stressed before, remember that you and your publisher are on the same side. Conflicts may arise over copyediting, money, schedules, and other matters, but they will be easier to resolve if you view them as arguments within a sound marriage rather than as flare-ups in a cold war. Be firm on important issues, but do not dig in your heels at every opportunity. Recognize your editor's expertise in publishing matters just as you expect your own professional knowledge to be respected.

Now that I have released the dove of goodwill, let me tell you how to keep it from treating you like a statue in the park. *Get it in writing.* Editors work on many books, and they change jobs a lot. They may also promise more than their bosses will want to deliver. Do not rely on phone conversations or casual assurances. Your basic guarantees are written into your contract. Beyond those, summarize in writing your understanding of subsequent promises and send it on. "It is my understanding that you will pursue permissions for the Lovejoy graphs," or "In our phone conversation yesterday, you agreed to deduct the indexer's fee from my royalties rather than having me pay it immediately," or "We agreed that the editorial changes in Chapter 4 to which I objected in my previous letter will not be made." If the editor disagrees with your interpretation, you will hear about it and you will be able to straighten out the matter quickly.

Be prompt about permissions and illustrations (see Chapter 10) and meet your deadlines. Do not agree to a deadline you know you cannot meet. Textbooks must be published on time, and the publisher must work out a realistic schedule. Honesty and realism on your side are vital. By the same token, if you are expecting proof or other material and it fails to arrive, call and check on it. Your editor should notify you of delays, but things do get lost in the mail or sent to the wrong address.

Finally, I urge you to express appreciation for work well done. If the copyediting was brilliant, say so. Tell the designer if you love the cover. When the graphs come out looking ten times better than you hoped for, send thanks. Praise the editor who saves you from mortification by spotting a factual error, and the typesetter who spots a misspelling. If you are like most people, you are quick to complain or criticize. It's nice to be nearly as quick to praise.

Teacher's Manuals and Study Guides

In some fields a teacher's manual for your textbook is nearly obligatory; in others, such supplementary material is rare. You and your publisher should share the decision on whether to prepare an instructor's manual and, if so, what kind.

A minimal teacher's manual provides answers to the problems given in the textbook if these are not printed in the book itself. Other possibilities include exam questions (essay, multiple choice, or true/false) with answers, discussion topics, take-home exercises, paper topics, and lecture outlines. You should also consider suggestions for collaborative learning exercises and group projects. Faculty are being encouraged to include such activities in their courses, and help will be welcomed.

Teacher's manuals are not elaborately produced. They are usually printed from typed or laser-printed copy, with only the simplest design and binding. The production does not take long and is usually begun at about the same time as the index. Nevertheless, you should have the material written well ahead of time. A teacher's manual will have to be copyedited, and it may take longer to write than you think. The rules for manuscript preparation still hold: double-spaced, laser printed, on 8½- by 11-inch bond; follow any specific instructions your publisher provides. Computers make it possible to improve on the usual appearance of these materials, if you are willing to spend the time (see Chapter 10).

The main consideration in an answer key is, naturally, accuracy. Check and double-check your answers, and proofread carefully, reading aloud with another person if possible. One reason for preparing the instructor's manual early is that you may find that the problems you wrote for the text itself contain ambiguities – or even that they are unanswerable. That is a good thing to discover before the problems are in print. In proof, check and recheck all cross-references to chapters, pages, and problems in the textbook. It is embarrassing to provide answers to thirty-two problems when the text contains only thirty-one.

You and your publisher may also decide that you should prepare a study guide for students using the textbook. This may offer general study hints, summaries, study questions, review outlines, and suggestions for supplementary reading. Study guides are produced in the same way as teacher's manuals, and on a similar schedule.

It is very tempting to regard supplementary materials like study guides and instructor's manuals as unimportant or even as minor nuisances. They certainly lack glamour. But if you have decided to prepare one, do it right. Write carefully, be accurate, double check all answers, and proofread scrupulously. Many instructors will ignore the manual, but those who rely on it expect it to be accurate and useful. If it is not, they may never use your text again.

Revised Editions

Textbooks are more likely to be revised and published in new editions than are trade and scholarly books. One reason for frequent revision is economic: There is a flourishing trade in used textbooks on which neither author nor publisher makes any money. This is not the only reason, however. In many fields, particularly the sciences, new information must constantly be assimilated into textbooks or they become obsolete. In other fields, such as history, methodological and sociopolitical changes require that texts be modified. For example, no survey of U.S. history is now marketable unless it includes material about the roles of women and minority groups; books on modern Russian and East European history must be updated. Sometimes books must be revised because of trends in teaching (such as increased use of discussions and collaborative learning in place of lectures) or because the students have changed. The most notable example of this last problem is the move toward simplified vocabulary and sentence structure in lower-level texts in response to reduced literacy.

You should begin working on a revised edition as soon as you have finished reading the proof of the current edition. You do not begin writing, of course, but you do begin a file of articles to be added to the bibliography, ideas for new topics, new illustrations, and so forth. You should not wait to do all your catching up at once.

When you and your publisher decide to prepare a revised edition, you should make sure you know the purpose of the revision. Your publisher's representatives will have been discussing your book with faculty members who use it and should have some ideas about which features are consistently praised and which are repeatedly criticized. Important omissions will have been noted. Your editor will also know what other publishers have been up to and how a revised edition might increase your competitive advantage. At the same time, you will have received criticism from colleagues and students, and you will have developed some ideas about what you wish you had done differently. You will also be aware of new research that should be reflected in your book.

You and your editor need to sit down and agree on what sorts of revisions should be made and how extensive they will be. You should discuss the need for new illustrations. If the book is to be redesigned and typeset from scratch, the production process is just as time consuming as if you were writing a completely new book. However, if the revisions are minor or are limited to a few parts of the book, only the affected parts may be reset, and the whole procedure will be a good deal less complicated (see Chapter 10 for instructions on preparing copy for a revised edition). If the revisions are extensive, your editor may want to have the new version reviewed all over again. And, of course, you must set a schedule for revision that you can follow and that will allow the publisher to get the book out on time.

Preparing a new edition is not just a physical task of cutting and pasting. Nor is it simply a matter of correcting errors. Even when you have made the revisions and additions that you and your editor have decided on, you must again read through the manuscript to make sure it is coherent. Details to watch out for include cross-references to pages, chapters, tables, and figures in the book that will change; time-related references ("this decade," "a few years ago," "in 2000 we will probably"); presidents who have become former presidents; the use of the present tense with people who have died or governments that have fallen; and language or allusions that have become dated. Tables and figures should be included in this check. The bibliography should be reviewed for outdated material. If you used a notation system with parenthetic author-date references in the text and a reference list at the end, you must make sure that new text references have corresponding entries in the list and that references completely omitted from the text have also been omitted from the list. Check, too, for books or articles that were "in press" or "forthcoming," and put in the dates of publication and page numbers.

Finally, sit down and read the whole book afresh (to the extent that's possible). Make sure you are happy with it. If you do not have the time, energy, or imagination to do this now, be sure to do it after the manuscript has been copyedited.

Textbook writing can be an intellectually and financially rewarding activity, but it is not as easy as it looks. It is very difficult to organize massive amounts of material, to simplify complex ideas, and to provide explanations, examples, and illustrations that help students learn. The review process can also be trying, both physically and emotionally, because accepting criticism and reworking what you thought was a finished product are rarely pleasant. Your investment in time and effort will be high. You may also have to make a significant financial investment in artwork if your book is heavily illustrated.

Because of the length of time and intensity of the involvement, you should make every effort to find a publisher with whom you can work comfortably. If you are writing with a coauthor or as part of a team, make sure you like and respect your colleagues. Be careful to see that everyone involved has compatible ideas about the project and that responsibilities are clearly assigned.

There are few publishing endeavors in which the gratification is delayed as long as it is in textbook writing. (The *Oxford English Dictionary* comes to mind, but not too much else.) Be prepared to work hard and to wait a while for both the praise and the royalties.

Chapter 9

Books for General Readers

In the idea of literature one essential element is some relation to a general and common interest of man – so that what
applies only to a local, or professional, or merely personal
interest, even though presenting itself in the shape of a
book, will not belong to literature.

Thomas de Quincey

Serious nonfiction – whether written by journalists, professional writers, or academics – has become very popular. Allan
Bloom's *Closing of the American Mind* and Stephen Hawking's
Brief History of Time both appeared on the *New York Times* best-
seller list for weeks on end (Hawking's for nearly two years),
and books by scholars such as Stephen Jay Gould, Deborah
Tannen, and John Kenneth Galbraith have made frequent, if
briefer, appearances. Still more books by academic writers,
though not best-sellers, have sold in respectable numbers,
sometimes for several years.

Academics have many reasons to write for general readers.
Trade books bring their authors more money than monographs do, though usually not as much as textbooks. They
also allow scholars to communicate with people other than
their colleagues and students. Writing for a nonspecialized
audience conveys a researcher's own discoveries, the state of
a discipline, enthusiasm for work, or the urgency of an issue
or cause to significant numbers of people. It is another way to
make a difference: to influence public policy, interest people in

an important subject, reduce ignorance about a discipline, or bring readers up-to-date on important research.

Because books for a general audience are usually published by trade houses, it is important to understand their acquisitions, editorial, and marketing practices. When trade books are published by university presses, they should be edited and marketed differently than monographs. And, most important, books for general readers must be written with a different audience in mind.

Economic Realism

By dangling *The New York Times* best-seller list in front of you, I may have created fantasies of wealth that – alas – I must now dispel. The nonfiction best-seller lists are dominated by books about diet, self-improvement, life after death, or the deeds and misdeeds of celebrities. Serious nonfiction rarely appears. No one can be sure which books will become best-sellers, but there are some fairly good predictors of success for academic authors. A nonfiction book is most likely to become a best-seller if the author has had a best-selling book before, has won a Nobel Prize, has a television show airing when the book is published, or receives extensive media coverage, usually because the book is timely and controversial. Few authors meet these criteria, and even if they do, their books may sell only moderately well. The author's previous best-seller may have been a fluke: *The Closing of the American Mind* was Bloom's only best-seller. A Nobel laureate in physics or chemistry may have little idea of what would interest a general reader. And even a much-discussed, highly controversial book may not sell as well as you might expect: controversial books are often discussed apparently knowledgeably by people who have read the reviews and news coverage, but not the book.

Of course, a publisher who believes a book has a good chance to become a best-seller will risk a great deal of money to acquire it. Some science books have brought their authors advances of more than $250,000, and in many cases the publisher has not regretted the decision. Advances of $50,000 to $100,000 are offered to significant numbers of authors in the sciences. For most first-time trade authors, especially those who are not scientists, an advance of $10,000 to $25,000 is more realistic, with university presses usually offering less. Of course, if a book with a small advance really takes off, the author will get additional royalties.[1]

I would encourage every writer who wants to reach a large audience to be optimistic, but it is a serious miscalculation to think that you can retire on the proceeds of one moderately successful trade book. Buying a new car, remodeling a kitchen, or paying a year's Ivy League tuition for one child is a more realistic financial goal. And you are unlikely to get a large advance unless you have a literary agent negotiating for you.

Finding a Literary Agent

Finding a literary agent is much like finding a publisher, and unless your manuscript shows strong promise of profitability you are unlikely to succeed. As explained in Chapter 4, literary agents charge fees that are a percentage of the author's royalties. They cannot afford to spend time trying to sell manuscripts that will bring them only a few hundred dollars. Nor are they likely to take on a project that will require a lot of editorial work before it can be submitted. Agents who handle nonfiction are looking for well-written, salable manuscripts on topics with a wide potential readership. As a result, most agents accept fewer than 10 percent of the manuscripts submitted to them. However, they almost always place the manuscripts they accept and are able to convince publishers to offer better terms and larger advances than an unrepresented author can negotiate.

---

[1] Information on advances and print runs is drawn from Laura Wood, "Targeting the Educated Lay Audience: Publishers' Perceptions and Strategies" (M.A. thesis, New York University, 1994).

To earn their 10 to 15 percent fees, literary agents submit manuscripts to publishers, negotiate contracts, persuade publishers to increase their marketing efforts, review royalty statements, either sell subsidiary rights or encourage publishers to pursue such sales more aggressively, and generally act as the author's advocate. Agents may offer editorial advice, but they do not do extensive revision. Some will refer an author to an editor, a coauthor, or even a ghostwriter, all of whom charge separate fees. In addition to their commissions, agents usually charge clients for expenses such as photocopying and long-distance phone calls.

A minority of agents charge fees to read manuscripts. Although such fees may be substantial, they are not meant to cover the cost of a thorough editorial review. Rather, the fee pays for a reading that determines whether the agent will take on the project and may include some general suggestions for revision. The more selective and better-known agents generally do not charge reading fees, and authors' associations recommend that their members avoid those who do.

If you think you need an agent, the first place to turn is *Literary Market Place, Literary Agents of North America* (both are in the bibliography and should be in your university or public library), or one of the online listings you can find on the Web. These directories provide names, addresses, phone numbers, and types of manuscripts handled; tell whether an agent accepts unsolicited manuscripts (more about this in a moment); and note whether an agent charges a reading fee. *Literary Agents of North America* is more detailed and generally lists commissions charged as well as typical or recent clients and books. It is indexed by subject, location, policies, and size.

Once you have identified a few agents who handle manuscripts in your field, you must note carefully what each expects as a first submission. Few agents accept unsolicited complete manuscripts. Rather, they want to see a query letter and a prospectus, an outline, or perhaps a sample chapter. They will want to know whether you have had other books published. Your letter or prospectus should not only describe the book but explain why it will appeal to a trade publisher and a lay audience. As in seeking a publisher, you may send queries to more than one agent at a time, but if you are asked to send a manuscript, you must send it to only one agent.

Reputable agents explain to prospective clients exactly what they will and will not do for them and spell out all commissions and fees. When they accept a client, they offer a contract that sets out all these matters. You should read such a contract even more carefully than you read a publisher's contract. You should clarify just how much advice an agent is prepared to offer on your writing. Most will offer general suggestions, and almost none make line-by-line corrections, but there are many possibilities in between. Some agents are very comfortable with the literary side of their work; others prefer to devote almost all their attention to the business side. You must understand the agent's obligations and your own, and you must be able to trust your agent with your money and your reputation. I strongly recommend a personal meeting with an agent before signing a contract.

Once you sign a contract with an agent, you must submit all manuscripts through the agency unless you and the agent have agreed otherwise. For example, the agent is unlikely to want to handle your submissions to nonpaying scholarly journals but will probably want to take care of submissions to popular magazines. Any requests that come to you for foreign rights, translations, or reprinting in anthologies must be referred to your agent. Other issues to be clarified include which communications with publishers may go directly to you and which should go to your agent. All financial matters are in the agent's province; copyeditor's queries are in yours. But many things fall in the middle, including review of catalogue and advertising copy and jacket design. Most agents will want to participate in decisions that relate to marketing.

The fact that most authors remain with the same agent throughout their careers testifies to the care that both parties must use in establishing the relationship and to the trust and respect it generates. If you plan to write more than one trade book in the course of your career, your agent will become a very important part of your professional life.

Agents may accept clients on the basis of book outlines or summaries, and they may secure a publication contract on that basis as well. If a book is on a salable topic and there is reason to think the author can live up to the promise of the outline, publishers are willing to make a commitment early on to secure the manuscript. Of course, established authors have an advantage here, but an agent may be able to get a contract and an advance for an inexperienced author with a good idea. If, however, your agent does not wish to seek a publisher until the project is further along, you should be guided by that advice.

Writing for General Readers

When you write a monograph, your audience is your peers and perhaps some graduate students. When you write a textbook, your readers are undergraduates. But when you write a trade book, the audience is harder to define. People who buy and read serious nonfiction are mostly college educated but not professional academics. They may have developed certain interests in college that they have retained but do not pursue in their careers. A lawyer, for example, may remember an astronomy course fondly, while an industrial chemist becomes an amateur archaeologist because of a particularly interesting freshman course. Other readers are seeking to fill in gaps in their education. Those who took physics as their laboratory science may wish to understand heredity and evolution better, or former English majors may want to catch up with their teenagers' more advanced knowledge of mathematics. Some serious nonfiction buyers are attracted to books simply because these books are being talked about, despite a lack of personal interest in the discipline of the author. Television series create spillover interest in their topics: viewers of *The Civil War* bought not only the book derived from the series but other books by Civil War historians and biographers.

It is vital to keep the audience in mind as you write, but how can you keep a steady vision of so disparate an audience?

One way is to think of them as alumni – your students of ten or twenty years ago, for instance, back for a reunion with your book instead of with you. As students, they varied in ability and interest, so you must now write to appeal to as many as possible. When they were students, of course, you had more power over them than you have now, and you cannot require them to buy your book. You must instead arouse their interest, pique their curiosity, answer their questions, and keep them reading.

Another way to think of your audience is to imagine a dozen or so real individuals who might read your book: a colleague in another field, your tennis partner, your child's teacher, a cousin, a neighbor, a colleague's spouse, your doctor, and so forth. When you have to make a decision about how much background to provide or how to explain a phenomenon, you can imagine speaking to one or two of these people and then write to meet their needs. You can even use them as guinea pigs occasionally.

How do you define a subject for a trade book? A monograph is usually the report of a research project, and a textbook's subject is defined by the courses in which it will be used, but the limits of a trade book are not set down anywhere. You cannot say that a book for "general" readers should be more "general" than a monograph: many successful trade books are extremely focused and specific. In history, for example, Natalie Davis's *Return of Martin Guerre* is simply a very effective recounting of a single legal case, and Laurel Ulrich's *Midwife's Tale: The Life of Martha Ballard* is an imaginatively edited diary from the turn of the nineteenth century. To determine what to write about, you must look at your reasons for writing and your audience's reasons for reading and then find a solution that satisfies both.

What are the possible intellectual motivations for writing a trade book? You may want to demonstrate the relevance of your field, explain recent developments and changes, set out competing theories (or argue in favor of one), alert readers to a serious problem that your work has uncovered, influence public opinion and policy, or simply share an insight or discovery. Each of these motivations would lead to a different kind of book.

Why might readers want to read what you have to say? Perhaps they want to educate themselves concerning a field about which they know nothing: they will be looking for a book that sets out the relevance, history, current approaches, and underlying knowledge of the field. Other readers may want to know what has happened recently in a field in which they have some background. They will be looking for books that set out new developments in evolutionary theory, the impact of computers on epistemology, or what "cultural studies" might be. Readers may want to know what researchers think about controversial public policy issues like race and intelligence, global warming, or international human rights. Some readers are looking for an inside view of research: How do geneticists, forensic anthropologists, or archaeologists go about their business, and what sort of people are they? Books designed to meet these needs are likely to succeed in a trade market.

Providing Context

Writing a trade book raises other questions that writing a monograph or textbook does not. The first is where to start. How much context must you provide? How much knowledge can you assume? The answer, of course, lies in that imaginary audience. One way to think about context and background is that it roughly substitutes for the literature review plus what you assume your peers know. Whether it is called an introduction or something else, the relevant chapter or chapters must provide all the information the reader needs in order to understand the heart of the book, including competing theories, underlying consensus, and basic terminology. It must also explain why your subject matters, perhaps because it is new, important for public policy, or just interesting.

"Humanizing" Your Subject

Many trade editors and authors emphasize the value of helping readers relate to your subject. In many fields, this comes easily. One reason for the popularity of biography and history is that they are full of characters with whom readers can develop relationships of admiration, empathy, disgust, or some other strong emotion. But if you are writing about physics or birds or fossils, creating an emotional connection requires more imagination.

One possibility is to focus on the researchers, giving the reader a sense of their excitement, doubts, ambitions, and rivalries. James Watson's *Double Helix* is the best-known book to use this approach. It is commonly used in accounts of medical discoveries, whose authors have casts of characters that include researchers, clinicians, and patients.

Another approach is to re-create imaginatively the conditions of life in an earlier era. Geoffrey Bibby, an anthropologist, did this in several of his very successful books, including *The Testimony of the Spade* and *Four Thousand Years Ago*. The latter book, published in 1961, was still in print when Bibby died in 2001. Richard Fortey took this technique one step further in *Trilobite!: Eyewitness to Evolution* by encouraging us to see the world as these primitive creatures once did.

Perhaps the most sophisticated narrative approach to humanizing material is to involve the reader in the search for knowledge. By using the quest motif beloved of fiction writers, and by making the reader a part of the expedition, nonfiction writers can engage readers both intellectually and emotionally. This approach also resembles the murder mystery, because it requires the author to disclose facts gradually, allowing the reader to engage in discovery. Jonathan Weiner's *Beak of the Finch* is a superb example of such a book.

A common and effective approach to attracting readers is to begin with a short, dramatic statement of the importance of the topic, perhaps opening with an account of a recent event or discovery and the controversy surrounding it or with the possibilities it creates. This becomes the introductory chapter, followed by a longer chapter or section of necessary background and explanations. Sometimes the first chapter wins over readers by showing the disastrous effects (on individuals or society) of failing to understand the subject of the book. However the problem is handled, the author of a trade book has only a few pages to attract readers and then perhaps a chapter to ensure that they do not drop out before they get to the important part.

Structure

Organization is important. Most serious nonfiction that succeeds in attracting readers and keeping them reading tells a story. It may be a single sustained narrative or a series of shorter ones, but it should have continuity and connections. Like a novel, the nonfiction story can use flashbacks to provide background, side plots to provide suspense and enhance interest, and hints about interesting things to come. Whenever possible, it should have well-developed characters and thoroughly described settings. In a scientific journal article, you might summarize an earlier study in one sentence, but in a trade book it might be worth several pages, including an analysis of the researchers' personalities and relationships, a description of the laboratory or its setting, and a sense of the excitement the results created among the researchers and, later, their colleagues. Indeed, you might begin with the excitement generated by the public announcement of the findings and then flash back to the work that went into the discovery. A historical or sociological monograph might summarize economic or demographic changes in a community with tables and explanatory text. In a trade book, the author would do well to choose a few individuals who experienced or typified these changes and tell their stories.

Not every book can be organized as a sustained narrative (although nearly every book can include "short stories" now and then). Other organizational schemes may be geometric. For example, you may think of your book as a pyramid, with a broad explanatory base underlying increasingly specific un-derstanding. Or perhaps your book is a series of concentric circles of diminishing diameter, beginning with a broad sweep and gradually focusing on particulars. Or perhaps you should begin at the center of the circles and work outward. Your book may be a group of circles that overlap one another, or perhaps a Venn diagram.

Your book may, in fact, not have very much unity. It may be the nonfiction equivalent of a collection of short stories shar-ing a very general theme. In that case, you can organize it by writing an introduction that sets out the theme, making that theme apparent in each chapter, and ensuring that each chap-ter is itself a coherent, interesting narrative. Mario Salvadori's *Why Buildings Stand Up* and *Why Buildings Fall Down* (written with Matthys Levy) are good examples of this approach.

If you have written only journal articles or monographs, the idea of "envisioning" a book in this way is probably new. With monographs, we generally think in terms of outlines and do not worry too much about the overall shape and motion of the book. Monographs are frequently rather static; geometrically, they look like rectangles. They are meant to convey informa-tion to people who need it and expect to find it in a predictable package, and both publishers and readers will be satisfied if they do this efficiently. Trade publishers and general readers expect something more attractive and original, and that expectation presents exciting opportunities for the writer.

Tone

The next important consideration is the tone of the book. How formal do you want to be? Trade books are supposed to be accessible, and to many writers that means informal, casual, or chatty. If you are comfortable with informality, and if it suits your subject, then this approach will work well. You can address the reader as *you*, for example, and throw in casual asides and humorous anecdotes. This will not work if it is forced or if it is inappropriate for your subject. Books about morally sensitive issues generally require a degree of formality to be credible. A casual, chatty approach to a book about genocide, for example, is unthinkable.

When the subject matter can be treated at any level of formality, the purpose of the book should help determine the author's approach. For example, John Allen Paulos's *Innumeracy*, a book that seeks to allay math phobia and show people that mathematics is useful and even necessary, works because it is casual, friendly, and funny. John D. Barrow's *Pi in the Sky*, which is mathematically no more difficult than Paulos's book, is also entertaining, but it is far more formal. Barrow assumes that his readers are already interested in (though not necessarily knowledgeable about) math and provides a history of counting and of approaches to mathematics. The two books cover many of the same topics, but reading them creates two completely different reading experiences and impressions of the authors.

You must also consider your own personality. If you are generally formal in your dealings with colleagues and students, it is unlikely that you can write convincingly in a casual, intimate style. The result would be forced and unnatural. If your usual approach to writing and speaking is relatively informal, an attempt to be more distant from your readers may end up reading like a parody. You must write in a style that is natural to you, or at least not uncomfortable.

Think about your subject, your audience, your purpose, and the kind of relationship you want to establish with your readers, and then decide how formal you wish your book to be. This decision, in turn, will determine the voice and tone you use.

How Much Is Too Much?

Trade book authors need to make certain mechanical decisions as well. In trade publishing, short is better than long. Although some historians and biographers find publishers for 500-page books, it is safer to aim for no more than 300 book pages (roughly 500 manuscript pages). If you write a long book, you need a very strong unifying principle, tight organization, and a continually magnetic presence (yours or your subject's) – a performance hard to sustain over several hundred pages. It is sometimes difficult to distill what you have to say, but many pages can be saved through discipline: finding a single, perfect example rather than offering two or three weaker ones; seeking out one crucial event to summarize or symbolize many; and keeping a tight rein on digression and verbosity.

Editors and writers generally agree that equations, tables, and diagrams deter readers. In the acknowledgments of *A Brief History of Time*, Stephen Hawking pokes fun at this idea, while at the same time following the advice it suggests:

> Someone told me that each equation I included in the book would halve the sales. I therefore resolved not to have any equations at all. In the end, however, I did put in one equation, Einstein's famous equation, $E = mc^2$. I hope that this will not scare off half of my potential readers.

There is no magic formula for determining how many equations or tables are too many. (If there were, I would have included the equation.) Although they probably should be minimized, do not lose sight of the fact that we use equations and other mathematical expressions because they are the most economical way of conveying information and relationships. As long as these elements are used for that purpose and are thoroughly explained, most readers can cope with a few numbers. The test is whether they are necessary for the reader's understanding, clearly explained, and better than a non-numerical alternative.

Footnotes and endnotes are also assumed to discourage readers, but a strict rule against them would be silly. The fact that you are writing for general readers does not reduce your obligation to give credit to others. However, credit can be given in the text, as I did with Stephen Hawking a moment ago, reducing the need for source notes. Other uses of notes should be avoided. Notes that amplify or qualify should either be brought into the text (if needed) or omitted (if merely nitpicking or overly finicky). Notes that are in fact brief bibliographical essays should also be eliminated. Some publishers suggest or accept note systems that eliminate superscripts but provide the sources in a commentary at the end of the book referring back to the relevant pages and lines. This allows readers to proceed through the text without being distracted but nevertheless provides the information they might want.

Drawings and photographs are generally considered to be assets in a trade book. They should be carefully chosen and executed to illustrate precisely the point you are trying to make. A picture can be worth a thousand or more words, if it is exactly the right picture. A trade publisher's editor will want to work with you, a photo researcher, or a graphic artist to develop the most useful art. Think carefully about where in your text illustrations can replace or enhance examples and explanations.

A bibliography is useful in a trade book, but it should generally be brief and suggest further reading for those who want to learn more about your subject. Supplementary materials like a glossary, chronology, or genealogical table should also be considered if they will help the reader. An index is almost always required. Indexes in trade books are usually shorter and less detailed than those in monographs, but the main consideration should still be the needs of the reader.

Language

In thinking about the needs of their readers, authors new to trade publishing tend to focus on avoiding technical language and jargon. That is a worthy goal, but it should not be overdone. Nor should it be regarded as a panacea. Some words that general readers will not understand must be used. You will not get very far in writing a physics book without using the word *mass*, but many intelligent, well-educated people do not remember exactly what it means. Use it, by all means, but explain it the first time you use it and put it in the glossary if you provide one. Use ordinary words when possible, but not at the price of clarity or specificity.

Trade editors say they are looking for writing that is accessible, lively, and engaging. You can help make your work accessible by avoiding or defining technical terms, but that alone will not do the trick. It is easy to write inaccessible prose in everyday words. Accessibility depends on clarity of thought and language. The words composing each sentence must relate clearly to one another; each sentence must have a logical connection to the sentences that precede and follow it; each paragraph must be a coherent whole and relate logically to the paragraphs surrounding it. All this must be accomplished without obvious signals, yet the reader must have a sense of motion – of getting from A to B to C – and of accomplishment. If people read serious nonfiction to learn something, then they should be able to stop at the end of each chapter (should they wish to do so) and explain briefly what they have learned. Imagine your reader as a passenger seated next to you in an airplane who puts your book down at the end of a chapter and says casually, "Did you know that...." If a reader can do that, your book is accessible: well organized, logical, and transparent.

Liveliness depends on a number of qualities. One is brevity: short books are usually livelier than long ones. Brevity depends on not repeating oneself more than necessary, avoiding unnecessary words, and sticking to what is relevant (even digressions should be purposeful). A second quality that promotes liveliness is precision of language. The most specific nouns should be chosen over more general ones, and adjectives and adverbs should be used to make nouns and verbs more precise. Specific words are usually livelier and more colorful than general words: *leap* is livelier than *move; anemone* is more colorful than *flower; Saturn* evokes a clearer image than *a planet.*

You can find all of these rules and suggestions in any good writing handbook. The point here is that these rules apply more strictly when you write for general readers than when you write for your peers. Academic readers are tolerant of (or resigned to) a certain degree of uniformity, or even drabness, in their professional reading. As long as a book conveys the information they need or explains the author's thinking clearly, they are satisfied. General readers are more demanding. Your book will have to compete not only with similar books but with other media. It has to be informative, but also entertaining enough to convince readers to spend a weekend reading it instead of watching television or going to a movie. You want them to buy your book, begin reading it, finish reading it, and recommend it to others. So you must choose words and put them together thoughtfully and carefully.

Writing a trade book is very different from writing a monograph. Most people find the actual writing, though not the research, far more difficult. Selecting and defining a subject, organizing and controlling the material, and expressing information and ideas clearly to nonexperts draw on skills that many academic authors have not developed. For most, however, the opportunity to reach thousands of readers makes the effort worthwhile.

Finding a Publisher for the Trade Book

Authors who have literary agents send their proposals or manuscripts to their agents and let them handle submissions and negotiations. Agents generally know which editors at which houses are likely to be interested in a project and can get quicker decisions from those editors than an unrepresented author can expect. Agents keep their authors informed about progress, though they do not report every detail. (Some authors, in fact, like having an agent because they do not want to hear about rejections.) Once an offer is made, the agent will discuss it with the author and give advice on whether to accept it. Even when represented by an agent, the author must make the final decision about whether to sign a contract.

Authors who are not represented by agents can also approach trade houses. In order to find the right editors to approach, you can ask colleagues who have had trade books published or you can look at the acknowledgments in trade books in your field. You should then send a carefully written query letter and prospectus to these editors. An editor may well ask to see the manuscript, and a contract may follow. The advice on contracts offered in Chapter 5 still applies, with some special cautions. A trade contract should always offer a royalty of at least 10 percent of retail or net on the casebound edition. Carefully read the provisions for paperback rights to see what royalty you will receive if the publisher exercises these rights (5–7.5 percent or a sliding scale is usual) and what percentage of the proceeds you will receive if paperback rights are sold to another house (at least 50 percent). Also look especially carefully at provisions pertaining to sales of subsidiary rights (serial rights, foreign rights, and so forth). If a television production is even remotely possible, look carefully at those provisions. If the book is to be illustrated, try to get the publisher to pay those costs. If you do not have an agent, you may wish to consult a lawyer about a trade contract.

Trade publishers are more likely than university presses to pay advances, and you should try to negotiate such a provision. If you are not an established author, and are not represented by an agent, you may have some difficulty getting a significant cash advance on the basis of an outline or a partial manuscript. It does no harm to ask, however, especially if a relatively small advance would allow you to work on the book during the summer and complete it more quickly. If you are writing on a subject of great public interest or if you are well known and respected in your field, publishers are more likely to make a financial commitment. Sometimes publishers will agree to pay a small portion of the advance when the contract is signed, with the balance to be paid when the manuscript is accepted. Occasionally, the advance will be divided into several parts, payable when specified deadlines are met.

Trade publishers frequently seek authors to write on subjects for which they feel books are needed. The advance then becomes, in essence, a commission to write the book. (Additional royalties will still be paid, of course, if they exceed the advance.) Trade editors will look for authors among the clients of the literary agents they work with, but they will look beyond that group by reading journal articles and news articles about research in the field. A publisher who commissions a book will provide a respectable advance and a great deal of advice and guidance on writing. As we shall see shortly, writing a trade book is almost always more collaborative than writing a monograph, but this is especially true for books initiated by publishers.

Even if your search for a trade publisher fails, your book may find a home with a university press that publishes books in your field for general readers. University presses publish many successful trade books, including those of Edward O. Wilson, John Rawls, and Peter Gay. In order to identify prospects, you should see who publishes books in your discipline that are reviewed in magazines like *The New York Times Book Review*, *The New York Review of Books*, *Harpers*, *Scientific American*, and the popular magazines in your field. Also examine the shelves of your local off-campus bookstores. Then follow the procedure described in Chapter 4, making it clear in your correspondence that you view your work as a trade book. At most presses, the acquisitions and review procedures are identical for trade and scholarly works. It is important, however, that you and your potential publisher have similar views on marketability and sales potential.

If a university press agrees that your book should reach a large general audience, you will be offered more generous royalty terms than would be offered on a monograph, and you may be able to get a modest advance. Your most important concern, however, should be with the press's commitment to selling subsidiary rights and to marketing the book. A royalty is simply a percentage of revenue, and a high percentage is worthless if the book does not sell. Before signing a contract, you should be convinced that the press will spend enough on marketing and that they have a track record of selling trade books. Publishers will not give you sales figures for a specific title (that is no one's business but the author's), but you can ask them how many copies they generally sell of their trade titles in your field, and you can ask for details of the marketing campaigns they have conducted for their trade titles. As we shall see, trade books are edited and designed differently than monographs, but the most important differences in their publication are in marketing.

Editing and Design

Editors take two approaches to trade books. Some look only for extremely well written books that require very little editorial work. Especially in large trade houses, few editors have time for painstaking reviews of manuscripts, and schedules are rushed. Other editors, especially those at smaller trade houses and at university presses trying to build their trade lists, seek out manuscripts that have sales potential because of their subject but may require editorial work to make them attractive to general readers. These editors may work directly with the authors or hire freelance editors who are skilled at this kind of effort. Each acquiring editor takes a different approach, and even editors who prefer to avoid extensive editing may make an occasional exception for an especially promising or interesting manuscript.

Trade book editors who prefer to be actively involved frequently ask to see early drafts so that they can provide suggestions for extensive revisions before authors have invested a lot of time on material that may not be included. These suggestions are like those made by developmental editors in textbook houses. New chapters may be suggested, and others may be deleted. Editors may want more (or less) background and context, more (or fewer) examples, more (or less) formality, and more (or fewer) personal asides. They may note that some features of the manuscript do not work. They may suggest reorganizing the whole manuscript or individual chapters. To the author used to dealing with university press editors about monographs, this level of editorial intervention will be unexpected and possibly insulting. Trade publishing is very much a collaboration, a melding of the talents and knowledge of the author and those of the editor. You know astronomy, history, or economics; your editor knows readers' expectations and how to meet them. The editor could not write your book, but without editorial help you cannot make it as salable as it must be. Expect a lot of advice and take it seriously.

You should consult your editor as you revise, whenever major questions arise. Do not be surprised if even a second or third version comes back with a lot of suggestions.

When your editor thinks the book is ready, it will go to a copyeditor who will do a sentence-by-sentence review. This editing is unlikely to require much revision on your part, but it may take a lot of time to answer the editor's queries and review the changes. The copyeditor may have been given a specific charge beyond the normal instructions. For example, if you have been unable to get the manuscript down to a desired length, that job may fall to the copyeditor. You will have an opportunity to review the copyeditor's work, and you will also have to review proof, as you would with a monograph or textbook.

While your book is being copyedited, it is also being designed. Trade books always have dust jackets, and these are generally more elaborate than those for monographs. For trade books, the jacket is a major marketing tool. It usually appears in advertising, and it must appeal to booksellers and to prospective readers. Your suggestions may be sought early in the design process, and you may get to see sketches of possible jackets. You will probably be asked to send a photograph of yourself for the back or flap of the jacket and for other publicity material.

The paperback edition of your book may use the same design or start over. If it is to have a new design (most likely if the paperback is issued by another publisher), you may again be consulted.

The inside of the book may be more elaborately designed than that of a monograph, too, with illustrated or ornamented chapter openings or part-title pages. Trade books are generally typeset professionally, so authors' disks are rarely used. A paperback edition will not be reedited, but it may be redesigned (less elaborately) for the smaller, less expensive format. At university presses, the paperback edition is usually identical to the original except for the binding. Larger format paperbacks are called "trade" paperbacks, as opposed to the smaller, cheaper "mass market" books. Some books eventually appear in all three formats – cloth, trade paperback, and mass market – sometimes with two or three different publishers.

The editorial, marketing, and design departments – and the author – will all be involved in creating a title. Titles are very important in trade publishing. A memorable title helps sales in many ways: the person who reads a review goes into the store and asks for the book by name instead of asking for "that new book on the Civil War" and possibly ending up with the wrong one. It is also easier to recommend a book to a friend if you can remember the title. Trade book titles must be memorable, but they must also be accurate and not promise more than they can deliver. This seems to be a special problem for university presses, which frequently use a title to grab the reader's attention and only in the subtitle disclose the book's limitations (an imaginary example: *The Meaning of Life: Deconstructing the Magazine's First Five Issues*).[2] You should contribute as many ideas as you can, offer your opinion on the short list, and object if the final choice does not really reflect what your book is about.

Marketing

A trade book is sold to readers in bookstores, where it competes with thousands of other new titles. The publisher's job is to get the book into the store, encourage the bookseller to promote it, and make sure that as many customers as possible walk into the store and ask for it. Marketing departments work at these tasks from the moment your book is accepted.

---

[2] Wendy Doniger discusses university press trade publishing, including titles, in "The Academic Snob Goes to Market," *Scholarly Publishing* 24, no. 1 (October 1992): 3–12.

The marketing department will solicit information from you about your book, who you think will want to read it, whether you have any contacts in the review media or among booksellers, whether any famous authors might be willing to say something complimentary about the book for the jacket, catalogue, and advertising, and so forth. Your literary agent's help will also be sought. You will probably be asked to write book summaries of different lengths that the marketers will use as the basis for jacket, catalogue, and advertising copy.

If the publisher has grand expectations for your book, you may be asked to participate more directly in its marketing. Authors are occasionally asked to address the publisher's salespeople, attend booksellers' conventions, or even make bookselling tours (autographing books in bookstores, for example). The marketing effort may include trying to book you onto radio or even television interview shows. An interview on NPR sells a lot of books. You can help by telling the publisher about media opportunities in your own city. But if you are not willing to do any of these things, say so early. Shy people can be successful authors, too.

Most of the marketing effort is less visible and demands far less of the author. Marketers focus on writing good catalogue and advertising copy, selecting the best places to buy advertising space, soliciting useful comments from well-known experts or public figures, getting review attention, and encouraging bookseller enthusiasm. Trade publishers may join booksellers in paying for local advertising, for example, or offering a cardboard display that can be placed near the cash register or in some other prominent place. When early reviews are favorable, marketers may mail or fax them to major bookstores. (For serious nonfiction, "major booksellers" often means the successful independent stores as well as the superstore chains.)

A minimum marketing budget for a trade book is about $25,000. That may sound like a lot, but advertising in the major review media is very expensive. What really sells books, though, is the kind of publicity that you cannot buy: lots of favorable reviews, word-of-mouth recommendations, and bookseller enthusiasm. Advertising can help all of this along, but it cannot guarantee results.

The best thing an author can do to help sell a book is to offer suggestions, cooperate with the marketing staff, and become sensitive to promotional opportunities. Use your campus news bureau to help generate local media interest. An interview in a local newspaper or on a local television program may attract national attention, and booksellers in your city talk to booksellers in other cities. Anything that gets the word out will be helpful.

Are You Ready for This?

Most academic authors wait until they are well along in their careers before writing for general readers. In part, this may be because they do not feel ready before then, but it is also because trade books do not usually help much in gaining tenure or promotion. Some people claim that they actually detract from one's chances for academic advancement. The disdain academics express for "popularization" may come from misunderstanding, snobbishness, or just plain jealousy, but it does discourage many younger writers. As universities become more sensitive to their public responsibilities and image, and more aware of the value of engagement with the community, this bias seems to diminish. Of course, actually writing a trade book is daunting. Yet most authors who write one successful trade book write at least one more. A few authors write many. Apparently the rewards are worth the difficulty.

Chapter 10

The Mechanics of Authorship

Describing the rhythm method of birth control in her latest book, . . . sex therapist Ruth Westheimer, Ph.D., incorrectly tells her readers that "the safe times [for sexual intercourse] are the week before and the week of ovulation." While proofreading, "I read the word 'unsafe' in my mind," says the tiny tycoon. "These things do happen."

Newsweek, January 13, 1986

Many of the tasks involved in publishing are mechanical, uninteresting, and frustrating. They are also crucial. This chapter does not make manuscript preparation, proofreading, indexing, and the like painless, but it will help the diligent author perform these jobs efficiently and well. If you yourself do not want to fulfill any of these functions, your publisher can help you find people to do them for you, but the cost of delegating all this work would probably be prohibitive. In many cases, too, the author is the best-qualified proofreader and indexer.

Manuscript Preparation

Almost all academic authors now use computers to prepare manuscripts for articles and books. Computers are easier to use than typewriters, and they provide the author with a great deal of assistance in writing and indexing. Publishers prefer to work with electronic material because it makes revision easier and in some cases permits them to save time and money on typesetting. Indeed, many publishers of scholarly journals and books now require that authors provide electronic manuscripts. Textbook publishers are less likely to require electronic manuscripts because of the complex layout and design of their books, and because typesetting is a small percentage of their production costs. They may well want to use electronic manuscripts for supplementary materials, such as study guides, however. Trade publishers usually rely on traditional production methods because, as in text publishing, typesetting is not one of their larger costs. (See Chapter 11 for a more detailed explanation of costs.)

However, even scholarly publishers may decide not to use the author's electronic manuscript for typesetting. A publisher may choose traditional typesetting for a number of reasons. It is generally impractical to use an author's disks for a book that is heavily illustrated or has an elaborate layout, because most of the cost and effort comes in laying out pages rather than in keyboarding. Even for a simple manuscript with nothing but straightforward text, using an author's disks may not be economical. The disks cannot simply be "plugged in" to a typesetting machine; they must be checked, coded, and corrected. The savings will be small if much coding or correction is needed because a typesetter's keyboarding staff is paid at lower rates than the staff that handles the typesetting of disks provided by the author and publisher. Even desktop typesetting provides only marginal savings if higher-paid members of the publisher's production staff (or the author!) do the work. And, as we will see in Chapter 11, the cost of typesetting is a fairly small percentage of the cost of publishing a book, particularly if the print run is large. The monetary savings may be inconsequential.

Nor is a great deal of time always saved. The actual typesetting time may be reduced from roughly four weeks to two, but over the nine months that it usually takes to produce a book, two weeks is not very much.

The decision to use the author's disks for typesetting is largely an economic judgment, and the publisher may simply decide that the savings on a given book will not be high enough. Nevertheless, you can improve the odds that your disks will be used by preparing them carefully. Whether the publisher uses them or not, you can save yourself and your editor some time in preparing the manuscript for publication, and you can reduce the chance that errors will be introduced. Assume that your electronic manuscript will be used for typesetting, but do not be too disappointed if it is not.

Planning

Because efficient use of computer technology requires compatibility of hardware and software, it is best to talk to your prospective publisher as early as possible about the practicality of typesetting from your disks. If you sign an advance contract before you have done much writing, you are in an ideal position to work successfully with your publisher on an electronic manuscript. You can agree on the word-processing program to be used and establish keyboarding rules and standard treatments for headings, block quotations, and so forth. You can decide how to handle the mechanics of editing, who will enter the typesetting codes, and how to handle other details. If you do not find a publisher until your manuscript is completed, all of this will be more difficult, but it is far from impossible. However, if you are going to do a significant amount of writing before finding a publisher, it will be especially important to follow the keyboarding rules given in the next section.

Publishers who are experienced in using authors' computer disks or tapes generally send authors questionnaires about the preparation of their manuscripts or instructions about their preparation; they may also ask you to send a sample disk. Figure 3 is the Cambridge University Press instructions. Such questionnaires, along with sample disks, provide

NEW YORK OFFICE
40 West 20th Street
New York, NY 10011-4211
U.S.A.

Some Notes for Authors
on Electronic Manuscripts

If the manuscript that you are preparing for the Press is being keyboarded on a computer, it is possible that we may be able to use your disks for conversion and phototypesetting, without total rekeyboarding. Or, if the output from your printer is of sufficiently high quality, in some cases we may be able to reproduce that output directly, photographing it page for page as camera-ready copy.

We would like to examine these possibilities as early as we can during the preparation of the manuscript, so that we can decide if either of these methods would offer more efficient and economical production of your book.

If you are using a computer, may we ask that you answer as many of the questions on this questionnaire as you are able. Send the completed form to your editor as soon as you can. Even if you do not yet have any of the materials typed into the system you plan to use, we would like to learn about that system.

Please enclose a sample page or two from your printer when you return the questionnaire, so that we can assess whether the output from your printer is sharp enough to be used for reproduction directly in your book, as well as examine the structure of technical or math displays, and quality of tables and charts.

When we receive the answers to these questions and if the system you are using might be compatible with that of our typesetter, we may ask you to send us a sample diskette. This will be tested by our typesetter to see if they can be used.

Please note that whether or not we use your electronic output for typesetting, your final manuscript should be sent to your editor in the form of two hard copies. Set your printer to print double-spaced with an unjustified right margin and there should be no wordbreaks at the end of lines. All the notes should be printed double-spaced in a separate listing by chapter at the end of the manuscript, and not be printed at the foot of the manuscript pages. Please refer to our 'Notes for Authors' for more information on manuscript preparation.

For some word processing systems it is possible that the Press can provide macros or stylesheets that automatically produce our house and series styles (eg. for TeX and LaTeX). Please indicate on the questionnaire if you believe that you could use one of these packages and the preferred format (disk size and format, electronic mail etc.).

Figure 3. Electronic manuscript instructions and questionnaire.

CAMBRIDGE
UNIVERSITYPRESS

Electronic Manuscript Questionnaire

Author_____

Title_____

Date_____ CUP Editor _____

Your Computer

Make and model (e.g. Mac IIci, NEC 386)_____

Word processing software (include version number)_____

Graphics software (include version number)_____

Peripheral packages (e.g. BibTeX, Formulator, MacEquation)

Your Disks

Size: 5.25"   3.5"

Density: single   double   high

Format (e.g. DOS, Mac) _____

Files: Formatted using the   ASCII   Both
             above listed software

Your Text

Does your text contain:
_____technical notation   _____foreign accents   _____other special characters

Has your text been:
_____spell-checked   _____grammar-checked   _____other special checking

Would you be willing to input CUP editorial revisions directly onto the disks yourself after the copyediting is complete? ___Yes   ___No   ___Uncertain at this stage

Other Information

Figure 3 *(cont.)*

the publisher with enough information to decide whether your disks can be used for typesetting.

The instructions for preparing a typescript are the same regardless of whether you are writing a monograph, textbook, or trade book. However, many publishers provide their authors with specific instructions on the preparation of the manuscript, especially if they are planning to use the author's electronic manuscript for typesetting. If your publisher gives you such instructions, follow them. If you have not received instructions, request them.

Producing a manuscript to be used for typesetting may require more work on your part than the traditional process. You will have to make all your changes on the disk – no more pencil corrections of typos or last-minute insertions. The disk must be letter-perfect. You may be asked to put in codes (abbreviations signaling the beginning and end of chapter titles, headings, block quotations, and other manuscript elements) and perform other tasks that authors in the good old days never knew were necessary. (A section later in this chapter explains how to do this.) If you are not prepared to do any of this extra work, make sure your publisher understands that.

In fact, discussions about your responsibilities for creating an electronic manuscript should be part of your contract negotiations. Some authors do not want to spend their time entering editorial changes or codes, and they must be sure that their contract does not require them to do so. At the other extreme, some authors prefer the kind of control this gives them and consider it to be worth the extra work. Similarly, the publisher may decide a book is publishable only if the author does a great deal of the work, whereas on another project no production work from the author beyond a typescript is desirable. After reading this chapter, you should have a clear idea of how much effort is required for various alternatives. If you do not want to do much of it, you will need to find a publisher who does not expect it.

Keyboarding

Whether your manuscript will be used for typesetting or not, you can follow some basic rules that will make manuscript preparation easier for you and optimize the usefulness of your disks for a publisher.

1. Select a commonly used word-processing program and, if possible, use the most recent version. Avoid systems specific to your campus or your department, as well as free experimental programs. The most popular programs are the ones that page-makeup and typesetting programs can adapt to most easily. Having chosen a program, do not switch software in mid-stream. If you begin a book using one program, stick with it, no matter how exciting a newer one may be. Even if material prepared with the old program can easily be exported into the new program, don't do it. This process can create a variety of minor, often unpredictable, problems later on.
2. Use disks sensibly. Label all disks to show your name, the names of the files, and the software used. Keep your electronic manuscript in order, with only contiguous chapters sharing a disk. In other words, do not put chapters 2, 5, and 8 on one disk, with 1, 3, and 7 on a second, and 4, 6, and notes on a third. Never divide a chapter between disks. Use as few files per chapter as possible; one file per chapter is best if length permits. Keep notes in a separate file (unless you're compiling a multiauthor book, in which case each chapter should have a separate note file). Do not embed the notes in the text unless your editor assures you that the press can cope with them. The bibliography, too, should be in a separate file, as should tables, captions, glossary, and any other special elements. Do not overload a disk. What constitutes overloading depends on your software, but make sure to leave plenty of space to edit what is there. Save your copy frequently and keep current back-up copies of all your disks. It does not do much good to have copies of only the unrevised disks if the ones with your revisions and the copyeditor's work are lost or destroyed.
3. Type carefully. Do not type zero for the letter oh, one for the letter ell, brackets for parentheses, zeros for bullets, or any other

substitutions. If you use any special character (e.g., asterisks before items in a list), use it for one purpose only. Use the word wrap feature, reserving carriage returns for places where lines must also end in the finished book – that is, at the ends of paragraphs, headings, lines of poetry, items in a list, formulas or equations set off on separate lines, chapter titles, epigraphs, and so forth. The publisher will expect all hard copy to be double spaced, including notes, bibliography, and block quotations. The publisher will also expect your manuscript to have adequate margins: An inch on the sides and at top and bottom is fine.

4. Avoid your program's bells and whistles. Under no circumstances should you use justification or hyphenation features. Do not break any words at the ends of lines except genuine compounds with permanent hyphens (e.g., English-speaking). Do not put notes at the foot of the page, even though your program can do it elegantly. Type notes in a separate file, paragraph style, with the numbers at line level rather than as superscripts. (You can use superscripts in the text itself, however.) The bibliography should be in a separate file, typed in a hang-indent style (first line at left margin and subsequent lines indented; select this option from your program's menu). Because page and line breaks will be different in the final book pages, any extra formatting commands will simply have to be removed anyway. You will save time and prevent errors by not using them in the first place.

5. Type consistently. If you wish to indent paragraphs, use the tab key to generate the same number of spaces for all paragraph indents (or use your program's special paragraph indent command). Otherwise, a hard return will do. Ask the publisher whether to use one space or two at the ends of sentences. (Opinions vary.) If you put extra spacing above or below headings (which is not necessary), always use the same number of spaces. Never add spacing to avoid an awkward page break.

6. Keep the manuscript simple. Do not put headings in italics, boldface, or all capital letters; capitalize only the initial letters of nouns, pronouns, verbs, adjectives, and adverbs. You can differentiate levels of headings by centering the major ones, placing the next level flush left on a separate line, and running the third level into the text. Do not use a different font or size for block quotations, notes, or any other special element. For

the sake of readability, it is all right (though not necessary) to center headings and to indent block quotations, but do not do anything more elaborate. Use italics or underlining only as necessary, for book titles, special terms, foreign words, and the like. (Remember that underlining will turn into italics when your manuscript becomes a book, because – in the absence of good reasons to do otherwise – the commands for underlining and italics will both be read as italics. To make the hard copy more attractive and consistent, use one or the other.) Do not add elements like running heads that are meant to make the manuscript look more like a book. A manuscript should look like a manuscript.

7. Print the manuscript out on a laser or inkjet printer on high-quality $8^1/_2$- by 11-inch paper. Manuscripts are subjected to a great deal of handling, and lightweight paper may not survive. Make a photocopy for yourself.

An editor may return the electronic manuscript to you if your disks have been prepared in a way that makes typesetting difficult. Failure to follow instructions (either the publisher's or those given earlier) might increase the amount of work for the publisher or typesetter to the point that the savings generated by using your disks would evaporate. In such cases, the responsibility for revision is clearly yours, just as it would be if you had submitted a single spaced or messy typescript. You might even be asked to make these changes before editing begins. At whatever stage this occurs, follow directions carefully.

What Software Can and Cannot Do

Although some word-processing features, such as automatic hyphenation at the ends of lines, should be avoided in preparing an electronic manuscript, many of them are helpful. If you can search the manuscript automatically, then you can correct misspelled names, replace one term with a more precise one, check for overuse of a word or expression, and check for consistency. A novelist, for example, can easily make sure that the hero's eyes do not change from steely gray to melting brown between chapters 2 and 5.

Remember, however, that the computer is not as smart as you are. Monitor your use of such functions as search-and-replace very carefully. At first glance, for example, it seems reasonable to tell the computer to replace, say, *man* with *human* – a quick and easy solution to one problem of sexist language. If you do not phrase your search precisely (in this case by searching for *man* surrounded by spaces), you will end up with such linguistic marvels as *comhumand, humandatory, ehumancipation,* and *rohumance.* Even if you tell the computer to make the change only when *man* stands as an independent word, you are likely to get strange sentences, such as those about the discovery of Peking Human and Shaw's play *Human and Superman.* It is safest to avoid such global commands in favor of searching out each use and making the individual decision to replace each use. (One instance in which the global replace command is useful is in coding, as I will explain later.)

Spelling checkers are also a boon to authors and copyeditors. If you are not a good speller or a good typist, the spelling checker will find your most embarrassing errors. It will not, however, correct the sort of spelling error most common among even careful writers – choosing the wrong homonym. Even a good spelling checker will let you use *discreet* when you meant *discrete* and allow you to "martial your resources," although the better ones will alert you to the possibility of error. Nor will a spelling checker find typos that happen to be correctly spelled words – though not the ones you intended. For example, if you type *casual* instead of *causal,* the checker will not take notice. Nor will accidental plurals be spotted.

One drawback to spelling checkers is that their vocabularies may be inadequate for specialized writing. Fortunately, most of them allow you to add technical terms, proper nouns, and so forth to their dictionaries. (Be sure to spell them correctly when you add them.) It is probably a good idea to turn off any automatic correcting features, because unfamiliar technical terms and names may be changed silently to a word that the computer recognizes but has nothing to do with your meaning. Spelling checkers remain too cumbersome to be of much use in manuscripts that contain material in foreign languages or that quote extensively from documents replete with inconsistencies or misspellings, such as seventeenth-century theological treatises. (This is another occasion when you *must* turn off automatic correction.) If large parts of your manuscript are in another language, you may be able to find a spelling checker for that language on the Web. These can be just as useful as English-language spelling checkers, and they have the same limitations.

Software versions of thesauruses are available, but – like their printed equivalents – they may not be very discriminating. Use them with caution.

Grammar checkers vary greatly in usefulness and sophistication. Most were designed for business correspondence and reports and are inadequate for scholarly writing. Before purchasing a grammar checker more elaborate than the one built into your word-processing program, read the reviews in computer magazines and test the alternatives carefully. The best test is to subject a brief manuscript to the checker. See how long it takes (some are extraordinarily slow) and how much of what it does is useful. For example, some programs claim to spot "unusual" words or words that are not readily understood by students in, say, their first year of college. Unfortunately, such a program may merely list every proper noun (e.g., Bosnia) along with everything else that is not in its vocabulary. Test, too, what it does when it finds a problem. Does it highlight it in some way, tell you specifically what is wrong (double negative, passive construction, or whatever), offer suggestions, or provide all of these kinds of assistance?

Neither spelling checkers nor grammar checkers will do any good if you turn them off or ignore them. There is really no excuse for turning in a manuscript with the kinds of errors that a spelling checker can avert, so use these features cautiously, but do use them.

What to Include

Make sure the manuscript includes the following elements:

1. A title page
2. A dedication if desired
3. A table of contents
4. A preface, acknowledgments, and foreword if needed
5. Lists of maps, illustrations, and tables if needed
6. The complete text
7. Maps, tables, and illustrations if needed
8. Glossary or list of abbreviations if needed
9. Notes
10. Bibliography

Note that the manuscript should not contain an index. Book indexes cannot be prepared in final form until you have at least preliminary page proofs, because entries must provide page numbers. The sole exception is a book that is indexed by numbered items or paragraphs, rather than by pages, such as a bibliography.

The title page should contain the title and subtitle (if any) and your name. It is advisable, though not vital, to include the standard copyright notice: Copyright ©1990 by Leslie J. Author.

Dedications are optional. If you want to dedicate your book to someone, by all means do so. But avoid flowery, overly personal, or cute tributes. A lot of people are going to read your book, and few of them need to be told in detail of your spouse's adoration, your parents' sacrifices, or your children's brilliance. Keep it short and simple. The dedicatees will be grateful for the recognition, no matter how few the words.

The table of contents can be brief (just chapter titles plus notes and bibliography) or more detailed. If your chapters are long and have major subdivisions with descriptive headings, include these headings if they will help the reader locate material more easily or determine whether the book is of interest. Only highly technical works need greater detail. When a manuscript is divided into parts as well as chapters, the parts should be included in the table of contents. *The Chicago Manual of Style* illustrates the varieties of tables of contents.

A preface is useful in explaining the inspiration for the book, origin and evolution of the project, and so forth. It should be regarded as optional reading, however, and should not include anything such as methodology or theoretical background that the reader needs to understand the book. Material essential to the reader's understanding belongs in the main text. A foreword is a preliminary essay written by someone other than the author. You and your editor may discuss whether it would be desirable to solicit one and, if so, from whom.

Acknowledgments, when included, should be brief and relatively formal. Personal thanks, particularly if effusive, should be handwritten in an inscription.

Be sure that your lists of maps, illustrations, and tables are accurate – that is, that they conform to the actual numbers, titles, and placement of the figures and tables.

The text should be complete. If you have left out a date, first name, or piece of data, fill it in. You do not want to give an impression of sloppiness or haste, and you are going to have to complete it eventually anyway.

Each table should be typed neatly, not handwritten, on a separate piece of paper, with correct alignment of columns. Tables should be numbered and titled. You can place the pages in the text where they belong or group them separately. For the latter alternative, be sure to indicate the number of the manuscript page where the table belongs. Short, simple tables can be typed within the text.

Instructions for preparing and mailing illustrations are provided shortly. When submitting a manuscript for consideration, however, you may simply send photocopies.

Type the glossary and list of abbreviations, if needed, in proper alphabetical order, double spaced. Make sure such elements are complete and accurate, and that they contain all the foreign words, technical words, or abbreviations as they are actually used in the book.

Notes should not be inserted at the foot of the text page. This is true no matter where the notes will appear in the finished book. Even if they are to be set at the foot of the page, the copyeditor and typesetter can deal with them more easily if you prepare them as a separate entity. Type them like the text, double spaced, each beginning as an indented paragraph with a number typed at line level followed by a period (i.e., 32., not ³²). Make sure you have the same number of notes as you have note numbers in the text. Number notes consecutively by chapter.

The bibliography or reference list should also be typed double spaced. Each entry begins at the left margin, with further lines indented three to five spaces; it is best to use your program's hang-indent formatting option to accomplish this. Although indentation can be added later, it is easier for the author and editor to check alphabetizing if the typescript is prepared in this format. Such lists are alphabetical, author's last name first, and entries are not numbered. When more than one work by the same author is listed, use three hyphens instead of the name for all listings after the first. *The Chicago Manual of Style* illustrates form and style of bibliographies and reference lists.

Submission

The manuscript you submit to a publisher has almost always been revised and reworked from an original draft. It should be carefully proofread and corrected. Send the manuscript (and disks, if requested) in a sturdy cardboard box (a padded bag is all right if you are not enclosing artwork or computer disks). When submitting a manuscript to a publisher for review, you will rarely be asked for the disks, which are needed only after acceptance. If you are mailing disks alone, use rigid cardboard mailers or plastic cases. Use first-class mail or a commercial delivery service. Overnight delivery is rarely necessary.

Coding

If your electronic manuscript is to be used for typesetting, the designer's decisions must be entered in the form of codes that provide instructions to the typesetting machine or laser printer. The copyeditor may enter codes, or you may be asked to undertake this task after the copyediting is complete. If your disks will not be used, you will not need to worry about this part of the process.

A basic understanding of the design and typesetting processes clarifies the need for coding. Each element of a manuscript needs to be designed. For the text itself, a designer must select the depth and width of the type page, the size of the type, the typeface, and the amount of space (or "leading") between lines. For each level of subheading, the size and face of the type must be chosen. In addition, decisions must be made about whether the heading will be italic, boldface, roman, or small caps; whether it should be centered, flush left, flush right, or in some other position; whether it will be set in initial caps and lowercase (as in book titles) or sentence style; and how much extra space will be inserted above and below it. Similar decisions must be made for running heads, page numbers, block quotations, equations, epigraphs, notes, chapter numbers, and titles – for every design element the manuscript contains. The purpose of the initial coding, which has been done for decades, independent of computer technology, is simply to identify each of these elements, regardless of the designer's decisions. That is, a first-level subheading is a first-level subheading, no matter what typeface the designer selects or whether it is to be centered or flush left. This part of the coding is frequently done by an editor before the designer looks at the manuscript, so that the designer can quickly see what elements must be designed. The editor writes simple codes of one to three letters on hard copy that is sent to the designer. Figure 4 is an example of one page of a manuscript coded by an editor for the designer.

The designer's choices are conveyed to the typesetter or the person setting up the page-makeup program in a list of

(CO)

(CN)
15
(CT) Coding a Manuscript

(TX) When an electronic manuscript is coded for typesetting--whether by the author, the publisher's production staff, or the typesetter--two types of elements must be coded. The first are design elements that designate parts of the text, such as chapter titles, subheadings, and lists. The second are typographical elements that occur within the text, such as italics, boldface, accents, and other special characters.

(A-HD) Design Elements

Every element that is to be designed must be coded. Beginning at the beginning (though after the frontmatter), most books will contain chapter numbers, chapter titles, first paragraphs of chapters, paragraph indents, subheadings at various levels, lists, extracts (sometimes called "block quotes"), tables, figures, figure captions, glossary, notes, bibliography, and index.

(A-HD) Typographical Elements

Some typographical elements that must be coded are special forms of type: italics, boldface, and small caps are the most common. Others are special characters, such as superscripts and accents. Others are characters that do not appear on the computer keyboard but are available in type, for example, dashes (--) and "opening and closing quotation marks." These, too, must be coded.

Some of the coding may take place without intervention. If the page-makeup or typesetting equipment can "read" your word-processing program's commands for italics, for example, then no coding is needed for italics.

(Drop FOL)

1

Figure 4. Manuscript page coded for the designer. Note that only design elements are coded. If the manuscript had included unusual typographic elements, such as a foreign alphabet, that would also have been noted.

specifications, which spells out the various elements the book includes and describes their design, and in the coding of the manuscript. Obviously, no one would like to have to write out in full the instructions for each element each time. (The description for a subheading, for example, might read: 10 pt. Baskerville, italic, caps and lowercase, centered, 12 points space above, 6 points below.) The codes convey this information in shorthand. Thus, on reading the code for level 1 heading, the typesetting machine or page-makeup program sets the words that follow in 10-point Baskerville, italic, caps and lowercase, and centers them, leaving 12 points of space above and 6 points below.

In the traditional typesetting process, when the typesetter receives the manuscript and the design specifications, more complex codes are substituted for the simple mnemonic codes and further codes are added for italics, accent marks, and other special characters within the text (see Figure 5).

When the author's disks are used, a similar system can easily be adopted. You have probably already recognized how a search-and-replace command could be used to change short mnemonic codes entered by an author or editor to the more complex typesetting codes. Once you know which elements need to be coded, it is relatively easy to code an electronic manuscript. However, unless you are trained in book design, you will need some help from your publisher. And you will need to be very careful about formulating and entering codes. If you undertake to code your manuscript, you can use three types of code: one you make up yourself, one specified by your publisher (or, if you are self-publishing or preparing camera-ready copy, by your page-makeup program), or the Standard Generalized Markup Language (SGML), an international standard code. Each has its requirements and its advantages, and each must be used exactingly.

Do-it-yourself Codes.   Making up your own code has the obvious advantage of allowing you to use a code that is easy to remember: If you make it up, you ought to be able to use it. It has the disadvantages of any idiosyncratic system: Perhaps no

15

Coding a Manuscript

When an electronic manuscript is coded for typesetting--whether by the author, the publisher's production staff, or the typesetter--two types of elements must be coded. The first are design elements that designate parts of the text, such as chapter titles, subheadings, and lists. The second are typographical elements that occur within the text, such as italics, boldface, accents, and other special characters. Each code must have forms for entering and exiting.

Design Elements

Every element that is to be designed must be coded. Beginning at the beginning (though after the frontmatter), most books will contain chapter numbers, chapter titles, first paragraphs of chapters, paragraph indents, subheadings at various levels, lists, extracts (sometimes called "block quotes"), tables, figures, figure captions, figure credits, glossary, notes, bibliography, and index.

Typographical Elements

Some typographical elements that must be coded are special forms of type: italics, boldface, and small caps are the most common. Others are special characters, such as superscripts and accents. Others are characters that do not appear on the computer keyboard but are available in type, for example, dashes (--) and "opening and closing quotation marks." These, too, must be coded.

Some of the coding may take place without intervention. If the page-makeup or typesetting equipment can "read" your word-processing program's commands for italics, for example, then no coding is needed for italics.

1

Figure 5. Manuscript page coded by a typesetter. Both design and typographic elements are coded.

one else will understand it. Certainly, nonhumans such as page-makeup programs and typesetting machines will not know what you are up to. However, you can use your own comfortable codes and then substitute more universal ones with your software's search-and-replace function.

Your own codes must follow certain rules. First, each must be unique. You cannot use the same code for a paragraph indent and a list indent. Duplication can be avoided by creating a complete list of elements to be coded and following it carefully, as I explain shortly.

Second, each code must be distinguished from text by symbols called "delimiters." These must be used uniformly and must be characters that are not used in the text itself. The most commonly used delimiters are angle brackets, which are rarely needed in ordinary text and which meet the criterion of providing an opening delimiter that is different from the closing delimiter. For mathematical text, where angle brackets are used to symbolize "less than" and "more than," other delimiters may be chosen.

Finally, you must remember to insert codes everywhere they are needed. If you have ever had the experience of forgetting the command for "end italics" when you typed a bibliography on your computer, you have experienced the havoc that such carelessness can wreak.

To avoid duplication, and to help create a code that has some internal consistency, you should begin by making a list of all elements that must be coded. The considerate and experienced publisher will provide a checklist, but if you do not get one, you can use the following list as a starting point. (Note that it covers only the text, not front matter like the title page and table of contents, which are especially complicated and for which the publisher should provide special instructions.)

1. Chapter number
2. Chapter title
3. Title without number (e.g., "Foreword")
4. Epigraph
5. Source of epigraph
6. First paragraph of chapter

7. Level 1 heading
8. Level 2 heading
9. Level 3 heading
10. Extra space (e.g., to substitute for a heading)
11. Prose block quotation
12. Poetry block quotation
13. Numbered list
14. List with bullets
15. Equations
16. Chemical formulas
17. Table numbers
18. Table titles
19. Table column headings
20. Table stub elements
21. Table text
22. Table notes
23. Figure numbers
24. Figure titles
25. Figure captions
26. Figure credits
27. Notes
28. Subheadings for notes section
29. Block quotations within notes
30. Bibliography
31. Subheadings for bibliography
32. Glossary text
33. Appendix number
34. Appendix title
35. Appendix text

Not all of these will be necessary in every book. For one thing, your book may not contain all of these elements. Equally likely, the book's design will be such that some of these elements will be identical. For example, subheadings may be the same in text, bibliography, and notes, so that a single set of subheading codes will be adequate. If your publisher provides a list of elements that need codes, your job will be made easier.

In addition to the codes for design elements, you will need codes for some characters within the text. The following list includes the most common such elements:

1. Italics
2. Boldface
3. Small capitals
4. Paragraph indent
5. Em dashes (those usually typed as two dashes)
6. En dashes (used for inclusive numbers and for other specific purposes that your copyeditor will mark)
7. 3-em dashes (used in bibliographies and occasionally in quotations)
8. Opening quotation marks
9. Closing quotation marks
10. Opening single quotation marks
11. Closing single quotation marks
12. Superscripts
13. Monetary symbols (dollars, cents, pounds sterling, etc.)
14. Accent marks (acute, grave, tilde, cedilla, etc.)
15. Greek letters
16. Cyrillic letters
17. Mathematical symbols

Again, not all of these codes will be needed in all books. In all likelihood, you are not using the cyrillic alphabet. More important, by testing a sample disk, your publisher can determine whether their typesetting program can understand your word-processing program's commands for such elements as italics, superscripts, accents, dashes, and paragraph indents. If it can, no special coding will be needed for those elements.

Once you have created a list of elements that you will need to code, you can make up opening and closing codes that are easy for you to remember. Enter them wherever needed, being sure to have a closing or exit code to end each coded command. Figure 6 shows a page coded in an author's code. It is an example, not a model: Your memory may work very differently than mine. Print out your manuscript and proofread the coding very carefully. (I would advise using a colored pen or pencil and marking each code with a checkmark as you go.) Correct any mistyped codes, delete any extra ones, and add any that are missing. Then, if it is your job to

(CN)15

(CT)Coding a Manuscript

(NOP)When an electronic manuscript is coded for

typesetting(DSH)whether by the author, the publisher's production

staff, or the typesetter(DSH)two types of elements must be coded. The

first are design elements that designate parts of the text, such as

chapter titles, subheadings, and lists. The second are typographical

elements that occur within the text, such as italics, boldface,

accents, and other special characters.

(SH1)Design Elements

(NOP)Every element that is to be designed must be coded. Beginning at

the beginning (though after the frontmatter), most books will contain

chapter numbers, chapter titles, first paragraphs of chapters,

paragraph indents, subheadings at various levels, lists, extracts

(sometimes called (OQ)block quotes(CQ)), tables, figures, figure

captions, glossary, notes, bibliography, and index.

(SH1)Typographical Elements

(NOP)Some typographical elements that must be coded are special forms

of type: (OI)italics,(CI) (OB)boldface,(CB) and (OSC)small caps(CSC)

are the most common. Others are special characters, such as

superscripts(OUP)1(CUP) and (AA)accents. Others are characters that do

not appear on the computer keyboard but are available in type, for

example, dashes ((DSH)) and (OQ)opening and closing quotation

marks.(CQ) These, too, must be coded.

(PI)Some of the coding may take place without intervention. If the

page-makeup or typesetting equipment can (OQ)read(CQ) your word-

processing program's commands for italics, for example, then no coding

is needed for italics.

1

Figure 6. Manuscript page coded by an author using an idiosyncratic mnemonic code.

enter the publisher's or typesetter's codes, you can do so by using the search-and-replace command.

Using the Publisher's Codes. Using the publisher's codes will ensure that your disks can be used easily in whatever typesetting process the publisher has chosen. It may or may not be significantly harder to assimilate than a code that you might invent. The publisher's code may in fact be the code set up for a page-makeup program. In this case, the codes will not be too complex, and you may find it easier simply to use them than to invent your own codes. If they are true typesetting codes, however, they will be more complicated, so that it may be worth the time it will take to make up your own codes and replace them electronically. Publishers who expect authors to enter their own codes will provide directions.

Generally, all you need is a list of elements and the corresponding codes. Read through the instructions, make sure you know what each element is, and call your editor with questions before you begin. Make sure there are codes provided for every element in your manuscript. Then study the codes more closely. Even the most complex codes are not arbitrary, and by spending some time with the code and instructions you can learn enough about how the code was designed to make memorizing easier. For example, exit codes are often identical to opening codes except for the addition of a single keystroke. Your word-processing program may also allow you to program the function or other keys so that you can use them for the codes that appear most frequently. Your editor can make your job easier by marking various elements to be coded on the hard copy of the manuscript, at least for the first chapter. Some publishers mark all the codes on hard copy for the author to enter. As noted in the instructions for using your own code, enter codes carefully and proofread thoroughly. Figure 7 is a page coded for Ventura, the page-makeup program used to produce the first two editions of this book.

```
@CN = 15

@TITLE = Coding a Manuscript

@FIRST PARA = When an electronic manuscript is coded for typesetting
<196> whether by the author, the publisher's production staff, or the
typesetter <196> two types of elements must be coded. The first are
design elements that designate parts of the text, such as chapter
titles, subheadings, and lists. The second are typographical elements
that occur within the text, such as italics, boldface, accents, and
other special characters.

@HEAD LEVEL 1 = Design Elements

@FIRST PARA = Every element that is to be designed must be coded.
Beginning at the beginning (though after the frontmatter), most books
will contain chapter numbers, chapter titles, first paragraphs of
chapters, paragraph indents, subheadings at various levels, lists,
extracts (sometimes called <169>block quotes<170>), tables, figures,
figure captions, glossary, notes, bibliography, and index.

@HEAD LEVEL 1 = Typographical Elements

@FIRST PARA = Some typographical elements that must be coded are
special forms of type: <MI>italics,<D> <MB>boldface,<D> and <>small
caps<> are the most common. Others are special characters, such as
superscripts1 and accents. Others are characters that do not appear on
the computer keyboard but are available in type, for example, dashes
(<196>) and <169>opening and closing quotation marks.<170> These, too,
must be coded.

        Some of the coding may take place without intervention. If
the page-makeup or typesetting equipment can <169>read<170> your word-
processing program's commands for italics, for example, then no coding
is needed for italics.
```

1

Figure 7. Manuscript page coded for the Ventura page-makeup program.

The Standard Generalized Markup Language. By now you are probably thinking that all of this would be much easier if authors, publishers, and typesetters could agree on a single, simple method of coding. Publishers, typesetters, and others have been cooperating in an effort to create such a method, and the result is the Standard Generalized Markup Language, or SGML, whose use is illustrated in Figure 8. It has been accepted as an international standard by the relevant agencies, but it has not yet been universally adopted by publishers and typesetters. (The agencies that create standards do so by convening international teams of experts, publishing their recommendations, and promoting them, but they have no enforcement powers. Their recommendations become truly "standard" only when they are voluntarily adopted by the relevant industries. The ISBN, or International Standard Book Number, which appears on the copyright page and back cover of this and virtually every book, is an example of a fully implemented standard.) SGML is undoubtedly more complex than a mnemonic code that an individual author might create, but it is not difficult to understand. If your publisher wants to use SGML, your editor will send you a list of the relevant codes, along with instructions. (If you are publishing your manuscript yourself and are having it typeset, your typesetter may use the SGML codes and can provide a list.)

If SGML is more widely adopted, it may become possible to eliminate altogether the need for coding manuscripts manually. Software is being developed that automates the insertion of SGML codes, and some major software manufacturers embed some of the SGML codes in word-processing software, so that the codes are entered automatically or optionally. That is, you can type the usual command for a paragraph indent or italics or click on the icon, and the program records the SGML command. This renders the task completely painless for authors and makes the use of author-coded disks much easier for publishers and typesetters.

SGML is commonly used by producers of electronic publications such as CD-ROMs. For such products the codes are used, not for typesetting, but for multiple uses of a single text,

```
<chp><no>15

<ct>Coding a Manuscript

When an electronic manuscript is coded for typesetting&mdash;whether

by the author, the publisher's production staff, or the

typesetter&mdash;two types of elements must be coded. The first are

design elements that designate parts of the text, such as chapter

titles, subheadings, and lists. The second are typographical elements

that occur within the text, such as italics, boldface, accents, and

other special characters.

<h1>Design Elements

Every element that is to be designed must be coded. Beginning at the

beginning (though after the frontmatter), most books will contain

chapter numbers, chapter titles, first paragraphs of chapters,

paragraph indents, subheadings at various levels, lists, extracts

(sometimes called &ldquo;block quotes&rdquo;), tables, figures,

figure captions, glossary, notes, bibliography, and index.

<h1>Typographical Elements

Some typographical elements that must be coded are special forms of

type: <it>italics,</> <b>boldface,</> and <scp>small caps</> are

the most common. Others are special characters, such as

superscripts<fnr>1</> and &aacute;ccents. Others are characters that

do not appear on the computer keyboard but are available in type, for

example, dashes (&mdash;) and &ldquo;opening and closing quotation

marks.&rdquo; These, too, must be coded.

<p>Some of the coding may take place without intervention. If

the page-makeup or typesetting equipment can &ldquo;read&rdquo;

your word-processing program's commands for italics, for example,

then no coding is needed for italics.


                          1
```

Figure 8. Manuscript page coded in SGML, the Standard Generalized Markup Language.

and for hypertext and other searching and organizing functions. This kind of SGML markup can become extremely complex and is best left to publishers. Again, however, software is being developed to make it easier to code and proofread electronic documents using SGML. (HTML, which is used to compose Web pages, is a subset of SGML.)

Camera-Ready Copy and Electronic Page Makeup

When sales of a book are expected to be small, it is not uncommon for publishers (especially university centers, professional societies, and specialized technical publishers) to request that the author submit camera-ready copy (a typescript that can be photographed for printing as is) or the electronic equivalent (an electronic manuscript formatted so that it is ready for printing without further work). Sometimes this is a condition for publication. Books that would be expensive to typeset because of technical material or foreign alphabets may also have to be provided in one of these forms, along with teacher's manuals and other materials supplementary to textbooks. Sometimes an author prefers to provide camera-ready copy to keep control over the material; this is particularly true for critical and documentary editions. And if you have decided to be your own publisher, designing and laying out your own book is usually the most economical alternative.

Preparing Copy for a Publisher. The well-equipped, computer-literate author can prepare camera-ready copy or the electronic equivalent that will end up looking nearly as attractive as that prepared by a publisher. One possible difference in quality arises from the equipment you have available. Typesetters use machines that print 1,200 or more dots per inch, far more than affordable laser printers. The differences in resolution are noticeable: The more dots per inch, the clearer the image. But for most scholarly books, the difference in cost outweighs the difference in clarity. If you are providing a formatted electronic manuscript, the publisher can use high-end typesetting equipment, so that the book will be indistinguishable from one produced more traditionally.

Most authors who prepare camera-ready copy use page-layout or page-makeup software. These programs have three major advantages over word-processing programs. First, most of them allow you to see a complete page on the screen in what is known as WYSIWYG form: What You See Is What You Get. Especially for people with little design experience, it is helpful to see how your design decisions are going to turn out before printing. Second, once you make your design decisions (or enter those provided by your publisher), most programs follow the instructions file after file, chapter after chapter, without your having to reinstruct them. Finally, page-makeup programs allow you to incorporate graphics directly into the text. Alternatively, they permit you a variety of choices for placement of figures by allowing you to create "windows" of different sizes. It is worth noting, however, that expensive page-makeup programs are not vital to preparing camera-ready copy, or to any other variant of desktop typesetting. Especially if the book is of simple design, a good word-processing program may be adequate – and you get to use some of the bells and whistles that are so dangerous when the book is to be printed using different software.

If you agree to prepare camera-ready copy or to provide a disk that the typesetter can use without further work, you should get very specific instructions from your publisher. These instructions may be electronic: Your publisher can select the desired options from those offered by your page-makeup or word-processing program, providing a sort of electronic style sheet. The same instructions can be provided in writing. For example, your program will ask you how many spaces to use for a paragraph indent; your publisher should tell you what to answer. If your manuscript is complex, these instructions will be complex, too, but it will be much easier to impart the publisher's decisions to your software and printer than it would be to make the design decisions yourself. The end result will be more attractive, too, if a professional designer has contributed expertise.

Also discuss with your publisher how graphics are to be handled. If you have created simple charts or maps on a computer, these can easily be incorporated into the text. Photographs or halftones can also be incorporated by using a scanner, but the quality may be poor. In most cases, you will be asked to leave a specified amount of space in the manuscript (in the form of a window, if you are using a page-makeup program) and to provide glossy black-and-white photos. The publisher will take care of incorporating the photographs into the text.

Allow yourself enough time to experiment with your software and printer. Read the manuals for both carefully and work through the tutorials. If you find the manual difficult to use, select one of the published guides to the program available in your bookstore. They can walk you through the process one more time, to give you some practice and confidence. It is a good idea to work through a shorter project before undertaking a book. Also, get to know what resources are available on your campus to provide assistance on your project. Some universities have desktop publishing experts on staff to provide consultation. Even if yours does not, you can probably find someone in a user's group who has a lot of experience using the same program you have chosen and who is willing to share the lessons learned.

There are many cheerful books about the joys of desktop publishing on the market, but I have included none of them in the bibliography. All of them make it sound as though you simply acquire the software and a printer, write the text at your keyboard (they usually allow three months for research and writing), create dramatic graphics, and produce a beautiful, highly illustrated book with no difficulty in a matter of days. It is foolish to assume that you can sit down with a new program and a book-length manuscript and work miracles. Plan to spend a significant amount of time learning to use your page-makeup program and assume that you will run into problems as you go along.

Alternatively, you can hire someone to turn your edited disks (with or without coding) into camera-ready copy. Someone experienced in desktop typesetting will produce pages ready for printing either according to your publisher's instructions or independently. Because they must invest in expensive software and hardware, and because their skills are much in demand, they will charge what may seem like a high hourly rate. However, they generally work quickly and efficiently and can save you both time and frustration.

Self-publishing. If you are preparing camera-ready copy to produce a book without the assistance of a publisher, you will have to do everything already discussed, but without expert help. In that case, you should consult one or two authorities on book design (see the bibliography) and, especially if you are not graphically talented or experienced, select a book that you find attractive to use as a model.

The basic design principles for a beginner to keep in mind are simplicity and symmetry. Keep the book simple by using only one typeface for everything except, perhaps, the title page and chapter numbers and titles. Distinguish levels of headings by using italics and by varying placement and spacing (locating one level flush left with extra space above and below, and the second flush left with extra space only above, for example), rather than by introducing new typefaces. Set off block quotations with extra space above and below, either in a smaller size of the same typeface or indented. Keep the notes at the back.

It is also a good idea for a beginner to select a symmetrical design. For example, you may decide that your design will focus on centered elements. In that case, the title and author on the title page will be centered, as will chapter titles and major subheadings. Or you may decide to base the design on placement of such elements flush left or, less conventionally, flush right.

Once you have chosen a design that you think looks good on the screen, print out some sample pages so that you can see the results in black and white, with the actual type fonts that will print out. (This is especially important if you are not using a WYSIWYG program, or if you are using one that does not place an entire page on the screen.) Try the first page of a chapter, a page of text with headings, and a page with a table or other special element. You can experiment with various changes easily until you are satisfied with the appearance of the sample pages. Record your decisions in writing for future revisions.

You should decide how elaborately you wish to produce your book according to its purpose. For example, if it is just for use in your own classroom, there is little reason to spend months designing and producing a professional-looking book. If you hope for a wider market, you may wish to spend more time at it.

Camera-ready Cautions. There is no reason why a book published from an author's camera-ready copy or coded disks cannot be as good a book as one published by more traditional methods. The author's research and writing are no different, and the refereeing process is the same. A manuscript editor can work equally carefully, and a designer can work within the limitations of the technology to help create an attractive, readable book. However, desktop publishing technology creates a temptation to take shortcuts that should be resisted.

If you can easily tell that a book has been prepared from the author's camera-ready copy, then the effort was not entirely successful. In some volumes of conference proceedings, for example, the papers have been produced individually by the participants, so that each article has its own typeface and layout. These books contain irregularities that publishers normally do not tolerate, such as facing pages of different lengths, or irregular spacing between text elements. All of these problems can be avoided, however, if the preparer of the copy knows the conventions of page layout and is willing to spend the time to prepare the volume carefully.

More disturbing is the quality of the editing in some camera-ready books. In some volumes, errors in grammar and spelling are frequent. (In one book I checked, a seven-line paragraph about the virtues of spelling and grammar checkers included two grammatical errors, one spelling error, and one stylistic error.) These problems are not inherent in the technology. Rather, they are indicative of procedural problems. When an author submits laser-printed copy using page-makeup software rather than an ordinary-looking double-spaced manuscript for the publisher to edit, the editing may be cursory. In the case of conference proceedings or other books that are difficult to bring together, require reasonably rapid publication, and attract only a small audience, the temptation to cut editorial corners is apparently strong.

If you are preparing camera-ready copy and wish to keep the editorial quality of your book high, make sure to submit an ordinary double-spaced manuscript to your publisher first, and make sure that the publisher is going to edit it. If you are working without a publisher, hire an editor to do the work. Once the manuscript has been edited and revised, you can proceed with the preparation of camera-ready copy. This need not slow down the schedule very much, because you can design the layout and learn to use the program during the editing.

The use of camera-ready copy prepared by authors makes practical the publication of much good work that might otherwise not be available to scholars. With a few precautions and no illusions about the speed or ease of the task, editorial and production standards can be maintained along with economy.

Preparing Revised Editions

The method used to prepare a revised edition will depend on the method used to prepare the previous edition. If the earlier edition was typeset traditionally (that is, not from your disks), then you can work from the existing book. If the publisher has unbound copies, ask for two. If not, you will have to cut apart two copies of the book (one for left-hand pages, one for right). Then, using paste, rubber cement, or tape – not paper clips or staples – put the new edition together on $8\frac{1}{2}$- by 11-inch paper, conserving as much of the original type as possible. For example, if you just need to change a word or two, paste up the old type and make the corrections by crossing out and writing in ink in the margin; indicate clearly where the correction belongs and use standard proofreaders' marks. If you are inserting material, cut the old page where the new information belongs and paste it and the newly typed addition onto a sheet of paper. To delete a paragraph or two, paste it up with the rest of the page and then cross it out. To delete whole pages, just leave them out. When changes are so extensive that cutting and pasting is cumbersome, retype the whole page, double spaced. (If your book was set in two or three columns, cut the columns apart and paste them up in sequence, each column on a separate sheet.)

Tables and figures to be retained should be pasted in place. Note the placement of new tables and figures in the margin and prepare new artwork just as for the original edition.

You must prepare new front matter (title page, preface, acknowledgments, table of contents, list of illustrations, and so forth). Renumber the pages of the manuscript. You will also have to redo the index when page proof is ready. If you were granted permissions that applied only to one edition, you will have to reapply. Check your files and ask your editor's advice.

It may be worthwhile to scan the earlier edition to generate electronic copy. Even with a good scanner, though, the copy will have a lot of typographical errors, and much of the formatting (including that for tables and italics) will vanish. You will have to read and correct the electronic version extra carefully, in addition to making the changes for the new edition.

If the previous edition of your book was set from your disks, you can revise on the disks. Ask your editor to send you copies of the disks from which the book was set in a form that is compatible with your software. Ask your editor whether it would be helpful to highlight changes by using the redlining (or "tracking") feature of your software program. Depending on how you work best, you may want to print out a copy of the unrevised manuscript, edit on that, and then enter the changes on the disk; or you may prefer simply to do your revisions only on the disk. In either case, your editor will probably want hard copy as well as disks, so you will have to print out the revised version of any chapter in which you made changes. Your manuscript editor can enter further changes directly on the disks as well.

You may receive files that include design coding. If you did not enter the codes for the previous edition, you can ignore them. If you entered the codes the first time, you will probably have to do this for any new material. Check with your editor.

No matter what system you use, you will need to proofread carefully and create a new index.

Illustrations

Whether your book is a biography with a frontispiece as the only illustration, an economics treatise with a dozen graphs, or a textbook with hundreds of illustrations, you need some basic understanding of the acquisition and preparation of the kinds of artwork you are using. If you are writing a heavily illustrated textbook, you must also figure out a way to keep track of all those graphs, cartoons, charts, and photographs.

You and your editor should discuss the number and kinds of illustrations to be included from the very beginning of your association, and before production of the artwork begins, you must agree on this. Compile a very specific list, chapter by chapter. Often the number and type of illustrations will be stipulated in the contract; certainly the use of color illustrations must be agreed on in writing, well in advance.

To work intelligently with your editor, you should learn the technical differences among illustrations, discover where artwork comes from, and understand exactly your responsibilities for providing illustrative material that is appropriate and of good technical quality. (Two excellent guides to developing and preparing illustrations are *Graphics Simplified*, by A. J. MacGregor, and the Council of Biology Editors' *Illustrating Science: Standards for Publication*, both listed in the bibliography.)

Types of Artwork

From the point of view of printing technology, there are three types of artwork: line drawings, halftones, and color plates. In all likelihood, the artwork in your book will be either line drawings or halftones. Line drawings are black and white, with no shading (cross-hatching or dots may be used to simulate shading, however). Examples are maps, graphs, and cartoons. Line drawings are the cheapest and easiest illustrations to reproduce. Halftones are illustrations with gray tones; examples include photographs and drawings with pencil shading. Some artwork can be reproduced as either a line drawing or a halftone, and the production editor will make this decision. Few books require color illustrations, and because they are extremely expensive, they are used only when absolutely necessary, most commonly in art books. (You will often see color printing in textbooks – headings in red or line drawings printed in brown or blue. This is not the same process as printing full-color photographs; it simply requires the use of two inks. It is more expensive than using just one color, but it is not nearly so costly as reproducing color photographs.)

Producing Artwork

Whether a given illustration is a halftone or a line drawing, it does not come from thin air. You must produce it yourself, have it produced, or acquire it from someone who already has it. Producing your own artwork is not a good idea unless you are an accomplished cartographer, graphic artist, or photographer. Sketches and snapshots will not do. Of course, you will have to provide the content of the artwork: the data for graphs, sketches for diagrams, subjects for photographs, and so forth. These must be complete, accurate, drawn to scale, and as detailed as necessary. You cannot just tell a cartographer that the Ohio River goes over here someplace. All keys, labels, numbers, names, and any other text that is part of the artwork must be legible and correctly spelled. It is a good idea to provide a separate, typed list of these as well. You should write out any additional instructions or explanations that the artist might find helpful, and, when possible, provide photocopies of similar art that shows what you have in mind. (Such photocopies should be marked clearly "Not copy.") Remember, the artist cannot be expected to do your research, check your facts, or clarify your data. If you submit inaccurate or vague sketches, incorrect or rough numbers, or maps with cities on the wrong bank of the river, you will not get good illustrations.

Computer technology facilitates the production of maps and graphs. Cartography programs are expensive, complex, and difficult to learn, so it is still best to have a professional produce maps. However, most graphs can easily be produced with software in common use. You can do these yourself, or hire someone familiar with a graphics program, and print them using a laser printer.

Textbook publishers usually prefer to have their own artists, or freelance artists under their supervision, produce the final illustrations. If this is the case, working from the list you and your editor developed, you must submit sketches of each illustration that is to be drawn from scratch.

The art editor and copyeditor will review and revise these, sometimes returning them to you with requests for further information or clarification. The artist will then draw the final art, and you will get photocopies for checking. Depending on the way your contract is written, you will be billed for all or part of the artwork or the fee will be deducted from your royalties.

If you are paying for the artwork, you would be wise to ask for an estimate before work begins and for an itemized bill when it is finished. As I suggested in Chapter 5, it is a good idea to try to get the publisher to share the costs of illustrations. This should be done at the contract stage. When the bill comes, it is a bit late to reopen negotiations.

If you decide to hire an artist on your own, that artist will have to follow the specifications set by the publisher. These vary, so you should get detailed instructions on size and type of paper, ink, style of lettering (typeset or hand-lettered? in what face or hand? supplied by whom?), and the size the artwork will be in the finished book. To avoid confusion, ask the editor to send specifications directly to your artist and to provide advice to the artist when questions arise. Do not have the artist begin work before your sketches have been edited. It is a good idea to have the artist submit to your editor for technical approval a sample of each category of illustration before proceeding. You should check the final artwork very carefully for accuracy.

Perhaps some of the line drawings you need have been drawn and published in other books or in journal articles. A very clear original from the journal may be adequate for reproduction, but only if it is highly contrasted, unsmudged, without ink from the other side showing through, and so forth. It is much better to borrow the original artwork from the author or the journal. In some cases, though, you will have to have it redrawn or scanned. No matter which of these courses you choose, you must get written permission from the owner of the illustration, a procedure explained in the section on permissions.

Photographs

Unless you have a large budget and a contemporary subject, the photographs you use will come from existing collections. Your publisher may have photo files, and you may have seen usable photographs in other books or articles.

Photographs should not be reproduced from publications if you can avoid it; you should obtain a black-and-white print (preferably glossy) or negative. When photographs are printed in books, they go through a process called "screening." This is obvious in newspaper photos, where visible dots appear, but you can see it in finer printing if you use a magnifying glass. If you take a screened photo and rescreen it, you get a moiré pattern that can obscure detail. Therefore, if you are using halftones, you must get prints from the original publisher, the photographer, the photo service, or the depository that owns them.

Finding appropriate, high-quality photographs can be very difficult. The World Wide Web is a convenient source for locating photographs, but not for producing them. Many photo collection catalogues can be searched online, and you may find useful artwork on sites related to your subject. Once you locate an image on the Web with the original source listed, you can go to the copyright holder for both permission and a usable print. However, although some illustrations can be downloaded from the Web, many are deliberately presented at too low a resolution to make them printable. If you do find high-resolution illustrations on the Web, check with your editor about the form in which they can accept them, and remember that you may still need to get permission from the copyright holder.

It would be impossible to list the sources for photographs in every academic field, but here are some general ideas, and I have listed further sources in the bibliography. First, if you have seen the perfect photograph already in print, consult the credit line or acknowledgments section of the book for the source. If none is listed, write to the publisher. Second, look through other books in your field and see where they got their photographs. You may not want to use the same pictures, but you will get some leads. Third, try free or inexpensive sources. These include federal agencies like the Library of Congress, the National Archives, the Smithsonian Institution, and NASA; public libraries, historical societies, and museums; and trade associations, businesses, and various countries' information offices. Fourth, commercial photo agencies will supply photos for a fee. United Press International, Black Star, and Magnum are examples of such companies. *Literary Market Place* provides a longer list.

To use any of these sources effectively, you must begin early. The Library of Congress, for example, always has a backlog of requests, and it may take several months to get your photographs. It is a good idea to call, write, or check the website to determine each collection's procedures: Must you send a deposit for reproduction and mailing costs? Do they have a catalogue? (Many photo catalogues are now online.) What information must you supply? What will they send initially – descriptions, photocopies, or glossies? (You will need glossy black-and-white photos for actual production, but photocopies may be adequate for making your selection.) Can they recommend a freelance photo researcher who knows their collection? Procedures vary, and advance preparation saves time.

The second key to success is to make your request as specific as possible, including all relevant details. Do not just ask for a picture of Franklin Roosevelt. Do you want an informal pose or a portrait? At what age? Alone, with family, or with the Cabinet? In the White House or elsewhere? Instead of asking for a photo of a mine, tell what sort of mine (coal? diamond? salt?), in what region (the American West? Appalachia? South Africa? Siberia?), with or without people, when (now? mid-nineteenth century?), and for what purpose (to show working conditions? technology? environmental impact?). The more specific you are, the more suitable the photos you receive will be.

You need to evaluate photographs not only for appropriateness of content but also for aesthetic qualities such as composition and for technical qualities such as contrast and clarity. Your editor, with help from the production staff, can provide guidance on these issues, and the books by MacGregor and the Council of Biology Editors offer good advice. Before paying agency or permissions fees, have your editor approve the photographs for inclusion in the book. Photo agencies may charge a great deal of money, and even the small reproduction fees collected by nonprofit agencies can mount up, so make sure photos are acceptable to the publisher before you invest. Also find out when permissions fees are due. Most agencies are willing to wait until publication.

A word of warning on photo fees is in order. Your publisher may volunteer to provide photographs, but you will still have to pay the fees (read your contract). When you are paying, the publisher may not be as motivated to seek out free or inexpensive photos. If you decide to let the publisher do your photo research, ask for a list of photos, sources, and fees well in advance. You can then take the time to find cheaper substitutes for expensive agency selections if necessary. If you do not do this, you may be in for a shock when the bill comes. It may also be less expensive for you to hire a freelance photo researcher who can find what you need and who will keep within a budget you set. *Literary Market Place* has a list of picture researchers, or try the New York or Washington, D.C., phone book. Experienced researchers can compile a list of free or inexpensive photos with amazing speed.

Keeping Track of Illustrations

Once you have identified the line drawing or photograph you need, you must make sure it is properly identified, placed, and credited. Your publisher may provide a form, checklist, or database program for this purpose. If not, and if you have many illustrations to keep track of, make up a form or use a database program that you own. Ideally, such a program should be able to renumber, reorder, and print out captions and credits separately. Figure 9 shows a form you may find helpful. Use pencil rather than ink to fill in whatever form you use.

First, number each illustration. Do not put the number on the front of a photograph. Use the back or a tissue overlay. If you mark the back of a photograph, use a fine, soft felt-tipped pen or write the number on a sticky label and then apply it to the back. Pressure on the back of a photo from a pencil or ballpoint pen will mar the front. Do not use paper clips; they, too, will mar the photo. It is all right to number a line drawing in the margin. If possible, though, be consistent about placement of numbers (e.g., back, upper right-hand corner) so that they are easy to find. If your publisher has a system for numbering, use it. If not, I recommend that you adopt a chapter-by-chapter double-digit system (1.1, 1.2, etc.) rather than try to number straight through the book. It is easier to make additions and deletions that way. Your working number system need

Working no.	Final no.	MS page	Description	Source	Final copy	Editor's OK	Perm. asked	Perm. rec'd	Caption written	Credit written

Notes:

Figure 9. Art inventory form.

not correspond to the published numbers, although it saves work if it does.

Now, go through the manuscript and note in the margin where each illustration belongs. On your form, fill in the manuscript page number. When you have finished this, the illustrations have been placed.

The next task is to write a caption for each illustration. A caption should be a brief identification of the subject of the illustration. In addition, it may have to explain the process being illustrated or identify detail. Perhaps it will state the conclusion drawn from the illustrated data. If the illustration is not vital but simply emphasizes a point in the text, then the caption may simply restate the point being made. The caption should include the final figure number (just leave space for this if you do not know it yet), and the working number should be written in the margin. When you have completed the caption, indicate that on your checklist.

Now write the credit lines. Check the permission letters. If a letter requires a certain form, use it. If not, adopt a simple formula: "Courtesy of the Library of Congress," "Used with the permission of National Sticky Wicket." Federal agencies or museums may provide photographs free, but you should nevertheless acknowledge their contribution.

Finally, type up the captions and credit lines, chapter by chapter, double spaced. Type or write your working number in the margin and leave space in the caption itself for the final number: Figure ___. George Washington, in a portrait by Charles Willson Peale. Courtesy of the Pennsylvania Academy of Fine Arts.

Preparing the art manuscript or art package for a textbook can be a nightmare if you are disorganized. Here is a summary of the procedure that may help you keep things straight:

1. Work with your editor to develop a list of illustrations, specifying whether a photograph or drawing is preferred.
2. Compile the artwork:
   (a) Prepare sketches of all new line drawings; submit them for editing; have them drawn to the publisher's specifications; proofread all final artwork.

(b) Locate existing line drawings; write for originals and permissions; make changes, redraw, or scan if necessary.

(c) Locate desired photographs; get the editor's approval; make sure you can afford fees; write for permission and glossy prints.

3. Organize artwork, using a checklist:
   (a) Number each illustration.
   (b) Indicate placement of each illustration in the manuscript.
   (c) Prepare captions and credit lines.
4. Pay permissions fees when due.

Permissions

Whenever you quote or otherwise draw on someone else's work, you must acknowledge the source. That is a simple matter of honesty and good scholarship. When your quotation exceeds what is vaguely defined as "fair use" (explained shortly), you must obtain the written permission of the copyright holder. Obtaining permission is vital for the writer of any book or article, and your contract will make clear that it is your responsibility. It is especially complicated for the textbook writer because textbooks are written for profit (one of the considerations mentioned in the copyright law) and because they tend to draw on a greater number of sources than do monographs.

When to Request Permission

Permission is not needed when your quotation is "fair use," but there is a good deal of debate about what this means. The copyright law is purposefully vague; because the provision is brief, I will quote it:

> §107. Notwithstanding the provisions of section 106, the fair use of a copyrighted work, including such use by reproduction in copies or phonorecords or by any other means specified by that section, for purposes such as criticism, comment, news

reporting, teaching (including multiple copies for classroom use), scholarship, or research, is not an infringement of copyright. In determining whether the use made of a work in any particular case is a fair use the factors to be considered shall include

1. the purpose and character of the use, including whether such use is of a commercial nature or is for nonprofit educational purposes
2. the nature of the copyrighted work
3. the amount and substantiality of the portion used in relation to the copyrighted work as a whole
4. the effect of the use upon the potential market for or value of the copyrighted work

These four factors are generally interpreted in terms of the nature of your use (a free class handout versus a profitable textbook); the nature of the quoted work (a speech versus an unpublished letter, a news release versus a limited-circulation investors' letter); the proportion – whether by length or significance – of the original work being reproduced (a single paragraph from a lengthy novel versus an entire sonnet; an example of an author's style versus the author's summary of an original theory or technique); and the potential economic effect of the use on the owner of the original work (will people decide not to buy the poet's own slim volume if the most famous poem is reproduced in your paperback anthology?).

The important point to note is that the law gives no maximum number of words or other hard-and-fast rules that you can rely on. Any such guidelines – including those that follow – are simply collections drawn from practical experience. Few, if any, have been tested in the courts.

Your publisher will give you at least rules of thumb about when you need to request permission, and the bibliography lists handbooks on copyright law. A brief summary follows that combines the variety of rules I have heard over the years. It is not a lawyer's advice, which you and your publisher should seek in difficult cases. The best general advice I can give is to remember that permissions are your responsibility, and when in doubt, err on the side of caution – especially if you are writing a textbook. Transgressions by authors of textbooks are considered much more serious than those committed by authors of unprofitable monographs.

1. When do you need permission for quotations?
   - In the case of a monograph, for quotations of a total of 500 or more words of prose from any published book or book-length document
   - In the case of a textbook, for quotations of a total of 150 or more words of prose from any published book or book-length document
   - For shorter quotations of prose from shorter works (e.g., 50 words from an article of 1,000 words)
   - For quotations of three or more lines of poetry or eight measures of a song
   - For any exact reproduction of a table, graph, or other illustration, including photographs of paintings or sculpture (data may be used without permission, though the source must be credited)
   - For any unpublished material (letters, diaries, manuscripts; recent court decisions have construed this very strictly) unless the author has been dead for at least seventy years. If the material was published for the first time seventy or more years after the author's death but before the end of 2002, it is protected until at least 2047
   - For material obtained in interviews (ideally, a release should be obtained from the subject at the time of the interview)
   - For examples, problems, or the like written by your students, friends, or relatives
   - For your own work published by another company
2. When do you definitely not need permission?
   - For quotations from material published in the United States whose author has been dead for at least seventy years
   - After 2002, for unpublished material whose author has been dead for at least seventy years
   - For quotations from material first published in a U.S. government publication (but watch for reports by individuals; these are sometimes protected)

3. When have you done enough?
   • When you have received written permission and paid any required fees

Remember: Be cautious, begin early, and keep good records.

How to Request Permission

Your publisher may provide a form letter for you to use in seeking permission. If not, *The Chicago Manual of Style* provides a sample letter. At a minimum, you must give the author, title, and publication date of the work from which you are quoting; the pages on which the material appears; any changes or deletions you propose to make in the quoted material; the author, title, and approximate length of your own book or article; and the publication date, price, and size and type of edition (paper and/or cloth) of your book. If a future paperback edition is likely, ask permission to quote in that, too. Ask your publisher whether the book is to be sold outside the United States. If so, you will have to obtain "nonexclusive world rights in the English language." If your book is likely to be translated into a foreign language, you can also ask for these rights so that you can sell foreign rights without complications. This can be postponed, however, until someone is actually interested in doing a translation. Figures 10 and 11 are permissions requests for a monograph and a textbook, with possible publishers' responses. Figure 12 is a permissions request for an anthology, also with a response.

Some publishers go through the manuscript and provide you with a list of material requiring permission. If your publisher does not do this, or does not do it early, you yourself should compile such a list. To make the job easier in the case of books requiring large numbers of permissions, use index cards or a database program instead of a single list. That way, you can compile the list as you go through the manuscript and then order the requests by publisher or journal to facilitate letter writing. After that, you can more easily check the status of each request. Make at least three copies of each letter: one for your files, one for the files of the publisher granting permission, and one for the publisher's signature, to be returned to you.

As in compiling illustrations, the keys to obtaining permissions are starting early and staying organized. Begin the permissions process as soon as you have a book contract in hand and send follow-up letters if you do not get responses. The author or publisher may deny permission (this is rare but possible) or ask an excessive fee, or you may have difficulty locating the person or company that holds the rights. You may have to send a copy of the pages in which the material appears, or the publisher may send you a form to complete. All this takes time. As soon as you run into trouble, ask your editor's advice; do not wait until the last minute.

Proofreading

If you want your book to appear with all the words spelled right and in the right order, with no words missing, and with the pages in the right order, you must proofread carefully. If the typesetter keyboards your book from scratch, then the typesetter proofreads, but that isn't enough. If the book is set from your disks, the typesetter does not read proof. Your publisher may or may not provide proofreading (university presses are more and more frequently leaving this entirely up to the author). In other words, if you don't do it, it is quite possible that no one else will.

Even if proof has been set from your disks, and regardless of who entered the codes, it must be read carefully. Many possibilities for error remain. After all, your manuscript may not have been error free, even after your careful preparation and your editor's careful reading. When you see the type set in its final form, the errors may be easier to catch. Also, this is the first time that you can actually see the results of coding errors. You must read carefully to see that headings, italics, chapter titles, block quotes, and other elements have been set

52 Sequoia Drive
Redwood, California 94444

May 10, 1995

Permissions Department
Ambleside Publishers, Inc.
2122 East Concorda Drive
Tempe, Arizona 85282

Dear Permissions Editor,

I have written a scholarly monograph, *Math Anxiety and Career Choice*, to be published by the University of Antarctica Press in September 1996. The book will be published in an edition of 1,500 copies and priced at $34.95.

I would like to quote approximately 750 words from pages 115-120 of *Psychology: Strategies for Success*, by David Cantrell, which you published in 1988. Although no paperback edition is planned at this time, I would like permission for a future paperback edition, as well as world rights in case the book is translated and published abroad. If you agree to this use, please sign and return one copy of this letter. I would be happy to include any credit line you specify.

Sincerely,

Leslie J. Author

We grant permission for the uses specified in this letter.

_____

for Ambleside Publishers, Inc.

_____

Date

Figure 10. Permissions letter for a monograph. The publisher granted permission by signing the bottom of the letter and adding one condition.

---

52 Sequoia Drive
Redwood, California 94444

May 10, 1995

Permissions Department
Ambleside Publishers, Inc.
2122 East Concorda Drive
Tempe, Arizona 85282

Dear Permissions Editor,

I have written a scholarly monograph, *Math Anxiety and Career Choice*, to be published by the University of Antarctica Press in September 1996. The book will be published in an edition of 1,500 copies and priced at $34.95.

I would like to quote approximately 750 words from pages 115-120 of *Psychology: Strategies for Success*, by David Cantrell, which you published in 1988. Although no paperback edition is planned at this time, I would like permission for a future paperback edition, as well as world rights in case the book is translated and published abroad. If you agree to this use, please sign and return one copy of this letter. I would be happy to include any credit line you specify.

Sincerely,

Leslie J. Author

We grant permission for the uses specified in this letter.

Susan Publisher
for Ambleside Publishers, Inc.

10 June 1995
Date

No special credit line needed - just usual note citation.

Figure 10 *(cont.)*

52 Sequoia Drive
Redwood, California 94444

May 5, 1995

Permissions Department
Ambleside Publishers, Inc.
2122 East Concorda Drive
Tempe, Arizona 85282

Dear Permissions Editor,

I am the author of a text in introductory psychology to be published by
Mammoth House. The first edition will be 50,000 copies,with a retail price
of $29.95. It will be published in cloth only, sometime in 1997.

I am writing to request world rights, in the English language, to quote the
section on reading statistics in David Cantrell's *Psychology: Strategies for
Success,* which you published in 1988. The section I wish to quote begins
with the first full paragraph on p. 116 and ends with the third full paragraph
on p. 118. This material will appear in a box.

If you agree to this use, please sign the form below and return this letter to me.
I have enclosed a second copy for your files.

Sincerely,

Leslie J. Author

We hereby grant permission for the use described above.

_____

for Ambleside Publishers, Inc.

_____

Date

Figure 11. Permissions letter for a textbook. The publisher in the
reply (facing page) attaches conditions to the permission. The fee is
undoubtedly negotiable.

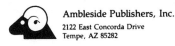

Ambleside Publishers, Inc.
2122 East Concorda Drive
Tempe, AZ 85282

June 2, 1995

Leslie J. Author
52 Sequoia Drive
Redwood, California 94444

Dear Professor Author:

Thank you for asking to use the section on reading statistics from David Cantrell's *Psychology*. We will grant the rights you requested with the following conditions:

1. Within the box containing this section, you must print the following credit line: From *Psychology: Strategies for Success* by David P. Cantrell, © 1988, Ambleside Publishers, Inc.

2. On publication of your book, you will send us a fee of $500 plus two copies of the book.

3. You will request renewal of this permission should you wish to use this section in subsequent editions.

Sincerely,

Susan Publisher

Susan Publisher
Permissions Editor

Figure 11 *(cont.)*

52 Sequoia Drive
Redwood, California 94444

April 4, 1995

Permissions Department
Ambleside Publishers, Inc.
2122 East Concorda Drive
Tempe, Arizona 85282

Dear Permissions Editor,

I am writing to request permission to include chapter 8, "Reading and Writing Papers in Psychology," of David Cantrell's book, *Psychology: Strategies for Success,* in an anthology I am compiling. The book, a reader for introductory psychology, will be titled *Winning Techniques for Understanding Psychology.* It will be published in paperback by Collegiate Publications in an edition of 10,000 copies. It is tentatively priced at $12.95.

If you agree to this use, please sign and return one copy of this letter to me.

Sincerely,

Leslie J. Author

We hereby grant permission for the use described in this letter.

_____
for Ambleside Publishers, Inc.

_____
Date

Figure 12. Permissions letter for an anthology. The publisher's response (facing page), which is perfectly reasonable, illustrates the need to develop alternative selections early in your planning.

Ambleside Publishers, Inc.
2122 East Concorda Drive
Tempe, AZ 85282

April 24, 1995

Leslie J. Author
52 Sequoia Drive
Redwood, California 94444

Dear Professor Author:

On March 22, you requested permission to reprint chapter 8 of David Cantrell's *Psychology* in your anthology, *Winning Techniques for Understanding Psychology.* I have consulted Dr. Cantrell, and I am afraid we must deny your request. Your anthology appears to be in direct competition with our book, which is still in print, and the chapter you want constitutes 16 percent of our volume.

Sincerely,

Susan Publisher

Susan Publisher
Permissions Editor

Figure 12 *(cont.)*

properly – and that they end where they are supposed to. Your editor will check all of these technical matters carefully, but you should look out for them as well. Remember, too, that electronic typesetting is prone to nonhuman errors, resulting from static electricity, faulty disks, gremlins, and other mysterious causes. Proofreading remains important. Always proofread hard copy. Proofreading on a screen does not work.

Proofreading is not intellectually challenging. It merely requires good eyesight and patience. *The Chicago Manual* provides detailed instructions, and I will explain when you have to proofread and what to expect, as well as offer some pointers.

You must read at least one set of proofs. If your book is first set in galleys (generally long sheets not divided into pages and without properly placed tables and illustrations), you will have to read both these and the subsequent page proofs. If the book is set directly into pages (as is usually the case when a book is set from the author's disks), you will receive only page proofs. Whichever form it takes, the first proof usually appears between one and three months after the edited manuscript goes to the compositor (another word for typesetter). Your publisher will give you as much advance notice as possible.

Proof will arrive either alone or with the edited manuscript, depending on the practice of your publisher. (If you know in advance that your publisher will not send the edited manuscript, you may want to make a photocopy when you review it.) You will also receive instructions, which you should follow to the letter. If you do not get the edited manuscript, then all you need to do is read the galleys very carefully and mark them for corrections. If you do receive the edited manuscript, then you must compare the manuscript and the galleys, to make sure the typesetter has reproduced the manuscript exactly. The best way to do this is to recruit a friend to read with you. The person holding the manuscript should read aloud, and the person holding the galleys should mark the corrections, using the standard proofreaders' marks found in *The Chicago Manual* or any good dictionary. No marks of any kind should be made on the edited manuscript. Nor should you attempt to rewrite your book. If you see an error that you should have caught earlier, fix it; but do not make optional changes. Such changes will cost you money (remember the contract clause about alterations to proof), delay the book, and increase the chances that new errors will be introduced when the corrections are made. In theory, vital changes can be made up to the last minute before the book is printed. In fact, they have to be awfully important to be done after page proof.

If your first proof is page proof, you can now fill in page numbers in the table of contents and the lists of maps, tables, and illustrations and possibly in the running heads for the notes section. Any cross-references to other pages of your book must also be filled in (these will usually be set as "see pp. 000 – 000" and can now be completed).

Some authors believe that the best way to proofread is to read backward – from the last line to the first – with the line above covered by a card or ruler. The theory is that you are less likely subconsciously to read in correct spellings or punctuation instead of accurately seeing errors. This practice (if, indeed, anyone has ever practiced it) is either masochism or sadism, depending on whether you read alone or with a companion. I do not recommend it. Reading frontward through the proof, checking carefully against the manuscript, is far more effective.

A few commonsense hints will improve your proofreading. Work at it for no more than two hours without a break, and when you take time off do something that does not tax your eyes or your concentration. Pay special attention to the following error-prone areas: chapter titles and headings, tables, numbers, proper names, foreign words, block quotations, footnotes, and bibliographies. If parts of your manuscript were heavily edited, read the proof set from them one extra time. Make sure all your corrections are legible and complete; for example, if you have deleted a word that has a comma after it, make sure that the comma is saved and put in the right place. Use a dictionary to check words that have been divided at the ends of lines.

The typesetter and your production editor will check type size and technical details, but if you see anything of that sort that looks peculiar – a heading that should be italic or larger or centered, for example – point it out in a query to the editor. Do not mark splotches or lines that are clearly the product of a dirty photocopying machine.

Finally – again – return the proof on time.

If you proofread galleys, you may also be expected to read page proofs. Your editor will let you know whether and when to expect them. If you are really pressed for time, you need proofread only those sections where corrections were made. Read from the galleys to the pages, and wherever a correction was to be made, check the new type. For safety's sake, read the whole paragraph, since several lines may have been reset and not all typesetters let you know where resetting begins and ends. You must also fill in cross-references to other pages of the book. Proofread running heads and folios. It is better, though, to read all of the page proof, because the more often proof is read, the fewer errors you end up with. If you can, when you have checked the corrections against the galleys and filled in the cross-references, read the whole thing through one last time.

Generally, the editor takes care of subsequent stages of proof – revised pages, bluelines (or the equivalent photographic proof), and folded and gathered pages. For a very few kinds of books, it may make sense for the author to check these as well. Books in this category might include documentary or critical editions, in which apparent errors are in fact correct. They might also include highly technical works with many symbols if galleys and page proofs contained many errors, or heavily illustrated books if the illustrations and captions did not appear in page proof. If you wish to read later proof, you should include such a provision in your contract. And because adding authorial readings for later proof extends the schedule by a week or two, make sure that you have reminded your editor about this well ahead of time.

At any stage in proofreading, if you have a major question, or if something appears to have been done consistently wrong, call your editor and discuss the problem. Sometimes the apparent error is just a technical shortcut (especially in galleys), and you can save yourself a lot of worry and time by checking. You can also avoid needless marking of the proof that will confuse and delay the typesetter.

Indexing

When page proof arrives, it is time to compile the index for your book. Almost every scholarly book and textbook has an index, although anthologies and collections of essays are sometimes exempt. You should decide whether you want to index the book yourself or hire an indexer. This decision should be based partly on whether you have the time to do it yourself and partly on whether you can afford to hire someone else. In part, however, the decision must be based on the nature of your book. If it is difficult and highly technical or theoretical, you may be the best indexer. If you want to hire someone, your publisher can recommend an indexer and let you know what the cost will be. You and your editor should let the indexer know the type of index you want, its approximate length, and its depth of coverage. You can provide a list of important topics, sample entries, and suggestions on how to handle difficult material. You may also want to review the completed index.

You must decide what kind of index is appropriate for your book: The main possibilities are a name index plus a subject index or an index in which names and subjects are combined. Sometimes a name index alone is adequate. The combined index is the most common, although the separate indexes may be helpful in a long, complex work. Separate indexes might also be added for titles of works (musical, literary, or artistic); first lines of works (as in poetry anthologies); or authors cited (separate from people as subjects). The nature of your book should determine which sort of index you compile, and your acquiring, manuscript, or production editor can provide guidance.

Preparing an index is not difficult, but it must be done carefully, sensibly, and quickly. It is usually due two weeks after you receive page proof. Your publisher can supply some guidelines, and *The Chicago Manual* and Judith Butcher's *Copy-Editing* have sections on indexes. Nancy Mulvany's *Indexing Books* is a thorough guide to the process. If you want to compile an index of professional quality, you should read it. You might also want to look at indexes of books similar to yours to see their general approach, strengths, and weaknesses.

I will not attempt to duplicate *Chicago* or condense Mulvany, but I can add some practical advice. Most authors overindex their own books. They include everything – even things that no one will look for – and they provide too much detail in modifications (e.g., "Communism, Reagan speaks frequently against" instead of "Communism, Reagan on"). If you compile your own index, here are some things to omit:

1. Items that people will not look for in that book. For example, a biology text tells the story of John Dillinger painting a gun carved out of a potato with iodine, so that the potato turned steel gray; iodine is a test for starch. You do not index Dillinger, John. (There is an argument for including it, however: this is a textbook, and Dillinger's name may be the only thing a student remembers.)

2. Items that will not give the reader any relevant information when looked up. For example, a book on Watergate has an index entry for the Taft-Hartley Act. When you look on the page given, it reads "Cox . . . had become close to John [Kennedy] when they worked together on revisions to the Taft-Hartley Act."

3. Mere mentions without content. For example, the only entry for Good Neighbor Policy turns out to be "Historians instinctively employ many insidious analogies without a second thought – or maybe even a first one. All of the following examples have caused trouble: [32 names], Good Neighbor Policy, [58 more names]."

4. People and institutions mentioned only in the acknowledgments.

5. Mere source citations, such as authors of articles cited in notes (in some disciplines these are included).
6. Tables and illustrations. These will be included in the entries for the text where they are mentioned. The exceptions are art books and any book in which the illustrations will be sought independently, as in a botanical manual or field guide.
7. Part and chapter titles.

Let me also offer some hints that make the process of generating the index a bit easier. First, use index cards or a good indexing program as your working tool. For example, if you have not decided which of two headings is better, put the alternative at the end of the entry. Or write possibilities for cross-references at the end of the entry as you think of them. Another possibility is to add your own symbols for such things as "this is marginal; use only if other entries turn up."

Second, if you are using cards, write very clearly, especially page numbers. You do not want to have to go back to the page proof to see whether you meant 91 or 97. Third, as you write each card, toss it upside down into a pile so that your cards are in page order. Then do your checking of page numbers, spelling of names, and so forth as you go along, every ten pages or so. Finally, in writing the entries, whether on cards or on a computer, err on the side of inclusiveness. It is much easier to discard entries than to go back through the proof to find what you left out. By the same token, write a "modification" (the descriptive part of the entry, as in "Democracy, *rise of*") for every entry even if you end up not using it. Otherwise you will find you have to go back to modify entries that you thought would not need modifications.

A computer can be an enormous help with the more tedious aspects of indexing. If the only index you need for your book is a simple, unmodified name index, the indexing feature of your word-processing program can generate one very easily. For a more complex index, you need a program that will at least alphabetize, order and combine page numbers, and combine entries. Many such programs are available, and the indexing feature of many word-processing programs is adequate for books of up to about three hundred pages. The search function is helpful for indexing names of people and places if you are working from electronic copy, and for checking on spelling of names and other details that may have sneaked through the proofreading process with inaccuracies or inconsistencies. Unfortunately, you will always have to do the hardest part yourself – selecting and phrasing the entries and modifications.

Computerized indexing has its hazards, particularly if you overestimate what it can do. The indexing features of word-processing programs are not as sophisticated as dedicated indexing software. They make it easy to index terms as they appear in the text, but they still require you to formulate entries and subheadings that differ from the text in any way. For example, you will have to type in a first name if only the last name appears and find the best noun to summarize a concept that is phrased variously throughout the book. When it sorts entries and subentries, the program is extremely literal minded, and it will combine them only if they are phrased identically and contain no typographical errors. You will have to read entries very carefully and supplement the program's work with your own combinations of entries and subentries. Also, the program will alphabetize by the first letter of the subentry, even if this is the beginning of a preposition or an article. Subentries are supposed to be alphabetized by the first *main word.* In other words, a subheading that reads "on communism" should be alphabetized under *c*, but the program will put it under *o.* You can outsmart the program by leaving out the prepositions until after the alphabetizing is finished, or you can enter the corrections by hand. In other words, an index generated by a word-processing program by an amateur indexer is essentially a first draft and needs a good deal of further refinement.

An index is worthless if it is not accurate, so proofread your typed copy against your cards very carefully; ask a friend or student to read aloud with you. If you used a computer program, proofread the final version as well.

Once you have sent in your index, your production responsibilities are probably over. Some publishers send authors index proof, but usually the editor will read it when it comes back from the typesetter, and the book will then go on to the printer. You can relax now.

Chapter 11

Costs and Prices

I always used to think that publishers had to be devilish intelligent fellows, loaded down with the grey matter; but I've got their number now. All a publisher has to do is to write cheques at intervals, while a lot of deserving and industrious chappies rally round and do the real work.

Bertie Wooster, in P. G. Wodehouse, *Carry On, Jeeves*

One of the questions publishers are asked most often is "Why are books so expensive?" The answer is not simple: It involves the interacting elements of production costs and overhead, pricing and discount policies, and markets. This chapter presents a simplified explanation of these topics that should console authors and book buyers – or at least quell their suspicions.[1] Another question that comes up very often is "Are books doomed to extinction?" For the scholarly monograph, this question is as much economic as cultural. In this chapter, we look at the financial implications of publishing without paper and ink. In the final chapter, we will explore the creative possibilities of electronic books.

---

[1] For an extensive, detailed discussion of the economics of scholarly publishing, see Herbert S. Bailey, Jr., *The Art and Science of Book Publishing* (Austin: University of Texas Press, 1970). The costs in this chapter are estimates based on figures provided by university press directors and production managers, book manufacturers, chambers of commerce, commercial-space realtors, and utility companies.

Costs

In publishing a book, a publisher incurs direct costs and indirect costs. Direct costs are those clearly attributable to publication of a specific title, such as the cost of having the book typeset.

Indirect costs are overhead items, including rent, utilities, salaries, and supplies. They are the publisher's general operating costs: costs that must be incurred to publish any books at all but that cannot readily be assigned to a particular title in a way that is not arbitrary. For example, how much office space and air conditioning are needed to publish a particular book? Or consider the time of an acquiring editor, who may review several hundred proposals and dozens of manuscripts in a year, in addition to traveling to conventions, calling prospective authors, attending meetings, reviewing budgets, and attending to administrative duties such as hiring and planning. Very little of this time can be shown to contribute to the publication of a given book, yet all of it is in some sense necessary to producing all the titles in the fields for which the editor is responsible.

Some costs may be either direct or indirect, depending on the circumstances. For example, if a publisher has a book copyedited and designed by freelancers (professionals who are not employees and are paid an hourly or per job rate), the freelance fees can easily be assigned to the book and are thus direct costs. However, if this work is done in-house, the costs can be assigned accurately only if the editor and designer keep track of the time they spend on the book, something they rarely do. Copyeditors may be doing a preliminary reading of one manuscript, copyediting a second, dealing with author's revisions on a third, checking proof of a fourth, writing summaries of books for the marketing department, helping an author with permissions problems, and attending to general administrative details – all in one week. It would be possible to record all this activity and assign most of the time to the relevant titles, but little useful information would be derived from the exercise. Keeping track of time in this way does not get books published faster, better, or cheaper, so no one bothers. Therefore, in-house copyediting and design are normally included in the publisher's indirect costs.

It is sometimes useful to allocate indirect costs to specific titles. To do this, a publisher takes the total of such items for some period, usually a year, and then, according to some formula, assigns a portion of the total to each book published during that period. The result is a somewhat artificial, but nevertheless illuminating, attribution of general operating costs to specific titles. For our purposes, this exercise helps to show what it really costs, taking everything into account, to publish a book. Accountants generally allocate overhead costs in proportion to revenue. In our example, however, I will simplify the technique and divide annual overhead costs by the number of books published in a year.[2]

Direct Costs

The most significant direct costs are production costs. They are also the easiest to estimate. Production costs divide into two types: plant costs and manufacturing costs. Plant costs include typesetting, the preparation of artwork for printing, and the preparation of printing plates; manufacturing costs (or "running" costs) include paper, printing, and binding. They differ in that plant costs remain constant no matter how many copies of a book you print, whereas manufacturing costs do not.

You might compare plant and manufacturing costs to the costs of typing a paper and having it photocopied. You will

[2] Harald Bohne and Harry van Ierssel provide accounting guidelines and sample balance sheets, profit-and-loss statements, and the like in *Publishing: The Creative Business* (Toronto: University of Toronto Press, 1973). *One Book/Five Ways: The Publishing Procedures of Five University Presses* (Los Altos, Calif.: Kaufmann, 1978; rept. ed, Chicago: University of Chicago Press, 1994) illustrates a variety of cost-estimating procedures and other worksheets that university presses employ. Chapter 7 in John Dessauer's *Book Publishing: A Basic Introduction* (New York: Continuum, 1989) also details accounting practices.

pay a typist perhaps $1.00 per page, no matter how many copies of a paper you eventually make; but you will have to multiply the photocopying charge, say 5 cents per page, by the number of pages and the number of copies. For a thirty-page paper, thus, the typing will cost $30.00, whether you eventually make one photocopy or one hundred. The photo-copying cost, by contrast, will be $1.50 for one copy but $150 for one hundred. To carry this analysis a few steps further, as we do shortly for publishing costs, the total production cost for the original plus one copy will be $31.50; if you make one hundred copies it will be $180. Now, suppose that you keep the original in a drawer and distribute the photocopies to your colleagues. Your total production cost per distributed copy, or unit production cost, is then $31.50 in the former case ($31.50 divided by 1) and $1.80 in the latter ($180 divided by 100). Clearly, the more copies you print, the lower the unit cost.

Let's return now to book publishing and consider an imaginary scholarly monograph of 300 finished book pages with no tables, illustrations, or other complications. The plant costs will be typesetting and plate preparation. A reasonable estimate for typesetting is $12.00 per page, for a total of $3,600. Plate making, changes in proof, and other one-time costs might total $1,500. Thus, total plant costs will be $5,100.

These costs can vary, of course, and we later examine the effects of production costs on prices and profits. Suppose, for example, that the publisher decides to use a less expensive typesetter (perhaps an on-campus computer system) who charges $10.00 per page, with correspondingly lower charges for author's alterations and page makeup. That might reduce typesetting to $3,000 and other costs to $1,000, for a total of $4,000. An even larger reduction might be achieved by setting the book from the author's computer disks. If the author supplies camera-ready copy, or disks ready for plate making, typesetting costs are eliminated altogether, although plates must still be made. (In the cases where the author supplies either disks or camera-ready copy, however, costs are really being transferred from the publisher to the author, not necessarily reduced.) At the other extreme, the publisher might decide to use a more expensive typesetter (e.g., for reasons of quality or speed), raising typesetting costs to $15.00 or more per page, with higher prices for other services as well. This could take the total plant cost up to $7,500 or more. A book that has a lot of tables, mathematical copy, or material in foreign languages would of course cost significantly more to set. For our purposes, we will use a middle estimate, $5,100.

To estimate manufacturing cost (paper, printing, and binding), we have to know how many copies of the book will be printed. Let's assume a print run of 1,000, which is a bit high for the average monograph but makes the math simpler. Paper would cost about $1,000 (obviously the quality and price of paper vary enormously) and printing about $1,000. For simplicity, suppose that we are publishing a clothbound book with a jacket and no paperback edition. On that assumption, binding would cost about $1.00 per copy, for a total in this case of $1,000, and jackets (depending on how elaborate they are) about 35 cents apiece, for a total of $350. Our total cost for paper, printing, and binding, then, is $3,350. To this we must add the cost of shipping finished books to the warehouse, say $500. (Freight costs, too, vary enormously. Sometimes printed pages must be shipped to a bindery, as well as the bound books to the warehouse. Distances also vary. If the printing and binding are done locally, there may be no shipping cost.) This brings our total manufacturing cost to $3,850 and our total production cost – plant cost plus manufacturing cost – to $8,950 ($5,100 plus $3,850). To simplify the calculations to follow, we'll call it $9,000.

We can now determine the unit, or per copy, production cost of each book sold. Of the 1,000 copies printed, 100 will be given away – to the author, potential reviewers, and the Register of Copyrights. We will therefore divide the total production cost ($9,000) by the number of copies available for sale (900), yielding a unit production cost of $10.00. This is an important figure, because many publishers take the unit cost, multiply it by some fixed number – anywhere from 4 to 8 – and use the product as a rough guide to determine how much to charge for the book. This calculation is supposed to allow, in an approximate way, for overhead and marketing costs, bookseller discounts, royalties, and profits – or, in other words, for all the factors that might bear numerically on the pricing decision.

Having determined the total and unit production costs of our imaginary monograph, we may now consider nonproduction direct costs – those costs for activities other than production that are easily assigned to a single title. Returning to that typed and photocopied paper, let us assume that you are selling the copies rather than giving them away. As you will recall, if you made one photocopy, the unit production cost was $31.50. This means that, if you wanted to break even on production costs, you would have to sell the copy for $31.50. If you made 100 copies to sell to your students and wanted only to break even on your $180 production cost, you would price them at $1.80. But suppose that you also wanted to cover your nonproduction direct costs: the costs of researching and writing that particular paper. If you are a philosopher or a theoretical physicist, you may have incurred no travel or equipment expenses (your time and office space we will consider as overhead or indirect costs). If you are a historian, your research for this paper may have included a trip to China that was devoted to nothing else. If you are a nuclear physicist or a radiologist, you may have to charge for, say, a week's use of a cyclotron or a CAT scanner. In other words, the nonproduction direct costs may be very small – or astronomical.

The range of nonproduction direct costs in scholarly publishing is not nearly so great, but the costs exist and must be calculated. We must include the costs of acquiring, editing, designing, and marketing a particular book. Suppose that the press paid two specialist readers $100 each to read the manuscript and that, after a careful consideration of editing requirements, it gave this work to a freelance copyeditor. If our 300-page monograph (about 450 manuscript pages) requires an average amount of editing, this might cost about $800, or $15.00 per hour for about 55 hours of the freelancer's time. (The freelancer's work will have to be reviewed, of course, and the manuscript finally readied for production, but we will treat in-house editorial time as part of overhead.) An equally common use of freelancers is for book design, that is, for the design of the text itself (what the pages look like), the binding, and the dust jacket. If the book is not unusually difficult to design, a freelance designer will probably charge about $400. (In-house design and production time are considered part of overhead.)

Marketing costs are another category of nonproduction costs. Under this heading, the costs of particular actions like running an ad in a journal are direct; the time of the marketing staff that designs and places the ad is part of overhead. Direct marketing costs can range from next to nothing to sky-high. We will assume that our imaginary book is displayed at conventions (sharing the cost of the booth with the other titles being shown), included in the publisher's catalogue (bearing a small portion of the cost of its production and distribution), advertised in two or three inexpensive journal ads, and sold through direct mail. The marketing budget for this book will then be about $3,000. (As a point of reference, note that a full-page ad in *The New York Times Book Review* costs about $25,000.) Our nonproduction direct costs thus total $4,400.

Indirect Costs

We must now estimate the indirect costs of publishing our imaginary monograph. Let's return again to your typed and photocopied paper. Suppose that you want to cover not only your direct costs (production and nonproduction) but also your indirect costs: the relevant portions of rent and utilities for your office, of your research assistant's salary and tuition waiver, of your salary and fringe benefits, and so forth. It is clear that these costs would vary from author to author (compare the salary of a full professor of law to that of an assistant professor of philosophy) and paper to paper (depending, for example, on how much of your time was devoted to it). It is also clear that you would have a hard time coming up with an accurate figure (how much office space was used to write the paper, as opposed to teaching your courses?). Similarly, indirect costs in scholarly publishing vary from book to book and publisher to publisher, and they are difficult to compute accurately.

The simplest way to calculate indirect costs is to estimate the total cost of operating the publishing house and allocate an appropriate portion of it to this book. The simplest way to allocate is to take the total operating cost for the year of publication and divide it by the number of titles published that year. This method is adequate for our purposes, but it is obviously oversimplified. Some manuscripts need more work than others, and both acquisition and copyeditors distribute their time accordingly. Similarly, publishers may spend more time marketing one book than another. An elaborately designed book with many illustrations will take more time in the design and production departments than a simple monograph. Also, if the press uses freelancers for some books and not others, this will further skew the distribution of in-house efforts. To cope with these factors, accountants employ a formula that allocates indirect costs in proportion to actual or projected revenues from book sales. We may evade these complications by supposing that our imaginary monograph is a representative product of the press, so that a crude per-book averaging of indirect costs will do.

Let us assume that our book is being published by a medium-sized press located in a middle-sized city in the center of the United States. It has 15 employees and publishes 40 titles a year. The salaries for the 15 employees, ranging from the director's $55,000 to the secretary's $15,000, total $350,000 per year. Fringe benefits amount to 25 percent of salaries, or $87,500. The press's total annual personnel cost is thus $437,500. Because of size, the press does not employ its own sales force or have many administrators (such as a personnel director, lawyer, or treasurer) that a larger house would need.

The press has adequate but not spacious quarters: It has office space of 3,000 square feet and warehouse space of 10,000. Office space in the city rents for $15.00 per square foot on average, with warehouse space going for $3.00. Using these figures, we can estimate that the press will pay $45,000 per year for office space and $30,000 for warehouse space, for a total of $75,000. Annual telephone expenses are $8,000, we assume, and other utilities total $12,000. Supplies and equipment cost $6,000. Postage and shipping (excluding shipping of books to customers, which customers traditionally pay, and mailing of advertising material, which is covered in our marketing estimate) run $4,000. The travel budget is $8,000. Association memberships, subscriptions, and book purchases add up to $4,000. (This includes membership in the Association of American University Presses.) If we add $5,000 for miscellaneous expenses (such as readers' fees for books not eventually published) and the inevitable unexpected expenses, the press's nonsalary overhead comes to $122,000.

We can now total these figures and allocate them to the 40 titles published annually:

Salaries and benefits	$437,500
Rent	75,000
Utilities	20,000
Supplies	6,000
Postage	4,000
Travel	8,000
Subscriptions, etc.	4,000
Miscellaneous	5,000
Total	$559,500

Dividing by 40 yields $13,987.50, which we may then allocate to each title. The indirect cost of publishing our imaginary monograph can be rounded to $14,000.

How much, then, will it cost to publish 1,000 copies of our 300-page monograph? A total of $27,400, summarized as follows:

Production costs	$9,000
Nonproduction direct costs	4,400
Allocated indirect costs	14,000
Total	$27,400

Dividing by 900 copies, this comes to $30.44 per copy, which we may call the *unit publication cost* (as distinguished from the unit production cost of $10.00). Unfortunately, this does not mean that the publisher can price the book at $30.44. If all costs had been figured accurately, and if all copies were sold, this price would enable the publisher to break even. However, it would not cover the author's royalty, bookseller discounts, publisher's profit, or margin for error. All these elements must be figured into the retail price.

From Costs to Prices

All the costs discussed so far are incurred by the publisher before publication; we may call them publication costs. But the sale of each copy of a book must repay not only the publisher but also others with an investment in it. These include the author and, in many cases, booksellers, both wholesale and retail.

The author's investment is repaid through royalties. As explained in Chapter 5, royalties are calculated as a percentage of either retail price or revenue. The publisher collects royalties when books are sold and pays them out annually.

Bookseller discounts are based on selling price. They represent a portion of the list price (what the customer pays for the book) that the publisher never receives. Publishers allow retail stores and book wholesalers (often called jobbers) to buy books at a discount. The jobbers and bookstores then charge customers more for the book (in the case of bookstores, the recommended retail price); that is how they pay their costs and make a profit. Each book publisher has a different discount schedule, and most offer a complicated variety of discounts, depending on the number of books ordered and the type of purchaser. For example, jobbers generally receive higher discounts than retailers, and large orders command higher discounts than do small ones. Some publishers vary their discounts according to the type of book in question, with trade titles that will be sold mainly in retail stores offered at a higher discount (usually 40 percent) than those expected to sell mainly to libraries and individuals (a short discount, usually 20 percent). Textbooks commonly sell at a 20 percent discount. In addition, some publishers hire commissioned salespeople who charge a fee of 5 to 10 percent of the list price. On the other hand, when copies of a book are sold directly to readers or libraries, generally through mail order, no discount is given. Rather than try to guess how many books will be sold at each discount, we will use an average discount of 30 percent.

Because royalties and discounts are calculated as a percentage of the book's price, we cannot estimate them without pricing our imaginary monograph. To do that, let us go back to our calculation of unit production cost ($10.00) and take the simplest pricing formula (which requires that we use an arbitrary multiplier, say, 5) to give us a first shot at a price. This yields a retail price of $50.00. Let us see whether that will allow us to cover our costs.

Now we can calculate the royalties and discounts. The author is receiving a royalty of 10 percent of the list (retail) price, or $5.00 per copy. We will figure an average discount of 30 percent, or $15.00 per copy. At $50.00, each sale would produce the following results:

Unit publication cost	$30.44
Royalty	5.00
Bookseller discount	15.00
	50.44
Price	50.00
Publisher's profit (or loss)	($ .44)

If the publisher is to make a profit, then, our monograph must sell for more than $50.00. If the publisher decided to price the book at $55.00, the figures would be:

Unit publication cost	$30.44
Royalty	5.50
Bookseller discount	16.50
	52.44
Price	55.00
Publisher's profit	$ 2.56

Note that increasing the price by $5.00 increases the publisher's net revenue by only $3.00; that is, the publisher gets slightly more than one-half of the increase.

In fact, the "profit" may prove to be simply a margin for error. Suppose, for example, that the publisher can actually sell only 800 copies of the book at $55.00. This small miscalculation will create a loss of $1,000 ($27,400 in publication costs against $26,400 in revenue, less discounts and royalties). Or, if the publisher underestimates costs even slightly, this can cut into the profit. For example, if typesetting costs $13.00 per page instead of $12.00, and an unusual number of alterations is required in proof, the typesetting cost per book could be 40 or 50 cents more; if the book runs a few pages longer than expected, requiring the printing of another signature (8, 16, or 32 pages), the per-copy printing bill might be 25 cents higher, and so forth. This may sound like nickels and dimes, but remember that the potential profit at $55.00 is only $2.56. It is clear that our imaginary monograph is not going to produce impressive profits.

In the absence of reliable ways to forecast the market, publishers must leave themselves some room for error, and prices must reflect that uncertainty.

Prices

Despite its crudeness, the method of setting the price by multiplying the unit production cost by 5 or 6 brings us surprisingly close to what a university press like the one we have imagined should charge. Many publishers do in fact use an arbitrary multiplier; those who must make a profit use 6, 7, or 8, whereas nonprofit houses use 4 or 5. Usually, however, the multiplier method is just a starting point, with other considerations coming into play.

Prices and Markets

Deciding to publish a book is one thing; deciding how to publish it is another. In scholarly publishing, the initial decision to publish is based mostly on the quality of the book, with costs and markets as subsidiary considerations. Once that decision is made, however, most of what a publishing house does turns on its perception of the market. In deciding how to proceed, a wise publisher looks carefully at who is likely to buy the book and at how prospective buyers will be influenced by such things as the book's appearance, price, and promotion.

Publishers who expect a title to sell almost entirely to libraries know a number of things. The first is the number of standing orders they have – that is, how many libraries automatically order everything they publish. They also know how many other libraries are likely to buy a book from them on this subject. They believe, with some evidence, that libraries will pay up to $50.00 or $60.00 for a monograph without protest. Finally, they know that libraries almost universally discard dust jackets and are not overly concerned with the design of the scholarly books they purchase. Publishers also know that certain prepublication reviews, particularly those in *Library Journal* and *Choice*, strongly affect library sales. If these reviews come out in time, publishers may alter their print run somewhat. For some titles with small print runs, library purchases account for more than half the sales, so this is an important market to understand.

Publishers who anticipate significant sales to individuals are somewhat more concerned about keeping prices down. If they believe that most such sales will be achieved through direct mail, they may not worry too much about design and dust jackets and spend money instead on attractive flyers. If, however, they expect to sell mostly through retail bookstores, they will want the books to be as eye catching as possible, so that prospective buyers will take them off the shelves to look at them. In setting the print run, publishers will also try to estimate the number of individual buyers. Such estimates are based on past sales of similar books or on the size of available mailing lists. The more specialized a book, the smaller the audience.

One of the things that makes publishing interesting is that predicting the market is so difficult. Most editors are confident of their ability to recognize good scholarship and good writing, but if a fairy godmother offered them a single (professional) wish, it would probably be the ability to predict sales. The prediction is both difficult and vital, because it determines how a book will be published. A prediction of poor sales is often a self-fulfilling prophecy, and it is impossible to know how many books have not been sold because a publisher underestimated the market. A prediction of high sales can in fact increase sales because it may result in a more extensive advertising campaign and more attractive design – though an upper limit is imposed by the book itself. For example, if you have written a monograph on the nematodes, a good marketing campaign can ensure that every nematologist hears about it. But no amount of advertising will increase the number of nematologists or create interest among purchasers of bodice rippers. Underestimating the market means losing money that one might have made; overestimating it means losing money, period. An accurate estimate is needed to establish both the print run and a price at which publication is financially worthwhile.[3]

To some extent, then, price is a marketing decision: Regardless of what it costs to produce this book, here is what we can sell it for. Some books – almost always those with higher print runs and, consequently, lower unit costs – can be

---

[3] Bailey, *Art and Science,* and *One Book/Five Ways* provide other examples of such calculations.

priced significantly in excess of what costs would require. Using similar reasoning, publishers sometimes raise prices for backlist titles (those published in earlier years that are still in print). A publisher may have issued a monograph several years ago, when both costs and book prices were lower, and priced it at $14.95. The book is still selling reasonably well and would continue to do so even at $19.95. Why not, then, raise the price? The only danger is miscalculation: By raising the price you may reduce sales to the point where you make less money overall, even while making more per copy. Another reason for raising prices on backlist books has to do with the costs of running a publishing house. Publishers must pay current costs out of revenues from books already for sale. Publishers that rely on backlist titles for much of their income must ensure that those revenues keep up with current costs. Thus, raising prices on backlist titles increases their profitability and enables the publisher to keep the books in print longer.

By contrast, marketing considerations sometimes require a lower price than would costs alone. Recall our example of the typed article. If we include in its price the cost of a well-paid full professor's trip to China, then even if we are distributing 100 copies, it might take a price of several hundred dollars per copy to break even. Although this price would be rational in the light of costs, no one would pay it. For a publisher, this kind of situation would mean that the book should not be published, that it must be published at a loss (a loss which must, in turn, be offset by greater profits from other books), or that costs must be reduced or underwritten.

If we are dealing with a nonprofit publisher, our imaginary monograph should, in theory, break even. It would be extremely difficult to make each book come out exactly with neither profit nor loss, and publishers do not try to do this. Instead, they set prices to make at least a small profit on each title. Some books will lose money despite careful projections; others may make more than expected. If a nonprofit publisher makes a lot of money on one title, that profit will simply offset the losses on others. What the publisher hopes for is to break even overall. This flexibility also allows the press to publish some titles that do not make economic sense, that cannot possibly sell enough copies at a reasonable price to break even. Similarly, profit-making publishers must make a profit overall. There is probably not a single publisher that has not lost money on at least one title. Publishers stay in business not by being right every time but by being right most of the time. Given the choice, any publisher would rather make money on a title than lose it. But for scholarly publishers, profit is not necessarily the only – or even the strongest – motive.

In setting prices, most publishers consider some combination of costs, what competing titles sell for, and what the market will bear. The notion of "competing titles" is not very useful in pricing monographs, which are generally not considered to compete with one another. (Each is, after all, unique.) For trade-oriented books and textbooks, however, this is an important concept. If, for example, you have a choice of three textbooks of roughly equal quality for a large undergraduate class, you will choose the $19.95 text over those priced at $29.95 and $34.95. Scholarly publishers do concern themselves, however, with what the market will bear. For small editions, libraries represent a large percentage of buyers. Publishers have a pretty good idea of what price will raise a librarian's eyebrows, and they may raise the price of a book to something just short of that figure. Similarly, they will think twice before setting the price any higher: If this is the sort of book that no university library can afford to pass up, the price can be higher; if it is likely to be considered an optional purchase, pricing it lower will produce more sales and greater revenue.

When publishers order a larger printing, they are anticipating sales to individuals through direct mail and bookstores. Individuals raise their eyebrows sooner than do librarians, so such books may be priced lower. This is partly a marketing decision, but it can be justified by the lower unit cost of books generated by printing more.

To see how this works, let's suppose that the press prints 3,000 copies of our imaginary monograph instead of 1,000. Its manufacturing (paper, printing, and binding) and shipping costs will increase; the other expenditures (plant costs, non-production direct costs, and overhead) are constant regardless of how many copies are printed. At 3,000 copies, the publisher is printing a sufficient number of copies to realize some economies of scale in manufacturing costs; they will increase from $3,850 to $7,800, for a (rounded) total production cost of $13,000 rather than $9,000. Because all other costs remain constant (with the possible exception of marketing costs), total publication cost will increase far less dramatically, from $27,400 to $31,400. This means that our unit publication cost will be much lower: Dividing $31,400 by 2,850 (we'll give away 150 copies) yields a unit publication cost of $11.02 – considerably less than the unit cost of 900 copies, which was $30.44. Also, with a printing of 3,000 the unit production cost will decrease from $10.00 to $4.56 and the price suggested by the arbitrary multiplier of 5 will drop to $22.80, which would probably end up as $25.00. If the multiplier of 6 were used, the book would be priced at $30.00.

Table 1 summarizes the relationships among print run, costs, prices, and profit. To show these relationships clearly, I have not used the arbitrary multiplier or rounded off the prices. Instead, I have added in a return to the publisher of a percentage of the unit publication cost. The price, then, is the unit publication cost plus the author's royalty, the discount, and the publisher's return. In most cases the return is 10 percent, but for the larger print runs I have given a second example of a higher per-copy return with, in consequence, a higher price. The publisher is taking greater risks on larger quantities and will expect higher returns.

This table illustrates the rapid reduction in unit cost produced by increasing the print run, and the way that reduction can be reflected in price. It also shows the interrelationships of market size, price, and costs. More prospective buyers mean larger print runs, lower unit costs, and the possibility of lower prices. The increased printings and lower prices are practical, however, only if the market estimate is accurate. If a publishing house prints 3,000 copies, lowers the price, and then sells

Table 1. *Print run, costs, prices, and publisher's profit*

Print run	Unit production cost	Unit publication cost	Profit per copy	Price
500	$16.67	$57.56	$5.76	$90.46
1,000	10.00	30.44	3.04	47.83
1,500	7.14	20.28	2.03	37.18
3,000	4.56	11.02	1.10	20.20
3,000	4.56	11.02	2.00	21.70
5,000	3.64	7.81	.78	17.18
5,000	3.64	7.81	2.00	19.62

Note: On each book sold, the author's royalty is 10% of the retail price. The average discount is 20% for 500 and 1,000 copies; 30% for 1,500 and 3,000; and 40% for 5,000.

only 1,500 copies, it will lose money – despite the lower unit cost. At a price of $25.00, for example, the loss would be $8,900 (net revenues of $22,500 against costs of $31,400). Not only does the publishing house lose money, but it has invested more scarce cash in production and is left with an inventory of unsold books to store. Table 2 shows how quickly a publisher's return shrinks (or turns into a loss) if sales are overestimated even slightly. Because the risk of overestimating the market increases with larger print runs, the difference between expected and actual sales in the table is higher for the larger print runs.

Why Prices Vary

With this understanding of costs, prices, and markets, let's look at the mystery of why some books that seem comparable are priced very differently. Everyone has had the experience of seeing two monographs on similar subjects and of the same length published by two different presses at astoundingly disparate prices – say, $19.95 and $49.95. When car prices vary

Table 2. *Expected sales, actual sales, and publisher's profit*

Print run	Price	Expected sales	Expected profit	Actual sales	Actual profit (or loss)
500	$90.46	450	$2,592	400	($ 574)
1,000	47.83	950	2,888	850	(355)
1,500	37.18	1,400	2,842	1,100	(3,851)
3,000	20.20	2,850	3,155	2,350	(2,905)
3,000	21.70	2,850	5,720	2,350	(790)
5,000	17.18	4,800	3,744	3,500	(7,423)
5,000	19.62	4,800	9,600	3,500	(3,153)

Note: In all cases, the author receives a 10% royalty. Average discounts are 20% for 500 and 1,000 copies; 30% for 1,500 and 3,000; and 40% for 5,000. Actual profit and loss are calculated by comparing publication cost and revenues net of royalties and discounts.

that much, consumers can point to differences in features such as horsepower, air conditioning, or four-wheel drive. In clothing, quality, style, and the cachet of a label account for the differences. In publishing, there are no such visible differences, but there are many possible explanations.

The most obvious explanation is that the two monographs are not, in fact, comparable. The examples in this chapter have been based on an imaginary 300-page monograph with no illustrations, no tables, no equations, and no foreign language material. Typesetting becomes much more expensive when tables, mathematics, or foreign alphabets are introduced. Costs for page makeup, or layout, are increased by the use of tables and illustrations of any kind. The use of photographs will increase printing costs and may require the use of more expensive paper. Color plates are extremely costly. In addition, two books that both end up at 300 pages may not really be the same length. One may have been set in a narrow typeface and smaller type, with wider lines of type, less white space, and more lines per page, while the other has larger type, more space between lines, wider margins, and so forth.

Table 3. *Costs and prices*

Typesetting cost per page	Unit production cost	Unit publication cost	Likely price
$ 8.00	$6.02	$19.16	$35.00
12.00	6.87	20.01	40.00
17.00	8.16	21.30	45.00
25.00	9.66	22.80	50.00

Note: Based on 1,500 copies printed, 1,400 sold.

Typesetting costs for the first book will be considerably higher because there are more characters per page, thus more labor per page. Table 3 shows the impact of differences in typesetting costs on price.

Another reason for the difference in price may be that the two presses estimated the market differently. This can happen because one publisher is more optimistic than the other for very good reasons. For example, the publisher with a series of books in the field, and a large number of standing library orders, can reasonably expect to sell more copies than the publisher that is new to the field. Or the more expensive monograph may be the revised dissertation of an unknown assistant professor, which is likely to sell fewer copies than the third monograph of an established scholar whose first and second books sold well. The preceding discussion of costs and prices illustrated the differences in price that would result from a variety of print runs. As you recall, the total cost of producing greater quantities is not much higher than the cost of producing fewer. It is the cost per book (the unit cost) that affects the price most dramatically. For this reason, the publisher's estimate of the market – a factor that is invisible to the book buyer – is crucial.

The nature of the market, as well as its size, affects price. Publishers who expect to sell most books directly to consumers at full price (publishers of professional books are a good example) may be able to price their books lower because

Table 4. *Bookseller discounts and prices*

Unit pub. cost	Average discount (%)	Price needed to break even
$30.44	0	$30.44
30.44	10	33.82
30.44	20	38.05
30.44	30	43.49
30.44	40	50.73

Note: Based on 1,000 copies printed, 900 sold; no royalty.

they do not have to allow for the bookseller's 40 percent; that leaves $22.00 worth of maneuvering space on our $55.00 book. (However, they may also have a smaller market, which keeps the price high.) By contrast, the publisher who anticipates mostly library sales through jobbers must price the book high enough to cover that discount. Table 4 illustrates the impact of discounts on the likely price of our imaginary monograph.

The publisher who anticipates selling few books at a discount, then, can afford to price books significantly lower. The $55.00 book could be sold profitably at $40.00; the $25.00 book, for $20.00. Even if the average discount turned out to be 20 percent, prices could be lowered several dollars. However, to sell large numbers of books, the publisher needs the help of jobbers and booksellers. Only a very small edition could be sold without discounts.

Another factor that affects price is the rate at which royalties are paid. Obviously, if an author is earning 10 percent of the retail price on every copy sold, then 10 percent of the price (and a greater percentage of the actual revenues) is not coming back to the publisher. The less the author earns, the lower the price can be. To illustrate these differences, Table 5 shows how royalties affect prices. Clearly, if the author will give up royalties, or receive them at a reduced rate, the price of the book can be lowered.

Table 5. *Author's royalties and prices*

Unit pub. cost	Royalty rate	Price needed to break even
$30.44	0%	$50.73
30.44	5% of retail	55.34
30.44	10% of retail	60.88
30.44	5% of net	53.40
30.44	10% of net	56.37

Note: All copies are sold at a 40% discount; 1,000 are printed, 900 sold.

Even if there are no differences in production costs, anticipated sales, discounts, or royalties, the two presses may have very different overhead costs. The one in Manhattan, New York, that is paying higher rent, utilities, and salaries may have to charge more for its books than the one in Manhattan, Kansas. Presses in desirable locations where there is a lot of competition for jobs may underpay employees. One press may do a more thorough – and costly – job of manuscript evaluation and copyediting. One press may have its costs more extensively underwritten by its sponsoring institution. Indeed, one monograph may have been underwritten by a foundation or a government agency. For our 1,000-copy edition, a $10,000 foundation grant would reduce the unit publication cost to $19.33, allowing the book to be priced at $40.00 or $45.00 instead of $55.00. Perhaps one press is more efficient than the other, with efficiency measured by the number of titles published per dollar of overhead expense. The more books you publish, the fewer overhead dollars you need to allocate to each title. To illustrate the possibilities, take one press with fifteen people and 3,000 square feet of office space that is producing twenty-five books per year and another that produces forty-five; the latter is more efficient and can apportion its overhead among more books. Using the total overhead figure from our example, the allocation in these two cases would be roughly $22,400 and $12,400 per title – a difference of $10.00 per copy if 1,000 copies are printed. This does not necessarily mean that one press is staffed by slow-moving incompetents. It may mean that the more efficient press includes reprints among its annual output, along with titles copublished with a British house that require almost no staff time. It may also mean that the less efficient publisher does not have the operating capital – the cash to spend on typesetting and printing – to utilize its staff and facilities efficiently.

Another explanation is that one press may publish a few trade-oriented titles that earn more money and can be used to offset the costs of less profitable monographs. Some university press catalogues include cookbooks, reference books, novels, anthologies that are used as texts, and other fast-selling items along with their monographs.

One possible explanation is that one press thinks – or has learned by experience – that buyers will pay higher prices for its books and therefore routinely charges more. This publisher can publish marginally profitable books that might be impossible for another press, and it can use its profits on some titles to subsidize others.

The $30.00 difference between $19.95 and $49.95, then, is no longer such a mystery. Look at the possibilities we have seen: a print run of 3,000 rather than 1,500 will let us reduce the price by $15.00 to $20.00; an average discount of 20 percent rather than 40 percent will reduce it another $5.00 to $10.00 (although these two strategies are probably not compatible); a lower royalty rate will save from $2.00 to $7.00; a subsidy from a foundation can reduce the price by $10.00 or $15.00; and even slightly greater efficiency on the publisher's part (or simply lower overhead) can be worth up to $5.00. Elementary.

Subtracting Paper and Ink

How does electronic publishing affect the cost and pricing of books? Now that we have calculated the costs of publishing a traditional monograph, it should be fairly easy to figure out which costs can be eliminated in paperless publishing.

Costs and Prices

Assuming that we are working from an author's disks, we will have no costs for typesetting or plate making. However, someone will have to encode the disks for online publication or put them into the chosen format. If the author does this, there are no plant costs at all for the publisher. Let us assume, however, that the publisher wishes to take responsibility for these tasks in order to control the appearance of the final product. We can budget $500 for design and coding. We will have no running costs, because there is no paper, printing, or binding. These are reduced from $3,850 to zero. Thus, production costs are reduced from $5,100 for traditional production (or $1,500 for production from the author's camera-ready copy) to $500.

However, we will have some new costs. Someone must put the book online in the chosen format, make sure that customers or distributors can actually download it from the site, and perform periodic maintenance. This will be a fairly well paid employee with a high-end computer. We can estimate this cost at $1,000 over the lifetime of the book (assuming that the press is producing many electronic books), with most of the cost at the beginning.

As is the case for traditional books, these costs are extremely variable. They can be reduced to nearly zero if the book is very simple and the electronic version is being published in addition to a print version, in a static format. This is the way books on electronic reserve are put online (see Chapter 12), and the result is a text that the user can read and print out but not manipulate or annotate. Such publications entail minimal costs for the publisher and minimal advantages for the reader. At the other end of the spectrum are electronic books that fully exploit the medium by providing hyperlinks, electronic annotation and glossaries, maps that can be overlaid, illustrations that can be enlarged, and so forth. These have extremely high production costs, they often are mounted on their own servers, and they require regular maintenance and customer service. For an ordinary monograph, the appropriate electronic enhancements might be footnotes accessed by clicking on the superscripts, similar treatment of terms in a glossary or other appendix, and ordinary maps and illustrations that did not appear in the print version. These would add to both the utility of the electronic book and its cost.

Our total manufacturing costs, then, will range from $1,500 on up. For a traditional monograph without "live" text or other features, $1,500 is the relevant figure. We thus save $7,500 over traditional production or $4,000 over production using camera-ready copy prepared by the author.

Nonproduction direct costs change little, if at all. The electronic book must be evaluated, edited, designed, and marketed. At best, we will save a few hundred dollars on jacket design. Indirect costs remain the same. Nonproduction costs total $18,000.

Our total publication costs are $19,500 instead of $27,400. *If* (and this is a big if) we can sell the same number of electronic books as traditional books, 900, then our unit publication cost is $21.50 instead of $30.44, a savings of nearly one-third.

How will this affect the price? As in the case of the traditional monograph, we must cover more than our costs. We must pay the author a royalty, and we must offer distributors a fee equivalent to the discount. If we price the electronic book at $40.00 (instead of $55.00), the author will receive $4.00. What will the distributor charge? At least 20 to 30 percent. True, the seller of electronic books need not warehouse, display, or ship books. However, the necessary technological infrastructure is at least as costly as warehousing and mailing, and salaries are higher for computer-literate employees than for warehouse workers. Retailers need not display books, but they will have to provide some sort of service and information – say, sample chapters or reviews easily accessible online – to bookstore browsers. We will estimate an optimistic 25 percent, or $10.00. That leaves us with a surplus of $4.50 – a reasonable figure if our publication cost is $21.50.

But will a consumer pay $40.00 for a virtual book? A library might, especially if the cost of printing out all or part of the book fell to the library patron. An individual buyer might feel that $40.00 ought to buy more than computer files. Should the reader prefer to read hard copy (as most do), printing out our 300-page book will cost about $20.00 for paper and toner. Printing out the book from the library copy might make sense (if that is permitted), but paying a total of $60.00 for unbound pages is not much of a bargain. (Remember, the bound and jacketed version was priced at $55.00.) Thus, if having the book in electronic form offers no functional advantages (such as linked footnotes and searchability), readers may expect a large price advantage. If the publisher must add such features to appeal to customers, the production costs – and the price – will go up.

If the publisher chooses the inexpensive option, and if such a publication appeals only to libraries, we will have to recompute the unit cost to reflect reduced sales. With a market of only 500 library purchasers, the unit publication cost rises to $39.00, and we would have to price the book at $70.00.

Perhaps we are using the wrong model here. The distributor's 25 percent may not be necessary. Possibly it would make more sense for the publisher to sell electronic books directly to the purchaser. Unfortunately, that would increase the publisher's outlay for fulfillment considerably. Publishers would find themselves handling phone calls from customers who cannot open the file or reset the margins, or who expected to be able to search or manipulate text. The distributor's 25 percent might soon look like a bargain. Nor would libraries be happy with this solution. They quite reasonably prefer to order from one or two wholesalers rather than from several hundred publishers.

All of these predictions are speculative. We do not yet know what scholarly book buyers expect from electronic books or what they might be willing to pay for them. It seems likely, though, that the most successful electronic books (like the already successful electronic journals) will provide features that traditional books cannot offer – searchability (beyond what an index provides), links, updating, reader annotations, and extensive illustration, to name a few possibilities. Electronic books that are no more than traditional books in virtual form are unlikely to save much money or attract enough readers to make economic sense. In order to exploit the market, e-books will have to exploit the technology.

Paperback and Reprint Editions

Most monographs are published originally in a hardcover edition. Sometimes a paperback edition is manufactured simultaneously, to be issued at the same time or after six months or a year. Sometimes the decision to publish a paperback edition is made later, and the book is then reprinted. Occasionally, a monograph is published only in paperback from the outset.

Paperback books are almost always priced significantly lower than casebound books. If you recall the manufacturing costs of our imaginary monograph, you will see immediately that this difference cannot be explained by the lower cost of paperback binding. We estimated casebound binding at $1.00 per copy, plus 35¢ for each jacket. The paper cover will cost about as much as the jacket, and paperback binding will cost anywhere from 10¢ to 25¢ depending on the quality and quantity. In other words, we are cutting costs by only 75¢ to 90¢ per copy. The lower price is made possible by a larger print run, which is in turn made possible by confidence in a larger market.

Publishers who manufacture cloth and paper editions simultaneously, increase the print run, and reduce unit costs generally maintain a higher casebound price and use the extra profit to reduce the price of the paperback, which may then be more attractive as a textbook. The decisions on how to price the editions are interrelated and are dependent on the view of the market.

When a publisher decides to issue a paperback edition after the casebound edition is out, the book will have to be reprinted. The cost of the edition will be lower than that of the first edition (excluding differences attributable to size), because plant costs (typesetting and plates) and such nonproduction costs as editing and design have been covered by the first edition. In addition, although our method of allocating indirect costs would require us to add the book's share in again, it will in fact require very little in the way of salaries and other expenses. These facts, plus the larger sales that the publisher presumably is counting on to justify a paperback edition, make a lower price possible.

A reprint of a successful book need not be a paperback, of course. If a first printing sells more rapidly than anticipated and the publisher thinks that the estimate of the market was too low, a second casebound printing can be issued. In this case, too, the publisher's costs will be reduced because the plant and other one-time costs have been absorbed and real overhead costs are small, but the manufacturing costs will be the same (again, disregarding differences attributable to the size of the print run). For practical reasons (including the need to avoid infuriating customers who paid the original price), the price will be the same or slightly higher. This means that the publisher must reprint a large enough number to make a profit at something close to the original price. It would make no sense to reprint five hundred copies of our $55.00 monograph six months later and try to charge $75.00.

Sometimes the demand for a small reprint edition arises years after original publication. The book is out of print, but some libraries and a few individuals would like to have it. Then the original publisher or a reprint house that has bought the rights may bring out a small casebound edition (a few hundred copies) at a relatively high price. Alternatively, the publisher might take advantage of recent technology and offer the book for sale on demand. That is, books can be produced from electronic files only when a customer places an order.

Another sort of reprint edition is justified by dramatically increased demand of the sort that occurs when a book is adopted for textbook use. This results in a large paperback edition with a price low enough to make it attractive as a text.

The publisher's decision to issue a paperback or reprint edition is based on demand. In the case of paperbacks printed at the same time as the original casebound edition, the publisher is relying on an estimate of anticipated demand. For reprints, no matter what their timing or binding, the publisher will want demonstrated demand: back orders, planned text adoptions, inquiries from prospective buyers of out-of-print books, and so forth. If you have evidence that a reprint or paperback edition of your book would sell, take it to your publisher, who can then do some market research and make a decision.

Your contract will spell out a royalty schedule for any paperback edition. A reprint edition that occurs while the book is in print or soon after it sells out is governed by the original rate unless the contract specifies a change. When a book has been out of print for years, however, the publisher may want to renegotiate the royalty rate before deciding to reprint. The nature of the edition is likely to be quite different – small and high-priced – and a lower royalty rate is appropriate.

Textbooks

The same principles we have examined for scholarly monographs apply to the costs and pricing of textbooks. Just as in scholarly publishing, text houses must price books to cover direct costs, indirect costs, royalties, and discounts – plus a profit. And prices must be comparable to those of competing titles. The main differences between the two kinds of publishing are in the scale: Textbook publishers spend much more money on each title and take far greater risks; they publish more elaborately and in much larger editions; if they do well, they and their authors make much more money.

Text publishers incur large developmental costs. They pay more readers higher fees for more detailed evaluations, and they spend much more of their acquisition editors' time and developmental editors' time working on each manuscript. Because the books are longer and more complicated, much more manuscript editorial time is required. It would not be surprising for a copyeditor to spend five or six hundred hours on a major textbook. Design and production are much more elaborate, and artwork – whether original or borrowed – is expensive. Print runs are much higher, and the books must be available for faculty examination long before the publisher can expect to sell a single copy. Teacher's guides and other aids must be produced and given away. In other words, the text publisher not only must spend much more money on typesetting and printing (because of the more elaborate format, greater length, and larger print runs) but must spend it well in advance of revenue. That means borrowing money and paying interest – a cost that scholarly publishers generally avoid. Textbook publishers also maintain large sales staffs and distribute large numbers of examination copies. It is common for a textbook publisher to spend $250,000 on a single text before selling a copy, and $500,000 is not unheard of.

Textbooks are sold at a short discount (20 percent) because the bookseller takes little risk and makes only a small investment. The retailer knows that the books will be sold because they are required for courses, and although textbooks take up a lot of space, they do not require elaborate display. This helps keep prices down somewhat. Real pressure comes from the sale of used textbooks, which provides no income to publisher or author. (Perhaps the availability of this source of revenue is some consolation to the bookstores for the short discount.) For a textbook to continue making money, the publisher must develop revised editions every few years. Costs are somewhat lower on the revised editions, and they prevent the sale of used books from cutting into profits – at least for one semester.

Trade Books

The same equations that apply to monographs and textbooks also apply to trade books. However, the various costs assume different proportions, and a high print run is the key to pricing and profitability. Marketing is extremely important, because it creates the demand that justifies the high print run. Finally, income from sources other than book sales can provide additional revenue.

When a book is published in a small edition, plant costs and overhead represent a large part of the costs. That is why, for example, an author's preparation of camera-ready copy can make a scholarly book financially viable. When a publisher expects to sell many thousands of copies of a book, by contrast, plant costs and overhead are divided among so many units that their significance decreases. The importance of spending in other areas increases, however.

Trade books must be more attractive than scholarly monographs because they must appeal to retail consumers. (Some scholarly monographs are extremely handsome and elegantly produced, but that is not their major selling point.) Trade publishers therefore invest heavily in design and production, sometimes commissioning more than one potential jacket design, for example. Four-color jackets are almost universal, and interior design may be more lavish. Paperback covers may feature metallic foil, die-cuts, and embossing.

The most important investment trade publishers make is in marketing. Trade publishers send out large numbers of complimentary copies to potential reviewers and to influential booksellers. Often they manufacture specially bound copies of page proofs for this purpose, to generate early enthusiasm and encourage advance orders. They advertise in trade and consumer magazines, which is far more expensive than advertising in scholarly journals. They may share the cost of advertising in local newspapers with an area's booksellers. The marketing department will also seek free publicity on radio and television, most often by booking authors onto interview programs. They may also sponsor regional or national author tours, or feature authors at booksellers' conventions. All of these efforts are time consuming, and many of them are expensive. The $3,000 allotted (rather generously) to marketing our typical monograph would be totally inadequate for a trade title; ten times that much is usual.

Much of the marketing done by trade publishers is directed at retail booksellers, because they are essential to the success of trade titles. The relationship with the bookseller influences design decisions, as we have seen, and it also affects pricing. Booksellers receive a discount of at least 40 percent on trade titles, so publishers must be able to make a profit (and pay royalties) on revenues of 60 percent or less of the retail price. Logically, that would push toward higher prices, but bookstore customers will not pay the prices that are acceptable to libraries or purchasers of professional books. So the publisher must price trade books at around $20.00 to $25.00, charge the retailer $12.00 to $15.00 for them, and still make money. The only way to do this is by printing and selling a lot of copies.

Another book industry practice creates pressure for high print runs but generally reduces the publisher's profits. Retailers are permitted to return unsold books to publishers for credit. This gives the retailer little incentive to order prudently or even realistically. As a result, returns on trade titles can run as high as 50 percent, leaving publishers with large numbers of unsold books in the warehouse after demand has peaked. These books end up on remainder tables and in discount catalogues. Although publishers have complained about the returns system for decades, it seems to be the best way to get booksellers to devote shelf space and sales efforts to new authors and risky titles. So publishers must factor returns into their financial projections.

Another significant expense for trade publishers is authors' advances. Although most trade authors receive modest advances of $10,000 to $25,000, a few authors with good track records or highly desirable manuscripts can demand advances of $100,000 or more. (Celebrity authors may receive advances in the millions.) Proceeds from the book must pay for these advances, and that means very high print runs and sales, and intense marketing efforts. Also, advances are paid well ahead of sales revenue, so publishers must either give up current income from the cash, or borrow and pay interest.

In most cases, revenues from clothbound books are not adequate to pay off multimillion-dollar investments, so trade publishers seek income from other sources. Even for books with more modest prospects, sales of rights can increase publishers' and authors' incomes significantly.

The most common additional source of income is paperback sales. The publisher may issue the paperback, thus realizing income from additional sales. But some trade publishers prefer to sell paperback rights to mass-market houses like Ballantine or Penguin. In this case, the paperback house pays a cash advance, sometimes even before the casebound book is published. The advance, shared between author and publisher, helps to offset the publisher's expenses, or adds to profits.

Trade publishers also try very hard to sell book club rights. Book clubs do not usually pay enormous sums to publishers, but they make their decisions on the basis of the manuscript, pay early in the publication process, and allow publishers to increase their print runs by thousands of copies, further reducing unit costs. Book clubs also help advertise their selections and, through their endorsements, increase bookstore sales.

Sale of serial rights can also boost income and provide additional publicity. Consumer magazines pay significant amounts for excerpts and bring books to the attention of thousands of potential readers. They may also generate television and radio publicity.

Foreign rights can also provide impressive revenues. There is a large market for American nonfiction – especially popular science – in the United Kingdom, Europe, and Japan. Foreign publishers are willing to pay for rights and, when necessary, to invest in translations. For the most part, however, sales of foreign rights do not affect the costs of the American edition (as book club sales do) or increase U.S. sales (as serial rights sales do); they simply bring in additional revenue.

Trade publishing is far riskier than scholarly publishing, but the potential profits are far greater. Trade publishers must put their efforts into marketing both the books and the rights attached to them. Their financial success depends on producing and selling large quantities, rather than on cutting costs or precisely targeting small audiences.

Financial Partnership

Throughout this book, I have described publishing as a partnership between author and publisher. The financial analysis in this chapter demonstrates that the partnership is more than an intellectual one. If authors are to make money, publishers must, too.

As the author of a scholarly book, your job (beyond writing a book that people will want to buy) is to help the publisher find the real market for your book by alerting your editor or the marketing manager to organizations, review media, and other outlets that the publisher might not know. You should also help your publisher to locate possible sources of grants. If your publisher is trying to cut costs, you should cooperate by giving up a dust jacket, resisting the urge to make changes in proof, and being realistic about royalties. If you are curious about how well your book is doing (and you certainly should be), you can find out what you need to know from your royalty statements, which often list the print run and current sales figures. Royalty statements are generally issued annually, so you might want to ask for interim sales figures at six months.

Sometimes, the nature of the book is such that neither author nor publisher will make any money. Usually, at least for scholarly books, they both will profit modestly. Sometimes they both will do very well. But unless a publisher has offered an unconscionable contract, and the author has accepted it, it is unlikely that one will profit at the expense of the other. Publishing cannot be played as a zero-sum game.

Chapter 12

Electronic Publishing

Reading off the screen is still vastly inferior to reading off of paper.... It's quite a hurdle for technology to achieve to match that level of usability.

Bill Gates

Technology has revolutionized scholarly communication, changing the way we study everything from Egyptian papyri to the human genome to musical composition. Using computers and the Internet, scholars have created new research tools and methods; in some cases, the innovations amount to entirely new modes of enquiry. Computers' capacity for storing vast amounts of data and manipulating them at extraordinary speeds has enlarged the scope of manageable research, and the Internet has admitted new minds and voices into scholarly discussions. Access to scientific data, archival material, and both established and recent scholarship has been expanded and accelerated. Ideas can be developed, tested, refined, or abandoned with the help of invisible colleagues around the world. Collaborative scholarship is taking hold in disciplines where it was rare or unknown.

Communication between faculty and students has changed, too. Many faculty members teach unseen students via the World Wide Web. Others enhance their on-campus courses with elaborate sites that provide access to readings, images, lectures, and laboratory demonstrations. Course sites are typically linked to other sites that provide opportunities for students to expand their reading, listening, viewing, and thinking. At least one major research university, the Massachusetts Institute of Technology, has announced that it intends to open all of the course material on its website free to everyone who wishes to use it.

Scholarly publishing lags behind research and instruction in embracing technology. The reasons are complex, and not technological. Indeed, publishers have been happy to replace old production and accounting technologies and to use the Web to publicize and sell their products. The resistance to change in publishing is rooted in economic and institutional causes, as well as a strong suspicion that in many cases paper and ink are actually better than their twenty-first-century alternatives. But the potential of electronic scholarly publishing is enormous.

This chapter explains electronic publishing forms that are already successful, though still evolving, along with some that remain experimental. I discuss how and why they work, the problems that remain, and some solutions now under consideration. The goal is not so much to describe the status quo as to encourage authors to consider electronic alternatives as they plan their research and writing and even perhaps to contemplate different kinds of projects that computer technology makes possible.

Electronic Journals

Electronic journals, and electronic editions of print journals, are an established medium of scholarly communication. These journals range from informal exchanges of developing ideas and research in progress to formal publications that are enhanced versions of traditional print periodicals. As noted in Chapter 2, authors can submit work to electronic journals, and revise and respond to queries, without altering their work methods very much. Indeed, electronic journals reduce the effort that authors and peer reviewers must expend. Although freelance writers and trade book authors continue to disagree with publishers about who should control electronic rights, this is at most a minor issue in scholarly journal publishing, where authors have never been paid for their work. (Some librarians and scholars argue that authors should retain *all* rights, but this is a separate economic dispute.) Most university administrators have come around to the view that what matters in evaluating faculty performance is the quality of publications, attested to by peer review, rather than the medium in which the results of research appear.

Electronic journals make life easier for their subscribers, who no longer need to visit the library or trudge through snow and sleet to retrieve the latest issue from their mailboxes. When speed is important, electronic journals can deliver information far more quickly than print journals. They can also make it easier for subscribers to select what to read by alerting them to articles that fit the profiles they provide, or by providing abstracts in advance.

Most librarians are comfortable with electronic journals, although they continue to hope and lobby for lower subscription prices. With electronic journals, librarians can serve their faculty and students more efficiently, and they do not need to provide shelf space. One issue of concern to librarians that remains unresolved is archiving: Can libraries rely on publishers to keep back issues accessible as technology alters, or is this a function the libraries must assume? Individual subscribers handle this by filing articles electronically or printing them out and filing the paper. However, researchers know that the article they want a year or two from now may not be among those in the drawer. For librarians this problem requires a systematic rather than an idiosyncratic solution.

Publishers, too, are happy with electronic journals. Small scholarly associations can reach their limited audiences without the expense of printing and postage. Publishers of journals with larger circulations have found a variety of business models that work for them. A few journals are offered free; some solicit voluntary donations; some provide electronic editions only to print subscribers; others allow subscribers to choose between print and electronic editions; and still others publish only electronically, charging subscription or document delivery fees.

One remaining issue for the scholarly community is the impact of electronic journal publishing on researchers in developing countries who may not have access to advanced technology, or even reliable electricity. This is a real concern, but the medium is not the problem. Impoverished libraries in much of the world cannot afford print journals and books, either. Any solution to issues of access will require an infusion of funds to developing nations through the efforts of international agencies and private foundations.

Electronic Reference Works

Electronic media are ideal for amassing, organizing, and disseminating large amounts of information that readers need to use for a variety of purposes and in a variety of ways. The material may be quantitative (census data, stock quotations, astronomical observations), visual (museum collections, MRI images, Mars photographs), textual (multiple versions of a literary text, historical documents, images of as yet undeciphered inscriptions), multimedia (music, animation, or video), or a combination of these elements in electronic encyclopedias or other compilations. Reference works may be accessible online or as CD-ROMs.

Online

Online publication is best for material that needs to be updated frequently or that users may wish to manipulate themselves, or for projects in which user interaction is desirable. Stock quotations need to be current; readers may wish to compare variant texts; and researchers working on newly discovered clay tablets may wish to collaborate in decoding them. Online publications can be designed to accommodate all such uses.

Many online collections of research materials are published by nonprofit groups and are made available free of charge.

Collecting the material, designing the publication, putting it online, keeping it up-to-date, and maintaining the site are not free, however. These invaluable tools rely on subventions from government agencies, private foundations, universities, museums, libraries, and individuals who volunteer their time. Other "free" sites are operated (often at a loss) by for-profit ventures that hope to pay for them eventually through advertising or by selling subsidiary products. Still others are not free but charge access fees of various kinds. The most successful of the for-profit research tools charge subscription fees to professionals or businesses that need the information they provide. Collections of legal research materials are the best-known example.

Primary sources and data are not the only candidates for online publication. Bibliographies and other reference materials, abstracts, and book reviews are frequently published online as well as (or instead of) in print. Some of these are provided free, while others are accessible only to paying subscribers. The annual fees range from a few dollars to a few thousand dollars.

Scholars who work in fields in which material more than a few years old is needed are less likely to find what they need online. Text that was not originally created in an electronic format must be scanned as text or images. If it is scanned as text, it must be proofread and corrected; if it is scanned as images, additional work is needed to make it searchable. There are also legal barriers to putting older material online: Because they did not anticipate electronic media, book and journal publishers did not acquire electronic rights from authors. Some journals have decided to take their chances and put back issues online, while others remain cautious. A number of projects are gradually putting back issues of humanities and social science journals online.

Publishers have become comfortable with online reference publications because they have found ways to make them profitable. At first, unable to sell online materials the way they sold books – as a one-time sale – they experimented with charging according to how long the user spent online (the taxi meter model). Now, most online reference products are sold by subscription, with rates often varying to reflect the number of potential users. For example, a law firm with five hundred lawyers pays more than one with fifty, and a library at a university with fifty thousand students pays more than one with three thousand. Because the institution pays for the subscriptions (like subscriptions to journals), users are generally unaware of the fees being charged.

Alternatively, the institution may pay a fee for partial access, with individual users paying for anything beyond that. For example, you may be able to read an abstract or table of contents online free, but in order to read or print out the full text, you must pay a fee. This is essentially an online document delivery service. Again, publishers are finding this method of dissemination profitable, and users are willing to pay for speed and convenience.

Concerns about archiving and access are similar to those for electronic journals. Also, the more commercial of these products tend to be used by more readers than scholarly journals. In addition to scholars, the readers may include high school students and elderly public library patrons. For such products, the user interface must be friendly, and navigation must be relatively foolproof. Servers must be capable of dealing with term paper rush hours, and help lines may be needed. Because users have a variety of software, uniformity of appearance and function cannot be guaranteed.

For scholars contemplating collaborative projects, projects in which images and sounds are important, or projects where nonlinear navigation is helpful, online publication is an exciting option. Nevertheless, these ventures should not be undertaken without a great deal of thought and planning. Even if a free website is available through your employer, there will be costs. You may have to pay permission fees for text and images, and you will either need to hire people to do the technical work or do it yourself. A forward-looking university administration *may* reward you for the intellectual achievement of online publication, but the routine trivia of HTML coding and the like is not what faculty members are paid to do. Some universities have funds to underwrite online research projects, and a number of foundations are investing in them. You should investigate these sources as part of your planning. If a foundation or federal agency helps to fund your project, that will provide legitimacy and publicity, as well as money.

If you are planning to create a commercial site, you will need a business plan, a home for your site, and a way of securing the site and limiting access. In this case, you should probably seek a publisher (traditional or Web-based) as a partner.

On Disc

CD-ROMs (compact disc-read only memory) are 4.72-inch disks similar in appearance to the ones you play music from. The user cannot alter the material on the disc (hence "read only"). CD-ROMs have enormous capacity. One disc can hold 275,000 typed pages of text (roughly forty-five shelf feet of books) or the equivalent of 1,500 magnetic diskettes. In addition to text and data, it can carry graphics, sound, and video images (although these take up more room than text or data). CD-ROMs are typically provided with highly sophisticated searching and indexing programs that make all sorts of creative applications possible and make the discs flexible and responsive to use, even though users cannot "write" on them.

CD-ROMs solve some of the problems of online publishing. For one thing, they do not require an Internet connection, so users do not need to worry about interruptions of service or connections. Sound, animation, and video are usually of higher quality. Because they are self-contained, they allow their authors more control over the way they are used than online products do. This makes them particularly attractive for instructional material, as we shall see shortly. Publishers were initially attracted to CD-ROMs because they seem to be more like books than online publications are. They are physical objects that can be packaged and sold in the same outlets as books, and they can be "finished" – at least until the next edition. And, unlike online publications, which are easily downloaded, copied, or sent on to others – they were hard to duplicate. Inevitably, however, the equipment needed to copy (or "burn") CDs has become far less expensive and may soon be standard equipment on medium-priced computers.

CD-ROMs are not the best medium for material that needs to be kept current, but they are nevertheless useful for some reference works. Compilations of print works (e.g., a disc containing a dictionary, thesaurus, short encyclopedia, and so forth) have done well. Some dictionaries have CD-ROM versions that include sound, allowing the user to hear words pronounced. Any product with its own search and navigation systems works well on CD-ROM. They can be updated in two ways. Some are licensed rather than sold, with new versions provided as often as monthly. More frequent updating can be done online.

Unless you are thinking of creating a CD-ROM purely for use in your own classes, you should be thinking about collaborating with a publisher. *Literary Market Place* includes a list of publishers who specialize in this medium. CD-ROMs are not difficult to produce physically (indeed, making multiple copies is cheaper than printing books), but they are very expensive to develop and design.

Electronic Instructional Materials

Instructional materials – textbooks, drills, supplementary materials, and simulations – are a natural application for computer technology. They require illustration and frequent updating; interactivity is essential for some subjects; instructors welcome greater flexibility; and cost and bulk are major considerations. Electronic media can respond to all these needs.

For science textbooks, online or CD-ROM publication can provide three-dimensional models of organs, cells, and molecules; they can provide animation or video images of biological, chemical, and physical processes; they can offer full color at negligible expense. They are easy to correct and update. Where desirable, laboratory demonstrations can be included as videos or simulations. The material can be used in any order the instructor desires, or it can be more tightly structured and directive. The student taking organic chemistry, physics, microbiology, multivariable calculus, and – for fun – the Victorian novel can carry all the course material without straining any muscles.

Students learning a language can use CD-ROMs on which native speakers model and guide their pronunciation, drills are automatically scored, and speaking dictionaries are built in. The language laboratory based on audiotapes has been replaced by electronic materials that allow the student to speak into a microphone and get automatic feedback on pronunciation. Students can listen to and learn songs, watch excerpts from movies, see the art and architecture of countries where the language is spoken, study maps, and plan imaginary tours. They can interact with simulated ticket agents, waiters, doctors, and police officers.

History students can re-create battles, learn to use census data and other statistics for their research, trace their genealogy, read original sources, see images of actual documents, locate and study historical photographs, and read periodicals from earlier centuries – all without leaving their computers.

Music students can use numerous programs to assist them in composition and orchestration, and synthesizers make it possible for them to hear their own works being "performed."

Computer simulations can help teach students to drive cars and pilot airplanes, sparing the nerves of their instructors until they have the basics in hand. Medical, veterinary, and dental students can begin to practice on simulated patients before they meet the real thing. Engineering and architecture students can test their building plans. (Many of these simulators are extremely realistic, with student errors resulting in crashes, bridge collapses, or extensive bleeding on screen.)

While pessimists may view the computer as the greatest threat to education since television, optimists are imagining ways in which this technology can make teaching and learning at all levels more exciting and effective. Many innovations are technically possible, but they require an enormous amount of intelligent planning and hard work in order to be put into action. Imagine an electronic "textbook" in your field for a freshman survey course. To exploit the full potential of the medium, and to achieve your teaching goals, you would need to do everything necessary for a traditional textbook. But you would also have to decide which teaching goals would benefit from interactivity, animation, incorporation of primary sources, games, video demonstrations, speeches, music, and possibilities no one has thought of yet. You would have to work with designers and technology experts to create all these features, and you would have to test and refine them.

Most faculty members prefer to start out on a smaller scale. A course website can guide students to images, documents, and the like that are already online. Well-funded institutions use video cameras in the classroom to make sure that every lecture or demonstration is available on the Web for students to view or re-view. Class chat rooms or discussion lists are easy to set up technologically, though often time consuming to monitor. Study questions and outlines can be put on the site before exams, and correct answers with detailed explanations can be posted afterward. Each semester, the instructor might add a new feature to the site, just as most instructors add new reading or classroom activities to their courses every time they teach. Over time, a course website may turn into the beginnings of an electronic text.

Some universities have funds for faculty members to develop technologically sophisticated courses. With funding, a graduate assistant, technological assistance, and release time, teachers can exploit their creative talents along with their knowledge and teaching experience. Whether such work makes economic sense remains to be seen. Universities are discovering that Web courses are a lot more expensive, and a lot less profitable, than they first imagined. In order to pay for themselves, these courses must either command high tuition fees from off-campus students or they must enroll enormous numbers – creating a drain on the time and energy of the faculty member and teaching assistants. And, although students in remote locations find Web courses a good alternative to correspondence courses, it is not at all clear that students will be happy with an education devoid of personal interaction with faculty and other students. Most faculty members suspect that – beyond a course or two, and unless supplemented by some intensive on-campus experiences, remote education, or distance learning, may be an oxymoron.

If the work that an author must invest in an electronic text is to pay off economically as well as educationally, it will have to be used by others – just as a printed textbook must be in order to make a profit. And this means that the author will have to find a publishing partner to help develop the work and to market and distribute it. Most of the large textbook publishers are working on electronic products either as supplements to their print textbooks or as independent products. Some smaller companies are devoted entirely to developing electronic instructional materials.

E-Books

People use the term *e-book,* short for *electronic book,* to mean many things. At the least technologically sophisticated level, an e-book is simply the electronic files of a book that can be input to a typesetting machine and turned into a paper-and-ink book. In that sense, virtually every book is an e-book. However, those same electronic files can be used in other ways.

Rather than generating an entire printing of a book, electronic files can be used to print books on demand. The publisher may wait for an order to come in before printing, or license a subcontractor to generate books as they are ordered. This is now done quite frequently with out-of-print books. Rather than risking the cost of reprinting and warehousing several hundred copies of a book that is generating only occasional orders, the publisher may stock none at all and incur no costs until the order is in hand.

Taking the process one step further, publishers can license retail booksellers to provide books on demand. In this model, a customer walks into a bookstore, asks for a book that has been reviewed or recommended, perhaps views a sample chapter on a computer screen, and then places an order. In minutes, the book has been printed and bound as a paperback, ready for the customer to take home. You may find such an on-demand kiosk in a bookstore near you. The technology has been available for a couple of years. Of course, it is also possible to sell on-demand books online. Online booksellers can take orders for as-yet-unprinted books as easily as they can for printed books, and they can either obtain copies from the publisher or subcontractor or they can generate them with their own equipment. The purchaser has no idea whether the book was sitting in a warehouse or in a computer file before it was shipped.

The problem with books on demand is that publishers and authors must somehow generate the demand. As you know from Chapter 11, publishers incur a lot of costs before a book is printed. These costs must be divided among the copies sold in order to break even or make a profit. The break-even point for books on demand may be lower than it is for traditional books, but it is bound to be more copies than the author has relatives. This means that publishers must print review copies and promote the books, probably by direct mail, limited advertising, and display at meetings. It is not enough simply to have the book listed in an online catalogue.

To see how such a system works without any investment in marketing, think of theses and dissertations. Nearly all of these are available on microfilm, as photocopies, or increasingly in electronic form. In order to acquire a dissertation, you must care enough about the topic to do a search of the relevant bibliographies and abstracts and then decide that you want it badly enough to order a copy without really knowing much about it. Few dissertations sell more than ten copies over their lifetime. That rate of turnover can be profitable when the supplier makes no investment in selection, editing, or design and can charge a fairly high price for a poorly bound photocopy or an electronic file. For a book, though, our expectations of editorial and production quality (to say nothing of content and writing) are higher.

The on-demand model of the e-book, then, works well for titles that have become known through their paper-and-ink editions but have since gone out of print, and for books that are identical editorially and physically to printed books for which the publisher has generated sufficient demand through normal marketing efforts.

Of course, books can be sold on demand without being printed and bound. A reader might prefer to purchase the electronic files and read them on the computer screen. This might be very useful for books not meant to be read cover to cover but rather to be searched and excerpted or annotated. Publishers are reluctant to provide this kind of service, because they lose control of the material. The purchaser could print out multiple copies, or simply send the electronic files on to someone else, in violation of copyright laws. Also, in order to make such material useful to the purchaser, the publisher must add electronic features to the text, which is costly.

In order to capitalize on the most technologically advanced possibilities of e-books, then, publishers have had to devise ways to provide readers with the books they want, at a price they are willing to pay, without allowing the books to escape into a market in which the publishers would receive no payment. (Avoiding this situation is exactly what the Napster litigation over online distribution of music is about.) From the publisher's point of view, the ideal e-book is one that can be sold directly to consumers or through retailers without ever being printed and that cannot be resold or given away. Such a book would be like a paper-and-ink book without the production costs and without the possibility of lending or resale. Publishers are very close to reaching this ideal.

For the reader, the ideal e-book would be the same size as a real book and feel as comfortable in one's hands. It would be as easy to read (that is, the print would be clear and the screen wouldn't scintillate or flicker). It would be completely portable (no wires) and could be read anywhere – on the beach, in bed, or in the bathtub. The reader could write notes in the margin. What makes it potentially better than paper-and-ink books is that it could hold hundreds of books in its memory that could be called up at the reader's whim, and those books could be searched. It could hold all sorts of books: a college student's entire reading list for the semester; the complete works of William Shakespeare, Charles Dickens, Stephen King, and Barbara Cartland; a reference library; and all the books reviewed in this week's *New York Times Book Review*. The reader could flip back and forth among these at will. Publishers are *not* close to reaching this ideal.

The difficulties are not technological. Current e-book readers do not have quite the capacity readers would like to have, but that shortcoming can undoubtedly be corrected. The tough problems are economic and human.

The publisher's ideal relies on providing e-books to customers on machines called readers. These may be devices designed to deliver only e-books, or they may be software for handheld computers created for other purposes, like Palm Pilots. The readers cost anywhere from $200 to $1,200, depending on memory, battery life, and other factors, and that does not include the cost of the books. This is an awful lot more than the paperback book that the machine emulates, but it is considerably less than what many of us spend on bookcases, which we will of course no longer need if we can rely totally on e-books.

Acquiring books for the readers may cost nothing if you acquire out-of-copyright texts from free online repositories. The (human) reader must download the text from the Internet using a computer and then load it into the reader. Depending on the compatibility of various software programs, the difficulty of this maneuver ranges from moderate to extreme. If e-books are to succeed commercially, though, consumers will have to purchase their e-books from publishers or booksellers. Some e-booksellers require that users download the book first into a computer (the purchaser's or the bookstore's). This allows the seller to record the computer's identification number for security purposes, preventing copyright violation. Other systems can send the book directly to the reader via telephone lines. E-book versions of many books cost as much as their paper-and-ink equivalents, or more.

The technical and security problems of e-books can be overcome, and presumably the price of both readers and books will fall if they become more popular. But other problems remain – problems that will be solved to suit markets quite different from those of scholarly books. Because publishers are not producing their own e-book systems, they must license works to providers. Some providers want exclusive licenses. That is, they want agreements with the publisher that do not allow other systems to provide the same title. Just as one publisher has a monopoly on the current Stephen King novel, one e-book manufacturer would have a monopoly on the electronic version. Publishers would prefer to license their titles to all manufacturers who can pay what they ask and provide adequate security. Readers will certainly be better off if the publishers win this argument.

Nor is it clear that anyone actually *wants* e-books very badly. Sales to readers have been negligible. Perhaps this is a chicken-and-egg problem in which consumer demand will not develop until more titles are available, and titles will not be made available until demand is demonstrated. So far, readers are not clamoring for e-books, and publishers are not rushing into the market.

If a market does develop for e-books, the trade publishers who own best-sellers will be able to negotiate profitable arrangements with e-book manufacturers, and so will textbook publishers. They own the content without which the hardware has very little value. But what about the scholarly publishers who control the rights to unprofitable monographs? If they believe that they belong in the e-book market, they will have to find e-book providers who are willing to do business on a small scale. In all likelihood, scholarly e-books will be slightly cheaper to create than paper-and-ink books (there is still the savings on paper, printing, and binding), but they will probably remain expensive for libraries and individuals to purchase. Possibly, nonprofit groups might band together to create an e-book reader and distribution service dedicated to scholarly books. That would be a good thing for libraries and academic readers, but it would keep the presses' publications out of the wider market that could make them both profitable and influential.

Some scholarly publishers have experimented with different forms of electronic books. Your library may have some volumes on the equivalent of electronic reserve. In addition to the real book, they have an electronic file of the book. Members of the university community, or members of the public using library computers, can read the electronic version for a fixed period of time. Only one reader can have access at a time. This is a very limited use and one that is not terribly popular with students or faculty. Students who live off campus cannot use the service unless they use their university servers; many prefer to use commercial services. And if another student is logged on, the book is not available. Often the student cannot keep the e-reserve book overnight, even if that student is the last borrower when the library closes. Most students prefer to read lengthy assignments on paper rather than on the screen.

In another experiment, a university press is issuing new books on controversial subjects as hardbacks and creating an online forum for comment. The authors publish their responses to these comments free online, and the publisher incorporates the responses into a subsequent paperback edition. This is an interesting hybrid experiment. It provides a sort of disseminated, midpublication peer review process that allows the author to polish the final product. And there is a final product, which is not the case for online publications that remain online and in flux. It is unlikely to satisfy those who advocate online publishing as an open forum – an ongoing, egalitarian discussion that does not privilege the author. One can easily make the argument that the author, having gone to the trouble of writing the book, is entitled to a fair degree of privilege.

The future of the scholarly e-book is very much up in the air. Publishers will presumably continue to experiment, encouraged by their concerns about the future of scholarly communication and by the willingness of private foundations to fund worthwhile innovations. I encourage academic authors to cooperate with these experiments thoughtfully, both as authors and as readers. Some observers of scholarly publishing believe that it cannot survive and continue to serve the academic community without embracing computer and Internet technology as its primary mode of distribution. Others believe that the future lies in a hybrid system of paper and screen. Still others think that paper-and-ink books will continue to dominate our reading and writing.

For scholarly books, best-sellers, and many books in between, paper and ink may well end up being the victor. We know that acid-free paper lasts for centuries, whereas electronic formats last only for a few years – and then only if someone keeps them technologically up-to-date. For archival purposes, paper is best. We also know that, at least for current generations of readers, the book is aesthetically more appealing than electronic devices for extended reading, whereas computerized text is vastly preferable for searching and selecting. Most of us spend our reading hours using both media, and we will probably continue to do so.

Thinking Big

I began this book by talking about the reasons scholars write and publish. I would like to end it by urging you to think about the ways both traditional and emerging media can help you meet the different goals you have as a researcher, writer, and teacher. Every idea can develop in myriad ways. That was true even when the media available for dissemination were limited to paper and ink. An idea might turn into an article for one of several journals; it might end up as a classroom lecture; it might expand into a book. Now, with sources easier to acquire and manipulate, and with potential collaborators as close as your computer terminal, research projects can be more ambitious and their outcomes can be disseminated in a variety of ways to multiple audiences. Academic authors must still think about – and work at – the small stuff: careful writing, proofreading, accurate citations, indexing, and all the other details that make their discoveries and ideas clear to others. But the source of academic writing has always been the big things: the questions, answers, alternatives, ideas, evidence, and arguments that scholars think and write about. Now the opportunities for creativity extend beyond the beginnings of a project through to its dissemination. Authors, and their publishers, can now be as creative in presenting knowledge as they are in discovering it.

Bibliography

Basic References

Association of American University Presses. *Directory*. Annual. Distributed by the University of Chicago Press.
   Names, addresses, and descriptions of the publishing programs of the member presses.
Butcher, Judith. *Copy-Editing: The Cambridge Handbook*. 3d ed. New York: Cambridge University Press, 1991.
   The British equivalent of *Chicago*, but more clearly organized and concise.
The Chicago Manual of Style. 14th ed., rev. and expanded. Chicago: University of Chicago Press, 1993.
   The bible of scholarly editors. The 15th edition is anticipated in 2002 or 2003. The website of the University of Chicago Press includes a *Chicago Manual of Style* FAQ feature that allows you to query the editors about matters of style that the manual does not cover or does not cover clearly.
Dessauer, John P. *Book Publishing: A Basic Introduction*. New York: Continuum, 1989.
   The third edition of a classic description of publishing, from acquisition through sales, that focuses on trade, textbook, and small press publishing.
Journal of Scholarly Publishing. Toronto: University of Toronto Press, quarterly. (Formerly *Scholarly Publishing*.)
   An excellent source of information on current problems, trends, and ideas in scholarly publishing, along with useful advice from editors on practical topics.

Bibliography

Literary Market Place (LMP). New York: Bowker, annual.
A directory of U.S. and foreign publishers that provides names, addresses, and other useful information. Also includes listings for translators, literary agents, awards, and review media. Limited access to this volume is provided on the World Wide Web, or you may subscribe to the full Web version.

Publishing Research Quarterly. New Brunswick, N.J.: Transaction Publishers. (Formerly *Book Research Quarterly*.)
This journal covers trade and textbook publishing, as well as scholarly journals and books.

U.S. Government Printing Office. *Style Manual, 2000*. 29th ed. Washington: GPO, 2000. Also available via the Internet from the GPO Access website.
Especially helpful for style matters involving government, international affairs, politics, and currencies.

Dictionaries

American Heritage Dictionary of the English Language. 4th ed. Boston: Houghton Mifflin, 2000.
An authoritative dictionary with helpful usage notes and illustrations. A CD-ROM edition is available with the print edition.

Chambers English Dictionary. Rev. ed. New York: Cambridge University Press, 1990.
Excellent for British spelling and usage and for archaic words. This dictionary is organized around root words and is the best of the lot for browsing.

Merriam-Webster's Collegiate Dictionary. 10th ed. Springfield, Mass.: Merriam-Webster, 1996. CD-ROM edition, 2000.
The most generally accepted desk dictionary.

Morton, Herbert C. "On the Differences of Dictionaries." *Scholarly Publishing* 20, no. 1 (October 1988): 23–34.
This article includes a lengthy review of the second edition, unabridged, of the *Random House Dictionary*, comparing it with the *Oxford English Dictionary* and *Webster's Third New International Dictionary*.

Oxford American Dictionary. New York: Oxford University Press, 1980. Paperback ed., New York: Avon, 1980.
A convenient dictionary with helpful usage notes.

Bibliography

The Random House Webster's Unabridged Dictionary. New York: Random House, 1999.
A larger, more thorough version than the earlier dictionary. CD-ROM available with print edition.

Webster's Third New International Dictionary of the English Language, Unabridged. Springfield, Mass.: Merriam-Webster, 1986.
The most generally accepted unabridged dictionary, but it does not give advice on grammar and usage.

Writing and Usage: General Guides

I have listed only a few of the many such guides available. If you find another that is both authoritative and helpful to you, use it.

Bernstein, Theodore M. *The Careful Writer: A Modern Guide to English Usage.* New York: Atheneum, 1995.
More detailed than Strunk and White, less difficult than Fowler.

Fowler, H. W. *A Dictionary of Modern English Usage.* 2d ed., rev. by Sir Ernest Gowers. New York: Oxford University Press, 1965.
Old-fashioned, opinionated, and fun to read.

Garner, Bryan A. *A Dictionary of Modern American Usage.* New York: Oxford University Press, 1998.

Maggio, Rosalie. *Talking About People: A Guide to Fair and Accurate Language.* Phoenix: Oryx Press, 1997.
Although you may occasionally disagree with the author's characterization of a word as biased, this book provides sensible guidance and alternatives.

Markland, Murray T. "Taking Criticism – and Using It." *Scholarly Publishing* 14, no. 2 (February 1983): 139–47.
How to benefit from criticism by colleagues and referees, including translations of standard cryptic referees' and editors' comments.

Schwartz, Marilyn. *Guidelines for Bias-Free Writing.* Bloomington: Indiana University Press, 1995.

Stainton, Elsie Myers. "Writing and Rewriting." *Scholarly Publishing* 10, no. 1 (October 1978): 75–83.
Sound advice on writing and revising.

Strunk, W., Jr., and E. B. White. *The Elements of Style.* 4th ed. Boston: Allyn & Bacon, 2000.
The one writing manual you must own.

Bibliography

van Leunen, Mary-Claire. *A Handbook for Scholars*. Rev. ed. New York: Oxford University Press, 1992.
Especially useful on citation, quotations, and the usage problems most common among academic writers.

Subject-related Writing Advice, Style Manuals, and Guides to Journals

Agriculture

American Society of Agronomy, Crop Science Society of America, Soil Science Society of America. *Publications Handbook and Style Manual*. 2nd ed. Madison, Wis.: ASA, CSSA, SSSA, 1998.

Art

Barnet, Sylvan. *A Short Guide to Writing About Art*. 6th ed. New York: Longman, 2000.

Biological Science

American Society for Microbiology. *ASM Style Manual for Journals and Books*. Washington, D.C.: ASM, 1991.
Atlas, Michel C. *Author's Handbook of Styles for Life Science Journals*. Boca Raton: CRC Press, 1996.
Council of Biology Editors. *Scientific Style and Format: The CBE Manual for Authors, Editors, and Publishers*. 6th ed. Edward J. Huth, ed. New York: Cambridge University Press, 1994.
Day, Robert A. *How to Write and Publish a Scientific Paper*. 5th ed. Phoenix: Oryx Press, 1998.
———. *Scientific English: A Guide for Scientists and Other Professionals*. 2d ed. Phoenix: Oryx Press, 1995.
Pechenik, Jan A. *A Short Guide to Writing About Biology*. 2d ed. New York: HarperCollins, 1993.
Zeiger, Mimi. *Essentials of Writing Biomedical Research Papers*. 2d ed. New York: McGraw-Hill, 2000.

Chemistry

American Chemical Society. *The ACS Style Guide: A Manual for Authors and Editors*. 2d ed. Janet S. Dodd, ed. Washington, D.C.: ACS, 1997.

Bibliography

Council of Biology Editors. *Scientific Style and Format: The CBE Manual for Authors, Editors, and Publishers*. 6th ed. Edward J. Huth, ed. New York: Cambridge University Press, 1994.

Day, Robert A. *How to Write and Publish a Scientific Paper*. 5th ed. Phoenix: Oryx Press, 1998.

———. *Scientific English: A Guide for Scientists and Other Professionals*. 2d ed. Phoenix: Oryx Press, 1995.

Ebel, Hans Friedrich, Claus Bliefert, and William E. Russey. *The Art of Scientific Writing: From Student Reports to Professional Publications in Chemistry and Related Fields*. New York: VCH, 1987.

Earth Sciences

Council of Biology Editors. *Scientific Style and Format: The CBE Manual for Authors, Editors, and Publishers*. 6th ed. Edward J. Huth, ed. New York: Cambridge University Press, 1994.

Day, Robert A. *How to Write and Publish a Scientific Paper*. 5th ed. Phoenix: Oryx Press, 1998.

———. *Scientific English: A Guide for Scientists and Other Professionals*. 2d ed. Phoenix: Oryx Press, 1995.

Papa, Gail, and Sharon Marsh, eds. *Writer's Guide to Periodicals in Earth Sciences*. 2d ed. Alexandria, Va.: American Geological Institute, 1986.

U.S. Geological Survey. *Suggestions to Authors of the Reports of the United States Geological Survey*. 7th ed. Washington, D.C.: Government Printing Office, 1991.

Economics and Business

Cabell, David W. E., ed. *Cabell's Directory of Publishing Opportunities in Accounting, Economics and Finance*. Beaumont, Tex.: Cabell, 1997.

———. *Cabell's Directory of Publishing Opportunities in Business and Economics*. 5th ed. Beaumont, Tex.: Cabell, 1990.

———. *Cabell's Directory of Publishing Opportunities in Management and Marketing*. Beaumont, Tex.: Cabell, 1994–98.

Miller, A. Carolyn, and Victoria J. Punsalan. *Refereed and Nonrefereed Economic Journals: A Guide to Publishing Opportunities*. New York: Greenwood, 1988.

Bibliography

Thomson, William. *A Guide for the Young Economist.* Cambridge: MIT Press, 2001.

Education

Algozzine, Bob, Festus E. Obiakor, and Jean N. Boson, eds. *Publish and Flourish: A Guide for Writing in Education.* Reston, Va.: Council for Exceptional Children, 1998.

Cabell, David W. E. *Directory of Publishing Opportunities in Education.* 5th ed. Beaumont, Tex.: Cabell, 1998–99.

Collins, Mary Ellen. *Education Journals and Serials: An Analytical Guide.* New York: Greenwood, 1988.

Dyer, Thomas G., and Margaret Davis. *Higher Education Periodicals: A Directory.* Athens: Institute of Higher Education, University of Georgia, 1981.

Henson, Kenneth T. *A Brief Guide to Writing for Professional Publication.* Bloomington, Ind.: Phi Delta Kappa Educational Foundation, 1998.

Judy, Stephen N., ed. *Publishing in English Education.* Montclair, N.J.: Boynton/Cook, 1982.

Loke, Wing Hong. *A Guide to Journals in Psychology and Education.* Metuchen, N.J.: Scarecrow Press, 1990.

Silverman, Robert J. *Getting Published in Education Journals.* Springfield, Ill.: Charles C Thomas, 1982.

Engineering

Balachandran, Sarojini. *Directory of Publishing Sources: The Researcher's Guide to Journals in Engineering and Technology.* New York: Wiley-Interscience, 1982.

Michaelson, Herbert B. *How to Write and Publish Engineering Papers and Reports.* 3d ed. Phoenix: Oryx Press, 1990.

Scull, Roberta A. *Publishing Opportunities for Energy Research: A Descriptive Guide to Selective Serials in the Social and Technical Sciences.* New York: Greenwood, 1986.

Health Professions

American Medical Association. *American Medical Association Manual of Style.* 9th ed. Baltimore: Lippincott, Williams & Wilkins, 1998.

Bibliography

The Author's Guide to Biomedical Journals. 2d ed. New York: Mary Ann Liebert, 1996.

Barnum, Barbara Stevens. *Writing and Getting Published: A Primer for Nurses.* New York: Springer, 1995.

Byrne, D. W. *Publishing Your Medical Research Paper: What They Don't Teach You in Medical School.* Philadelphia: Lippincott, Williams & Wilkins, 1997.

Cormack, Desmond F. S. *Writing for Health Care Professions.* Boston: Blackwell Scientific, 1994.

Council of Biology Editors. *Scientific Style and Format: The CBE Manual for Authors, Editors, and Publishers.* 6th ed. Edward J. Huth, ed. New York: Cambridge University Press, 1994.

Daly, Jeanette M. *Writer's Guide to Nursing Periodicals.* Thousand Oaks, Calif.: Sage, 2000.

Fondiller, Shirley H. *The Writer's Workbook: Health Professionals' Guide to Getting Published.* 2d ed. Sudbury, Mass.: Jones & Bartlett, 1999.

Fondiller, Shirley H., and Barbara J. Nerone. *Health Professionals' Stylebook: Putting Your Language to Work.* New York: National League for Nursing Press, 1993.

Huth, Edward J., M.D. *Medical Style and Format: An International Manual for Authors, Editors, and Publishers.* Philadelphia: ISI Press, 1987.

———. *Writing and Publishing in Medicine.* 3d ed. Baltimore: Williams & Wilkins, 1999.

Morgan, Peter. *An Insider's Guide for Medical Authors and Editors.* Philadelphia: ISI Press, 1986.

Sheen, Anitra Peebles. *Breathing Life Into Medical Writing: A Handbook.* St. Louis: Mosby, 1982.

Excellent advice on writing clearly and precisely. Although the examples are medical, the book is useful to all academic writers.

Zeiger, Mimi. *Essentials of Writing Biomedical Research Papers.* 2d ed. New York: McGraw-Hill, 2000.

History

Marius, Richard. *A Short Guide to Writing About History.* 3d ed. New York: Longman, 1999.

Steiner, Dale R., and Casey R. Phillips. *Historical Journals: A Handbook for Writers and Reviewers.* 2d ed. Jefferson, N.C.: McFarland & Co., 1993.

Bibliography

Language and Literature

Mackesy, Eileen M., and Karen Mateyak, comps. *MLA Directory of Periodicals: A Guide to Journals and Series in Languages and Literatures.* New York: Modern Language Association of America, biennial. Also available online via SilverPlatter and as a CD-ROM.

Modern Language Association. *MLA Handbook for Writers of Research Papers, Theses, and Dissertations.* By Joseph Gibaldi. 5th ed. New York: MLA, 1999.

Olson, Gary A., and Todd W. Taylor, eds. *Publishing in Rhetoric and Composition.* Albany: State University of New York Press, 1997.

Law

The Bluebook: A Uniform System of Citation. 17th ed. Compiled by the editors of the *Columbia Law Review,* the *Harvard Law Review,* the *University of Pennsylvania Law Review,* and the *Yale Law Journal.* Cambridge: Harvard Law Review Association, 2000.

Joyner, Al. *Directory for Successful Publishing in Legal Periodicals.* Charleston, Ill.: Qucoda, 1987.

Library and Information Science

Alley, Brian, and Jennifer Cargill. *Librarian in Search of a Publisher: How to Get Published.* Phoenix: Oryx Press, 1986.

Schroeder, Carol F., and Gloria G. Roberson, eds. *Guide to Publishing Opportunities for Librarians.* New York: Haworth, 1995.

Mathematics

American Mathematical Society. *A Manual for Authors of Mathematical Papers.* 7th ed. Providence: AMS, 1980.

Krantz, Steven G. *A Primer of Mathematical Writing: Being a Disquisition on Having Your Ideas Recorded, Typeset, Published, Read and Appreciated.* Providence, R.I.: American Mathematical Society, 1997.

Bibliography

Music

Basart, Ann Phillips. *Writing About Music: A Guide to Publishing Opportunities for Authors and Reviewers.* Berkeley: Fallen Leaf Press, 1989.

Irvine, Demar. *Writing about Music.* 3d ed., rev. and enl. by Mark A. Radice. Portland, Or.: Amadeus, 1999.

Wingell, Richard J. *Writing About Music: An Introductory Guide.* 2d ed. Englewood Cliffs, N.J.: Prentice Hall, 1996.

Nature Writing

Heintzman, James, Michael Gross, and Ronald Zimmerman, eds. *Making the Right Connections: A Guide for Nature Writers.* Stevens Point, Wis.: UW-SP Foundation Press, 1988.

Philosophy and Religion

Dawsey, James M. *A Scholar's Guide to Academic Journals in Religion.* Metuchen, N.J.: Scarecrow Press, 1988.

Hoffman, Eric. *Guidebook for Publishing Philosophy.* Bowling Green, Ohio: Philosophy Documentation Center and the American Philosophical Association, 1997.

Watson, Richard A. *Writing Philosophy: A Guide to Professional Writing and Publishing.* Carbondale: Southern Illinois University Press, 1992.

Physics

American Institute of Physics. *AIP Style Manual.* 4th ed. New York: AIP, 1990.

Council of Biology Editors. *Scientific Style and Format: The CBE Manual for Authors, Editors, and Publishers.* 6th ed. Edward J. Huth, ed. New York: Cambridge University Press, 1994.

Day, Robert A. *How to Write and Publish a Scientific Paper.* 5th ed. Phoenix: Oryx Press, 1998.

———. *Scientific English: A Guide for Scientists and Other Professionals.* 2d ed. Phoenix: Oryx Press, 1995.

Bibliography

Primack, Alice Lefler. *Journal Literature of the Physical Sciences: A Manual.* Metuchen, N.J.: Scarecrow Press, 1992.

Psychology

American Psychological Association. *Publication Manual of the American Psychological Association.* 5th ed. Washington, D.C.: APA, 2001.

Bellquist, John Eric. *A Guide to Grammar and Usage for Psychology and Related Fields.* Hillsdale, N.J.: Erlbaum, 1993.

Journals in Psychology: A Resource Listing for Authors. 5th ed. Washington, D.C.: American Psychological Association, 1997.

Loke, Wing Hong. *A Guide to Journals in Psychology and Education.* Metuchen, N.J.: Scarecrow Press, 1990.

Mullins, Carolyn J. *A Guide to Writing and Publishing in the Social and Behavioral Sciences.* New York: Wiley, 1977. Reprint ed. Malabar, Fla.: R. E. Krieger, 1983.

Sternberg, Robert J., ed. *Guide to Publishing in Psychology Journals.* New York: Cambridge University Press, 2000.

Wang, Alvin Y. *Author's Guide to Journals in the Behavioral Sciences.* Hillsdale, N.J.: Erlbaum, 1989.

Social Sciences

American Sociological Association. *ASA Style Guide.* 2d ed. Washington, D.C.: American Sociological Association, 1997.

Becker, Howard S. *Writing for Social Scientists: How to Start and Finish Your Thesis, Book, or Article.* Chicago: University of Chicago Press, 1986.

Mendelsohn, Henry N. *An Author's Guide to Social Work Journals.* 4th ed. Washington, D.C.: NASW Press, 1997.

Mullins, Carolyn J. *A Guide to Writing and Publishing in the Social and Behavioral Sciences.* New York: Wiley, 1977. Reprint ed. Malabar, Fla.: R. E. Krieger, 1983.

Political and Social Science Journals: A Handbook for Writers and Reviewers. Clio Guides to Publishing Opportunities, no. 2. Santa Barbara, Calif.: ABC-Clio, 1983.

Bibliography

Journals: General Information

Axtell, James. "Twenty-five Reasons to Publish." In his *The Pleasures of Academe: A Celebration and Defense of Higher Education*, pp. 48–68. Lincoln: University of Nebraska Press, 1998.
An articulate discussion of the relationship between research and teaching, and the rewards of writing.

Budd, Louis J. "On Writing Scholarly Articles," in *The Academic's Handbook*, ed. A. Leigh DeNeef, Craufurd D. Goodwin, and Ellen Stern McCrate,   pp. 201–15. Durham, N.C.: Duke University Press, 1988.
A well-written essay on working with editors of humanities journals, with much practical advice.

Irizarry, Estelle. "Redundant and Incremental Publication." *Journal of Scholarly Publishing* 25, no. 4 (July 1994): 212–20.
A discussion of the ethical issues and suggestions for editors and authors.

National Science Foundation. "Federal Support of Scientific and Technical Publication." *Publishing Research Quarterly* 14, 4 (Winter 1998/99): 9–23.
Reprint of a 1976 report on regulations relating to page charges and a survey of practices.

Page, Gillian, Robert Campbell, and Jack Meadows. *Journal Publishing: Principles and Practice*. Rev. ed. New York: Cambridge University Press, 1997.
A thorough introduction to journal publishing that is concerned with nuts and bolts.

Penaskovic, Richard. "Facing Up to the Publication Gun." *Scholarly Publishing* 16, no. 2 (January 1985): 136–40.
Good advice on finding ideas and publishers for journal articles.

Scal, Marjorie. "The Page Charge." *Scholarly Publishing* 3, no. 1 (October 1971): 62–9.
An explanation of journal financing and the role of page charges. Includes a discussion of rates and policies on waivers.

Strain, Boyd R. "Publishing in Science." In *The Academic's Handbook*, ed. A. Leigh DeNeef, Craufurd D. Goodwin, and Ellen Stern McCrate, pp. 216–25.
A concise summary of considerations for authors of scientific articles.

Bibliography

Thyer, Bruce A. *Successful Publishing in Scholarly Journals*. Thousand Oaks, Calif.: Sage, 1994.
A brief guide to submitting and revising articles.

Zink, Steven D. "Journal Publishing in the Field of U.S. History." *Scholarly Publishing* 11, no. 4 (July 1980): 343–59.
Suggestions for improving communication between authors and editors of scholarly journals.

Refereeing

Banner, James M., Jr. "Preserving the Integrity of Peer Review." *Scholarly Publishing* 19, no. 2 (January 1988): 109–15; "Guidelines for Peer Review of Sponsored Book Manuscripts." *Scholarly Publishing* 20, no. 2 (January 1989): 116–22.
Banner offers suggestions to improve the peer review process, including the provision of a description of the process for authors. The second article includes the description provided by Banner's own press.

DeGeorge, Richard T., and Fred Woodward. "Ethics and Manuscript Reviewing." *Journal of Scholarly Publishing* 25, no. 3 (April 1994): 133–45.
A good review and discussion of the obligations of authors, editors, and publishers.

Forscher, Bernard K. "The Role of the Referee." *Scholarly Publishing* 11, no. 2 (January 1980): 165–9.
What journal editors expect from referees.

James, M. R. "Casting the Runes." In *The Ghost Stories of M. R. James*, pp. 235–7. 2d ed. London: Arnold, 1974.
A memorable argument for referees' anonymity.

Stieg, Margaret F. "Refereeing and the Editorial Process: The AHR and Webb." *Scholarly Publishing* 14, no. 2 (February 1983): 99–122.
A case study of how refereeing and editorial evaluation actually work.

Zuckerman, Harriet, and Robert K. Merton. "Patterns of Evaluation in Science: Institutionalization, Structure, and Functions of the Referee System." *Minerva* 9 (1971): 66–100.
A classic study of the history of refereeing, a case study of *The Physical Review*, and conclusions about the system.

Bibliography

Reviewing Books

Budd, John. "Book Reviewing Practices of Journals in the Humanities." *Scholarly Publishing* 13, no. 4 (July 1982): 363–71.
How journals select reviewers.
Cortada, James W. "Five Ways to Be a Terrible Book Reviewer." *Journal of Scholarly Publishing* 30, no. 1 (October 1998): 34–7.
A warning against bad practices in refereeing and reviewing.
Hoge, James O., ed. *Literary Reviewing*. Charlottesville: University Press of Virginia, 1987.
This thoughtful volume discusses the duties, problems, and ethics of literary reviewing. Topics covered include reviewing criticism, literary history, literary biography, bibliographies, and editions of letters, journals, and diaries.
Simon, Linda. "The Pleasures of Book Reviewing." *Journal of Scholarly Publishing* 27, no. 4 (July 1996): 237–41.
Why and how to be an active reviewer.
Walford, A. J. *Reviews and Reviewing: A Guide*. Phoenix: Oryx Press, 1986.
A discussion of the art of reviewing and a guide to review media in various fields.

Dissertations

Fox, Mary Frank. "The Transition from Dissertation Student to Publishing Scholar and Professional." In *Scholarly Writing and Publishing: Issues, Problems, and Solutions*, ed. Mary Frank Fox. Boulder, Colo.: Westview Press, 1985.
A very short essay on developing habits of work and of thought that will contribute to scholarly productivity.
Harman, Eleanor, and Ian Montagnes, eds. *The Thesis and the Book*. Toronto: University of Toronto Press, 1976.
An indispensable guide for revisers of dissertations, helpful for referees and, particularly, for those who are not sure how writing for book publication is distinguished from other writing.
Zerubavel, Eviatar. *The Clockwork Muse: A Practical Guide to Writing Theses, Dissertations, and Books*. Cambridge: Harvard University Press, 1999.
Excellent advice on disciplining oneself to write and revise.

Bibliography

Finding a Publisher

Day, Colin. "The University Press: An Organic Part of the Institution." *Scholarly Publishing* 23, no. 1 (October 1991): 27–44.
An excellent review of the state of university presses.

Funk, Robert W. "Issues in Scholarly Publishing." *Scholarly Publishing* 9, no. 1 (October 1977): 3–16; 9, no. 2 (January 1978): 115–29.
Publishing by learned societies.

Halpenny, Francess G. "Of Time and the Editor." *Scholarly Publishing* 1, no. 2 (January 1970): 159–69.
A cogent explanation of why university press reviewing and editing take so long and some suggestions for authors.

Hawes, Gene R. *To Advance Knowledge: A Handbook on American University Press Publishing.* New York: American University Press Services, 1967.
Although written in a period of rapid university press expansion and optimism, this book remains an articulate exposition of the purpose and workings of university presses.

Johnson, William Bruce. "Ethical Procedures for Authors and Publishers." *Scholarly Publishing* 7, no. 3 (April 1976): 253–60.
A discussion of multiple submissions, rejections, refereeing, objectivity, and reviews.

Kerr, Chester. "One More Time: American University Presses Revisited." *Scholarly Publishing* 18, no. 4 (July 1987): 211–35.
Kerr reports on the state of university press publishing, a task he performed in 1949 and 1969 as well.

Metro, Judy. "Is It Publishable? The Importance of the Editorial Review." *Journal of Scholarly Publishing* 26, no. 3 (April 1995): 168–72.
A brief description of the manuscript review process at a university press.

One Book/Five Ways: The Publishing Procedures of Five University Presses. Los Altos, Calif.: Kaufmann, 1978. Reprint ed. Chicago: University of Chicago Press, 1994.
An illustration of how five university presses would have handled the same manuscript, including sample contracts. Note, however, that the financial estimates and technology all date to the 1970s.

Parsons, Paul. *Getting Published: The Acquisitions Process at University Presses.* Knoxville: University of Tennessee Press, 1989.
A study of decision making at a university press.

Bibliography

Legal Issues

Bunnin, Brad, and Peter Beren. *The Writer's Legal Companion: The Complete Handbook for the Working Writer.* 3d ed. New York: Perseus, 1998.

Crawford, Tad, and Tony Lyons. *The Writer's Legal Guide.* 2d ed. New York: Allworth, 1998.

Goldfarb, Ronald L., and Gail E. Ross. *The Writer's Lawyer: Essential Legal Advice for Writers and Editors in All Media.* New York: Times Books, 1989.
A guide to First Amendment rights, copyright, libel, contracts, privacy, and other legal matters, with clear discussions of recent cases. It also includes a chapter on obtaining research material under the Freedom of Information Act.

Harvey, William B. "The Publishing Contract." *Scholarly Publishing* 8, no. 4 (July 1977): 299–314.
The standard contract's provisions, with comments.

Jassin, Lloyd J., and Steve C. Schechter. *The Copyright Permission and Libel Handbook: A Step-by-Step Guide for Writers, Editors, and Publishers.* New York: John Wiley, 1998.

Norwick, Kenneth P., and Jerry Simon Chasen. *The Rights of Authors, Artists, and Other Creative People: The Basic ACLU Guide to Author and Artist Rights.* 2d ed. Carbondale: Southern Illinois University Press, 1992.

Patterson, L. Ray, and Stanley W. Lindberg. *The Nature of Copyright: A Law of Users' Rights.* Athens: University of Georgia Press, 1991.

Sanford, Bruce W. *Libel and Privacy.* 2d ed. Englewood Cliffs, N.J.: Prentice Hall Law & Business, 1991.

Scarles, Christopher. *Copyright.* New York: Cambridge University Press, 1980.
A clear, brief guide to U.S. and British copyright.

Strong, William S. *The Copyright Book: A Practical Guide.* 5th ed. Cambridge: MIT Press, 1999.
The classic in the field.

Wincor, Richard. *Rights Contracts in the Communications Media.* New York: Law and Business, 1982.
An explanation of contracts directed at publishers but useful for authors.

Bibliography

Subventions

Jones, Barbara G. "Changing Author Relationships and Competitive Strategies of University Publishers." *Journal of Scholarly Publishing* 31, no. 1 (October 1999): 3–19.
A survey of publishers that included questions about cash subsidies as well as increased author responsibilities.

Kameny, Fred. "Authors with Deep Pockets: The Ethics of Subsidies." *Journal of Scholarly Publishing* 29, no. 2 (January 1998): 65–70.
A survey of practices and a discussion of the ethical issues.

Smith, Datus C. "An Anatomy of Subsidies." *Scholarly Publishing* 6, no. 3 (April 1975): 197–206.
Explains the variety and importance of subsidies to publishers, as well as the problems they raise.

Smith, John Hazel. "Subvention of Scholarly Publishing." *Scholarly Publishing* 9, no. 1 (October 1977): 19–29.
A survey of university press subvention policies and practices.

Multiauthor Books

Black, Cyril E., and Carol Orr. "'E Pluribus Unum': Symposia and Publishers." *Scholarly Publishing* 5, no. 2 (January 1974): 145–52.
Shortcomings of symposia, criteria for good ones, and publication thereof.

Horowitz, Irving Louis. "The Place of the Festschrift." *Scholarly Publishing* 21, no. 2 (January 1990): 77–83.
Useful ideas to improve the genre.

James, Rowena G. "Et Alia." *Scholarly Publishing* 2, no. 1 (October 1970): 59–65.
Helpful suggestions for early planning of multiauthor books.

Meyers, Jeffrey. "On Editing Collections of Original Essays." *Scholarly Publishing* 17, no. 2 (January 1986): 99–108.
A first-person account by the editor of three such volumes.

Textbooks

Arnold, David L. "Faculty Perceptions of the Scholarship and Utility of Writing College-Level Textbooks." *Publishing Research Quarterly* 9, no. 2 (Summer 1993): 42–54.

Bibliography

A study that surveyed faculty and department chairs to determine their evaluation of the scholarship required to write a textbook and the likelihood that such work will be rewarded.

Heilenman, L. Kathy. "Of Cultures and Compromises." *Publishing Research Quarterly* 9, no. 2 (Summer 1993): 55–67.
A discussion of the conflicts between the culture of academe and that of textbook publishers, with suggestions for resolving them.

Trade Books

Callenbach, Ernest. *Publisher's Lunch: A Dialogue Concerning the Secrets of How Publishers Think and What Authors Can Do About It.* Berkeley: Ten Speed Press, 1989.
A series of conversations between an acquiring editor and a prospective author in which each sets out typical concerns and attitudes.

Knauer, Joyce. "Scholarly Books in General Bookstores." *Scholarly Publishing* 19, no. 2 (January 1988): 79–85.
Although directed toward university press staff, this article is a useful description of the lay audience and the bookseller's role in reaching it.

Luey, Beth. "University Press Trade Books in the Review Media." *Scholarly Publishing* 25, no. 2 (January 1994): 84–92.
An evaluation of presses' effectiveness in getting their books reviewed in the popular media.

Agents

A web search for "literary agents online directory" will lead you to web resources in addition to these print sources.

Dickerson, Donya. *Guide to Literary Agents.* Cincinnati: Writer's Digest Books, annual.

Dorn, Fred J. "Do Scholarly Authors Need Literary Agents?" *Scholarly Publishing* 14, no. 1 (October 1982): 79–86.
Sometimes, and if so, how to find one and what to expect.

Literary Agents of North America. New York: The Associates, annual.
A detailed guide.

Bibliography

Mechanics

Desktop Publishing, Design, and Camera-ready Copy

Lee, Marshall. *Bookmaking : The Illustrated Guide to Design, Production, Editing*. 2d ed. New York: Bowker, 1979.
Although this book provides more detail than an amateur designer needs, it is easy to follow.

Tibbo, Helen R. "Specifications for Camera-Ready Copy: Helping Authors Be More Productive." *Journal of Scholarly Publishing* 25, no. 4 (July 1994): 221–32.
What publishers need to tell authors so that they can produce camera-ready copy efficiently.

Williamson, Hugh. *Methods of Book Design: The Practice of an Industrial Craft*. 3d ed. New Haven: Yale University Press, 1983.
This book is meant for professional designers, but it does provide an introduction to the principles of book design.

Illustrations

Brouwer, Onno. "The Cartographer's Role and Requirements." *Scholarly Publishing* 14, no. 3 (April 1983): 231–42.
How to work with a professional cartographer.

Council of Biology Editors. *Illustrating Science: Standards for Publication*. Bethesda, Md.: CBE, 1988.
An excellent guide to preparing, submitting, and producing high-quality illustrations of all kinds. Despite its title, it is useful for authors in all disciplines.

Cox, Stephen. "The Editor and the Photograph in the Age of Zing! And Bam!" *Journal of Scholarly Publishing* 27, no. 1 (October 1995): 12–21.
A discussion of the changing uses of photographs with guidelines for gathering, selecting, and handling them.

Eakins, Rosemary, and Elizabeth Loving, eds. *Picture Sources U.K.* London: Macdonald, 1985.
A subject guide to picture collections in the United Kingdom, including addresses, coverage, and procedures. It also contains a brief introduction to doing picture research.

Evans, Hilary and Mary. *Picture Researcher's Handbook: An International Guide to Picture Sources and How to Use Them*. 5th ed. New York: Van Nostrand Reinhold, 1992.

Bibliography

MacGregor, A. J. *Graphics Simplified: How to Plan and Prepare Effective Charts, Graphs, Illustrations, and Other Visual Aids*. Toronto: University of Toronto Press, 1979.
A brief, clear book that delivers fully on its subtitle's promise.
Robl, Ernest H., ed. *Picture Sources*. 4th ed. New York: Special Libraries Association, 1983.
Provides descriptions of 980 picture collections, including subject coverage, people to contact, and procedures.
Tufte, Edward R. *The Visual Display of Quantitative Information*. Cheshire, Conn.: Graphics Press, 1983.
An elegant, detailed book about the use and abuse of graphs. More extensive than MacGregor; vital for the writer in statistical fields and fascinating for others.
———. *Envisioning Information*. Cheshire, Conn.: Graphics Press, 1990.
Another superb volume, this time with more color and discussions of electronic media.

Copyright and Permissions

Harman, Eleanor. "On Seeking Permission." *Scholarly Publishing* 1, no. 2 (January 1970): 188–92.
Practical advice that emphasizes an early start.
Mesrobian, Arpena. "Banditry, Charity, or Equity." *Scholarly Publishing* 1, no. 2 (January 1970): 179–87.
An excellent, balanced explanation of publishers' permissions policies, with examples of requests granted and denied.
U.S. Library of Congress. Copyright Office. "Copyright Basics." Washington, D.C.: U.S. Government Printing Office, n.d.
Available free on the Copyright Office website.
An official summary of the law.
———. "How to Investigate the Copyright Status of a Work." Washington, D.C.: U.S. Government Printing Office, n.d.
Available free on the Copyright Office website.
An explanation of how to determine whether a work is still protected by copyright and who holds the rights.

Proofreading

Butcher, Judith. *Typescripts, Proofs and Indexes*. New York: Cambridge University Press, 1980.
A good, brief handbook.

Bibliography

Harman, Eleanor. "Hints on Proofreading." *Scholarly Publishing* 6, no. 2 (January 1975): 150–7.
Very practical, detailed suggestions.

Indexing

Butcher, Judith. *Typescripts, Proofs and Indexes*. New York: Cambridge University Press, 1980.
A good, brief handbook.
Mulvany, Nancy C. *Indexing Books*. Chicago: University of Chicago Press, 1994.
For the author who wants to learn more about the theory and practice of indexing.
Spiker, Sina. *Indexing Your Book: A Practical Guide for Authors*. Madison: University of Wisconsin Press, 1987.
Very helpful advice on how to compile an index.

Economics

Bailey, Herbert S., Jr. *The Art and Science of Book Publishing*. Austin: University of Texas Press, 1970.
A detailed analysis of the business side of publishing.
Broderick, John C. "The Cost of a Bad Book." *Scholarly Publishing* 18, no. 2 (January 1987): 83–8.
Broderick computes the costs of researching, writing, publishing, cataloguing, and storing a monograph.
Potter, Clarkson N. *Who Does What and Why in Book Publishing: Writers, Editors and Money Men*. Secaucus, N.J.: Birch Lane Press, 1990.
The last chapter is a very clear explanation of some publishing business practices.

Electronic Publishing

Benford, Tom. *Welcome to CD-ROM*. New York: MIS Press, 1993.
Botto, Francis. *Multimedia, CD-ROM, and Compact Disc: A Guide for Users and Developers*. Wilmslow, Eng.: Sigma, 1992.

Bibliography

Crane, Gregory. "'Hypermedia' and Scholarly Publishing." *Scholarly Publishing* 21, no. 3 (April 1990): 131–55.
A description of the conception and development of the Perseus Project, originally a CD-ROM for the study of classic Greek texts, now available online as the Perseus Digital Library.

Helgerson, Linda W. *CD-ROM: Facilitating Electronic Publishing.* New York: Van Nostrand Reinhold, 1992.

LaGuardia, Cheryl. *The CD-ROM Primer: The ABC's of CD-ROM.* New York: Neal-Schuman, 1994.

Myers, Patti. *Publishing with CD-ROM.* Arlington, Va.: Meckler Publishing Corp. and the National Composition Association, 1986.
A useful and accessible introduction to CD-ROM.

Ohi, Debbie Ridpath. *Writer's Online Marketplace: How and Where to Get Published Online.* Cincinnati: Writer's Digest Books, 2001.

Raimes, James. "Developing a CD-ROM." *Journal of Scholarly Publishing* 25, no. 2 (January 1994): 107–13.

Ressler, Sanford. *The Art of Electronic Publishing: The Internet and Beyond.* Upper Saddle River, N.J.: Prentice Hall PTR, 1997.

Robbins, Robert J. "Biological Databases: A New Scientific Literature." *Publishing Research Quarterly* 10, 1 (Spring 1994): 5–27.
A thorough, thoughtful analysis of the impact, advantages, and problems of scholarly database publishing.

Sherman, Chris, ed. *The CD-ROM Handbook.* 2d ed. New York: Intertext/McGraw-Hill, 1994.

Index

Index

e-books, 280–86; *see also* electronic publishing

editing, *see* copyediting; developmental editing

editorial boards, 20, 49, 65, 70, 110

editorial consultants, 60–61

editors

author's, 60–61

developmental, 133, 140–45, 170–71

freelance, 99, 237, 241–42

production, 50, 96, 99–100

series, 58

of textbooks, 128–29

titles of, 50

of trade books, 170–71

see also copyediting; journals

electronic journals, 9–10, 28–30, 271–73

electronic manuscripts

and author's alterations, 86

benefits of, 175–76

coding of, 82–83, 180, 189–201, 208

contract provisions for, 70, 85, 180

and costs, 239

editing of, 99

of journal articles, 18–19, 176

limitations of, 176–77

of multiauthor books, 108, 111

planning of, 177–80

preparation of, 181–85

proofreading of, 100–101, 221–28

for revised editions, 207–8

and royalties, 82–83

transmission of, 19

see also camera-ready copy; computers

electronic publishing

advantages of, 29, 271–73, 286–87

of anthologies, 119, 121–25

of e-books, 280–86

economics of, 6, 29, 258–60, 274–75, 281–84

expectations for, 6, 260–62

prices of, 260–61, 284

of reference works, 273–77

and self-publishing, 56–57

see also CD-ROMs; electronic journals; electronic rights

electronic rights, 77, 78–79, 271–72, 274, 284

encyclopedias, 110–11, 115

equations, in trade books, 164

errata, 104

ethics, 13, 16–17, 21, 30, 58, 65, 87–90, 155–56

excerpts, sale of, 77

"fair use," of copyrighted material, 88, 117, 217–20; *see also* copyright; permissions

fees

agents', 154–55

artists', 210–11

of author's editors, 60–61

in lieu of royalties, 84, 114–15

page charge, 26–28

for permissions, 77–78, 120–21, 132–33, 213–15, 220, 221

submission, 26

footnotes, *see* notes

foreign rights, 59, 75–76, 220, 268

foreword, 187

314

Index

Index